Presidents from
Washington through Monroe,
1789–1825

**Recent Titles in
The President's Position: Debating the Issues**

Presidents from Theodore Roosevelt through Coolidge, 1901–1929
Francine Sanders Romero

PRESIDENTS FROM WASHINGTON THROUGH MONROE, 1789–1825

Debating the Issues in Pro and Con Primary Documents

AMY H. STURGIS

The President's Position: Debating the Issues
Mark Byrnes, Series Editor

GREENWOOD PRESS
Westport, Connecticut • London

Library of Congress Cataloging-in-Publication Data

Sturgis, Amy H., 1971–
    Presidents from Washington through Monroe, 1789–1825 : debating the issues
in pro and con primary documents / Amy H. Sturgis.
        p.   cm.—(The president's position : debating the issues)
    Includes bibliographical references and index.
    ISBN 0–313–31387–3 (alk. paper)
        1. Presidents—United States—History—18th century—Sources.   2. Presidents—
    United States—History—19th century—Sources.   3. United States—Politics and
    government—1789–1815—Sources.   4. United States—Politics and
    government—1815–1861—Sources.   5. Washington, George, 1732–1799—Political and
    social views.   6. Adams, John, 1735–1826—Political and social views.   7. Jefferson,
    Thomas, 1743–1826—Political and social views.   8. Madison, James, 1751–1836—
    Political and social views.   9. Monroe, James, 1758–1831—Political and social
    views. I. Title II. Series.
    E176.1.S927   2002
    973.4'092'2—dc21   2001023312

British Library Cataloguing in Publication Data is available.

Library of Congress Catalog Card Number: 2001023312
ISBN: 0–313–31387–3

First published in 2002

Greenwood Press, 88 Post Road West, Westport, CT 06881
An imprint of Greenwood Publishing Group, Inc.
www.greenwood.com

Printed in the United States of America

The paper used in this book complies with the
Permanent Paper Standard issued by the National
Information Standards Organization (Z39.48–1984).

10 9 8 7 6 5 4 3 2 1

For Larry
with love
in the grand way

CONTENTS

SERIES FOREWORD

When he was running for president in 1932, Franklin D. Roosevelt declared that America needed "bold, persistent experimentation" in its public policy. "It is common sense to take a method and try it," FDR said. "If it fails, admit it frankly and try another. But above all, try something." At President Roosevelt's instigation, the nation did indeed take a number of steps to combat the Great Depression. In the process, the president emerged as the clear leader of American public policy. Most scholars see FDR's administration as the birth of the "modern presidency," in which the president dominates both domestic and foreign policy.

Even before FDR, however, presidents played a vital role in the making of public policy. Policy changes advocated by the presidents—often great changes—have always influenced the course of events, and have always sparked debate from the presidents' opponents. The outcomes of this process have had tremendous effects on the lives of Americans. The President's Position: Debating the Issues examines the stands the presidents have taken on the major political, social, and economic issues of their times as well as the stands taken by their opponents. The series combines description and analysis of those issues with excerpts from primary documents that illustrate the position of the presidents and their opponents. The result is an informative, accessible, and comprehensive look at the crucial connection between presidents and policy. These volumes will assist students doing historical research, preparing for debates, or fulfilling critical thinking assignments. The general reader interested in American history and politics will also find the series interesting and helpful.

Several important themes about the president's role in policy making emerge from the series. First, and perhaps most important, is how greatly the president's involvement in policy has expanded over the years. This has happened because the range of areas in which the national government acts has grown dramatically and because modern presidents—unlike most of their predecessors—see taking the lead in policy making as part of their job. Second, certain issues have confronted most presidents over history; tax and tariff policy, for example, was important for both George Washington and Bill Clinton, and for most of the presidents in between. Third, the emergence of the United States as a world power around the beginning of the twentieth century made foreign policy issues more numerous and more pressing. Finally, in the American system, presidents cannot form policy through decrees; they must persuade members of Congress, other politicians, and the general public to follow their lead. This key fact makes the policy debates between presidents and their opponents vitally important.

This series comprises nine volumes, organized chronologically, each of which covers the presidents who governed during that particular time period. Volume one looks at the presidents from George Washington through James Monroe; volume two, John Quincy Adams through James K. Polk; volume three, Zachary Taylor through Ulysses Grant; volume four, Rutherford B. Hayes through William McKinley; volume five, Theodore Roosevelt through Calvin Coolidge; volume six, Herbert Hoover through Harry Truman; volume seven, Dwight Eisenhower through Lyndon Johnson; volume eight, Richard Nixon through Jimmy Carter; and volume nine, Ronald Reagan through Bill Clinton. Each president from Washington through Clinton is covered, although the number of issues discussed under each president varies according to how long they served in office and how actively they pursued policy goals. Volumes six through nine—which cover the modern presidency—examine three presidencies each, while the earlier volumes include between five and seven presidencies each.

Every volume begins with a general introduction to the period it covers, providing an overview of the presidents who served and the issues they confronted. The section on each president opens with a detailed overview of the president's position on the relevant issues he confronted and the initiatives he took, and closes with a list of suggested readings. Up to fifteen issues are covered per presidency. The discussion of each issue features an introduction, the positions taken by the president and his opponents, how the issue was resolved, and the long-term effects of the issue. This is followed by excerpts from two primary documents, one representing the president's position and the other representing his opponents' position. Also included in each volume is a timeline of significant events of the era and a general bibliography of sources for students and others interested in further research.

As the most prominent individual in American politics, the president receives enormous attention from the media and the public. The statements, actions, travels, and even the personal lives of presidents are constantly scrutinized. Yet it is the presidents' work on public policy that most directly affects American citizens—a fact that is sometimes overlooked. This series is presented, in part, as a reminder of the importance of the president's position.

Mark Byrnes

PREFACE

I learned to read by devouring biographies. The first dog-earing sessions I remember included *Meet George Washington* by Joan Heilbroner and *Meet Thomas Jefferson* by Marvin Barrett. The founding period seemed larger than life to me, and I was fascinated by the leaders who acted in a moment of change and gave substance to the hopes of a nation. As I grew, *The Federalist Papers* replaced Dorothy Clarke Wilson's novels of the First Ladies, but my fascination with the era never waned.

The calm and idyllic young nation of children's stories, however, does not reflect the true complexity of the early national era. The Virginia Dynasty presidents enjoyed a consensus about a number of subjects, but they also disagreed about key issues and made difficult decisions with important repercussions for the nation. These early debates illustrate fundamental tensions in U.S. political thought. This book investigates the issues of the time and the positions each president took regarding them. The introduction at the beginning of the book offers an overview of the men, their era, and the questions they faced. The timeline helps to anchor the topics in a concrete chronology. Each chapter, which includes its own introduction, further explores the vital, contested issues of a president's administration. These discussions, organized chronologically, provide context for the debates and opposing primary sources that allow the historical actors to speak for themselves. I hope my introductions and analyses make the original documents interesting and accessible to students and other readers. May the questions raised, along with the primary sources and suggestions for further reading offered here, guide interested individuals to new and fruitful avenues of research.

My thanks go to Mark Byrnes for inviting me to participate in this series and Barbara Rader and Heidi Straight for guiding this project. I am indebted to the staffs of the Belmont University and Vanderbilt University libraries for their assistance. I appreciate the ongoing support of my parents, sister, grandparents, friends, and colleagues. Most importantly, I am grateful to my very own political scientist, my husband Larry M. Hall, for kindnesses too numerous to count. Any errors remaining in this work are my own.

TIMELINE

1789

April 14   Charles Thomson, secretary of Congress, visits Mount Vernon to inform George Washington that he has been elected president of the United States. Washington accepts the position. John Adams is elected vice president.

April 30   George Washington is inaugurated as president in New York City.

May 14   The U.S. Senate votes to address the executive as "Mr. President."

1790

January 9   Alexander Hamilton presents Washington with his "Report on Public Credit."

July 16   Washington signs the bill moving the national capital to the Potomac (the future Washington, D.C.) in ten years.

1791

February 25   Washington signs the bill creating the Bank of the United States.

1793

February 13   Washington is unanimously reelected to a second term as president. John Adams is reelected as vice president.

March 4   Washington is inaugurated for his second term.

April 22   Washington presents his Proclamation of Neutrality.

1794

July 15   The Whiskey Insurrection begins when armed citizens oppose a U.S. marshal in Westmoreland County, Pennsylvania.

November 19   The Jay Treaty is signed between the United States and Great
               Britain.

1796

December 7   John Adams is elected president and Thomas Jefferson is elected
               vice president.

1797

March 4   Adams is inaugurated as president.

1798

April 3   Adams sends the XYZ documents to be read to both houses of
               Congress.

July 4   Adams signs the appointment of George Washington as lieuten-
               ant general and commander in chief of the U.S. Army.

July 6 and 14 Congress passes the Alien and Sedition Acts, respectively.

December 24   The Virginia Senate adopts the Virginia Resolution protesting
               the Alien and Sedition Acts.

1799

December 14   Former president George Washington dies of a throat infection
               at Mount Vernon. His will frees his slaves.

1800

November 1   John Adams becomes the first president to move into the White
               House.

1801

February 17   Thomas Jefferson is elected president and Aaron Burr is elected
               vice president, after a tie sends the decision to the U.S. House
               of Representatives.

March 4   Thomas Jefferson is the first president to be inaugurated in the
               new capital.

May 20   Jefferson sends a naval squadron to the Barbary Coast after the
               pasha of Tripoli declares war against the United States.

July 22   Foreign envoy Pichon reports to French minister of foreign af-
               fairs Talleyrand that Jefferson is willing to cooperate with France
               against Toussaint L'Overture in Santo Domingo.

1802

October   Juan Morales, Spanish intendant at New Orleans, issues a proc-
               lamation closing the port to all foreign shipping.

November 3   Jefferson assures Handsome Lake that the U.S. government will
               not take native American land without proper consent.

               The Georgia Compact of 1802 cedes Georgia lands in the West
               to the national government in return for the United States extin-
               guishing native American land titles within the Georgia state
               borders.

1803	*Marbury v. Madison* goes to the Supreme Court. Its decision sets the precedent of judicial review.
April 30	James Monroe, special envoy, and Robert Livingston, ambassador to France, make the Louisiana Purchase with French officials according to Jefferson's directions.
	Toussaint L'Overture dies in France.
1804	
July 12	Alexander Hamilton dies the day after being shot in a duel by Vice President Aaron Burr.
November	Jefferson is reelected to the presidency and George Clinton is elected vice president in the first national election under the Twelfth Amendment, which separated voting for presidential and vice presidential candidates.
1805	
March 4	Jefferson is inaugurated for his second term.
1807	
June 22	The British *Leopard* attacks U.S. vessel *Chesapeake* off the Virginia coast.
December 22	Congress passes the first of the Embargo Acts.
1808	
December 7	James Madison is elected president and George Clinton is elected vice president.
1809	
March 4	James Madison is inaugurated as president.
May 6	Madison pardons General Michael Bright and other Pennsylvania militiamen for their protection of the Rittenhouse sisters against U.S. marshals.
1810	
October 27	Madison issues his Proclamation on West Florida, describing his decision to occupy the land in the name of the United States.
1812	
June 1	Madison delivers his "War Message" to Congress.
December	James Madison is reelected to the presidency and Elbridge Gerry is elected vice president.
1813	
March 4	Madison is inaugurated for his second term.
1814	
August 24	British forces sack and burn Washington, D.C.
November 23	Elbridge Gerry becomes the first vice president to die in office.

December 15	The Hartford Convention signals the end of the Federalist Party.
December 24	The Treaty of Ghent is signed, ending the War of 1812.

1815

January 30	Madison vetoes the charter of the bill for the Second Bank of the United States.

1817

January 1	The Second Bank of the United States opens for business.
February 12	James Monroe is elected president and Daniel D. Tomkins is elected vice president.
March 3	Madison vetoes the "Bonus Bill" for internal improvements.
March 4	Monroe is inaugurated as president.

1819

February 22	Spain sells the Floridas to the United States after General Andrew Jackson's seizure of Pensacola.

1820

March 3	Maine is admitted as a state according to the provisions of the Missouri Compromise.
March 6	Missouri is authorized to create a constitution and state government according to the provisions of the Missouri Compromise.

1821

March 4	James Monroe is inaugurated for his second term after running unopposed and winning reelection along with Vice President Daniel Tomkins.

1822

December 3	In his sixth annual message, Monroe underscores his support for a constitutional amendment regarding internal improvements.

1823

December 2	In the president's seventh annual message, he articulates the Monroe Doctrine.

1825

February 9	John Quincy Adams is elected president and John C. Calhoun is elected vice president, thus ending the Virginia Dynasty in the White House.
March 4	John Quincy Adams is inaugurated as president.

1826

July 4	Thomas Jefferson dies at his Monticello home. Hours later, John Adams dies at his home in Quincy. His last words are "Thomas Jefferson survives."

1831

July 4   James Monroe dies—the third of the first five presidents to die
                on July 4.

1836

June 28   James Madison, the last of the Virginia Dynasty presidents, dies
                at his home.

INTRODUCTION

The first five presidents of the United States are often called the Virginia Dynasty. Of the five—George Washington (president from 1789 to 1797), John Adams (president from 1797 to 1801), Thomas Jefferson (president from 1801 to 1809), James Madison (president from 1809 to 1817), and James Monroe (president from 1817 to 1825)—only one was not a native Virginian. John Adams hailed from Massachusetts. Also, he served merely one term, as opposed to the two terms served by each of the other four men. Adams, then, was the exception to the rule of the early executives. As a whole, the first administrations formed a coherent phase of development for the new office. The five men and their staffs faced a unique challenge in bringing the presidency and its powers, responsibilities, and personality to life. Their positions not only changed the nation at the time, but also set precedents for policies and procedures that continue to the present day. The original five presidents and their administrations are the first and best key to understanding the U.S. presidency as a whole.

BACKGROUND

For a useful perspective on the early presidents, these men must be placed in the greater context of their times. The nation over which they presided had only recently broken, as a series of separate states, from the colonial power Great Britain. Just fifteen years before George Washington's inauguration as president, he was leading troops against his former countrymen from Great Britain in the War of Independence. The British began colonizing North America in 1607, and soon possessed thirteen colonies along the Atlantic. For years relations between the colonies and homeland remained cordial. Beginning in 1763, however, Britain passed a series of measures intended to strengthen their authority on the colonies. The Stamp Act of 1765, for example, imposed a direct tax on North American colonists for the first time. The Townshend, Tea, and Intolerable Acts followed. Colonists opposed these measures and sought representation in the British Parliament to no avail. In 1775, the battles of Lexington and Concord pushed events toward war. Future president Washington, an experienced soldier, led the colonial troops. Future president James Monroe, barely more than a boy, was wounded and awarded a medal for bravery.

The experience of shared suffering and fighting drew the disparate colonies together. On July 4, 1776, the Continental Congress adopted a Declaration of Independence severing the tie between the colonies and Great Britain. The chief architect of the document, Thomas Jefferson, was also a future president. By signing the document—an act of heroic patriotism if the colonies won the war, and a lethal act of treason if they did not—the representatives of the various colonies united the people's hopes and futures. The Treaty of Paris in 1783, negotiated by a diplomatic team including future president John Adams, formalized independence after General Washington's victory in the war. The newly independent states did not seek close alliance, however. Instead, they chose to organize themselves in a loose confederation that allowed each state sovereignty and only the broadest cooperation among states for mutual benefit. The Articles of Confederation served as the mechanism to hold but not bind the states together.

The confederation seemed doomed from the start. Postwar complications, most related to debt and other financial woes, plagued the government. In less than a decade it was obvious that the problems would not solve themselves. After several smaller meetings, a Constitutional Convention convened to alter and correct the Articles of Confederation. The representatives of the states took their limited authority and ran with it; rather than modifying their current system, they devised an entirely new one. The result was the U.S. Constitution, fashioned largely by future president James Madison. After the convention released the document to the public, the next step was ratification. Critics and supporters debated the Constitution tirelessly. One sticking point for the opposition, in fact, was the power of the president under the new compact. The general consensus was that the hero of the War of Independence, George Washington himself, would lead the nation as the first chief executive. This, and the promise of a Bill of Rights, satisfied a number of concerned citizens. By the end of 1788, enough states had voted for the Constitution to make it the law of the land. Washington was quickly and unanimously elected president.

PERSONALITIES

The lives of the first five presidents, then, were inextricably linked to powerful events that predated the formation of the United States as a nation. Their service as military, political, and diplomatic leaders provided them with experience and credibility that led directly to the presidency. The infant country they inherited faced difficult questions about its own identity and purpose. As distinct individuals, each of the early presidents was suited by personality and intellect to address issues of the new nation somewhat differently. In turn, U.S. citizens responded to each of the gentlemen in unique and telling ways.

George Washington consciously groomed himself to fit the role of national figurehead. Handsome, gallant, aloof, and ever-cool, Washington impressed and intimidated men and charmed and dazzled women. He played to his strengths: appearance and action. He dressed impeccably and conducted himself with an almost royal formality. He chose to express himself in symbolic actions rather than in stirring speeches or detailed treatises, trusting his instinct for drama and timing. As for policymaking, the military man found he was not a natural. He preferred to delegate decisions to specialists or allow opponents to debate before him and try to convince him of their positions. As president he leaned on his cabinet, most heavily on his most trusted advisor, Alexander Hamilton, and allowed others to be the mouthpiece, arms, and legs of his policy. Though considered a Federalist, Washington's own bias ran against parties altogether. His well-developed sense of morality trumped a shallower grasp of statecraft. In short, Washington was less of a politician than a leader. He served as a unifying force when it was needed most. The breadth and depth of Virginia Dynasty political thought, however, would have to come with another president.

John Adams the man was something of an anti-Washington. Smaller in stature than the celebrated Washington and pudgier as well, Adams did not create the same royal image of leadership that his predecessor did. Due to age and health he did not trust himself as he once did in his fiery orator or precise diplomat days, and the lack of self-confidence showed. His efforts to provide stability in leadership placed his own administration at a disadvantage. In a position without self-appointed advisors or allies, Adams retreated. Washington drew respect, even adoration, for his distance from the citizenry; Adams drew fire for his own distance from the people and even physical distance from the capital. A partisan Federalist, the New Englander simply did not fit in the mold of Washington.

If Thomas Jefferson did not fit in Washington's mold, then he simply stretched it to his comfort. Jefferson was physically tall and impressive like Washington, but as comfortable and disheveled as the first executive was proper and staid. Jefferson thrived on control and exerted it in every facet of his life. More than any other of the five, Jefferson reflected an aggressive, distinctly southern ideal of masculinity. Washington's minimalist personality intrigued, but Jefferson's energetic presence captivated; he did with charisma even more than Washington had done with reputation. Behind the leader was a political theorist. He trusted a few close and equally brilliant advisors, but made final decisions on his own. Democratic-Republican ideology permeated his actions and created a popular, comprehensive, and long-lived vision for the country. Washington may have been the first president, but Jefferson was the intellectual father of the Virginia Dynasty presidents.

James Madison and James Monroe, both friends and neighbors of Jefferson's, provided equally interesting contrasts to the so-called Sage of Monticello. Jefferson visualized the big pictures; Madison did the details. Nearly as gifted a theorist as Jefferson, and definitely a more sophisticated constitutional mind, Madison lacked the vigor and force of personality of his predecessor. He had served as a politician but preferred to work behind the scenes in advising capacities. He was short and slight and quiet, a plain and bookish scholar. Monroe, on the other hand, the youngest of the five, evoked an old-fashioned appeal in outdated dress and uncomplicated personal appearances before the public. Monroe came full circle in terms of taste; he replaced Jefferson's egalitarian style and Madison's Spartan image with a Washington-like formality. And like Washington, Monroe placed his faith in his hard work rather than his intellect. His experience on the international stage as a diplomat and envoy also made him more accessible than his unassuming predecessor. Both Madison and Monroe remained dedicated to the Jeffersonian platform and proved to be consistent and successful executives.

CONSENSUS

The five men's differences in personalities, abilities, and experiences paled in comparison to their similarities. Four of the five were born into the landed Virginia aristocracy; Adams himself was considered gentry in his own Massachusetts. Each had intimate knowledge of the states' struggle to define themselves as independent and self-governing after the break with Britain, as each had served in some vital capacity during that process. All were in their late fifties or early sixties when they took office, as well. The early presidents also came to power during an era of consensus about a number of key issues that would be hotly contested in later generations. At the time the five gentlemen served as chief executive, general convictions about republicanism, suffrage, slavery, and manifest destiny were rarely if ever questioned.

Firstly, mainstream consensus among leaders and citizens alike supported a government composed of representatives of the people: a republic. Mechanisms such as indirect elections of senators allowed those with more specialized knowledge to make choices on higher positions. In the same vein, the electoral college emphasized that states, not individuals, chose presidents. There was a spectrum of opinion running from the views of the more elitist Federalists such as John Adams, who believed some representatives deserved lifetime positions and near-royal power, to the views of the more egalitarian Democratic-Republicans like Thomas Jefferson, who encouraged the participation of the people, but no one seriously questioned the fact that the nation was organized as an extended republic instead of a monarchy or pure democracy.

If most U.S. citizens accepted a republican form of government, they also accepted limitations on suffrage. Women and black men, for example, were denied participation. Abigail Adams wrote to her husband John and exhorted him to remember the women of the nation and the issues dear to their hearts, but nothing like an organized campaign for voting rights emerged. In the same sense that most men held women to be inferior in legal as well as social terms, most whites also accepted the idea of their own racial superiority over blacks and other minorities. An African-American man, even if he were free and not enslaved, could not vote in elections, and the idea did not receive widespread attention at all.

Racial assumptions did not lead all leaders and citizens to accept slavery, however. Many actively opposed it. Most arguments against slavery, however, were directed at its expansion across western territories; the ideal of abolishing it wholesale across the nation seemed impossible. The South was too dependent on the slavery system financially to let it go without a fight. Individual southerners made personal choices—Jefferson condemned the practice in his writings though he owned slaves himself, and Washington freed his own slaves in his will—and certain religious groups opposed it publicly, but no widespread movement threatened slavery where it was entrenched in the South. The general consensus in the nation was that slavery was in the South to stay.

Lastly, most people in the early republic assumed that it was their manifest destiny as citizens to expand the United States to natural borders such as the Gulf of Mexico and the Pacific Ocean. This meant expansion not only in the physical sense, but also in the racial (white) and religious (Christian) senses. In other words, a semispiritual nationalism swept the young country and convinced its people that they justifiably could remove and/or conquer, convert and/or kill, whatever peoples (Amerindian, Spanish, etc.) they encountered as they claimed North America. At its best the impulse was progress, and at its worst it was imperialism. Either way, few contested the belief that the United States was destined to control the continent.

DEBATES

Though the mainstream shared assumptions about republicanism, suffrage, slavery, and manifest destiny, the infant nation faced other issues that were quite controversial. Throughout the first five administrations, the presidents encountered recurring debates about the relationship among the branches of national government, the relationship between national and state governments, the growth of the domestic economy, the protection of civil liberties, the nature of international trade, the nature of diplomacy, the size of the military, the expansion of territory, and the policy toward native Americans. These issues, and the presidents' positions on them, formed the major themes of the early national presidency.

The executive, legislative, and judicial branches of the young country first had to determine how to relate to one another. In terms of the presidents, this raised three questions: How should the president relate to the people? The Congress? The Court? Washington addressed the question of the people very early in his first term, when John Adams and others pressed him to add elaborate titles to his name in the manner of royalty. Washington demurred and his supporters eventually agreed on "Mr. President" as the way to address him. Washington insisted on formality to prove he took the position and the nation it represented seriously; he feared that additional titles, however, would injure the republican nature of the government by placing one elected citizen too high above the others.

The presidents also had to determine how to work with the legislature. Washington began the trend of working closely with some congressmen, such as James Madison, when developing policies. At times Congress played watchdog against the president and pointed out when he seemed to overstep his constitutional authority, as when legislators protested James Madison's military actions in West Florida. At other times, though, the president checked overzealous representatives when they tried to expand their own power. James Monroe, for example, vetoed an internal improvements bill because he believed it could not be justified under a strict reading of the "general welfare" clause in the U.S. Constitution. The executive and legislative branches developed a sometimes-close, sometimes-adversarial relationship based on checks, balances, and common goals.

The Court also had a unique relationship with the presidents. The judiciary asserted its power during the Jefferson presidency, when the Court, led by Chief Justice John Marshall, set the precedent of judicial review in *Marbury v. Madison* in 1803. The Court claimed the right to review legislation to be certain each law was constitutional. The executive gained new power during the Madison administration, when the president pardoned militiamen obstructing the execution of a Court decision. The Court could determine constitutionality, it seemed, but the presidents could act on common sense. As one branch grew more powerful, the other moved to restore balance between them.

The presidents not only had to navigate the relationship of the three branches in the national government, but also had to determine the relationship between the national and state governments. Since the U.S. Constitution provided a federal system of governance, the national and state governments shared power and sovereignty. When should each dominate? How should they resolve differences? Washington and Adams chose to err on the side of the national government. Washington supported the assumption of state debts, effectively penalizing fiscally responsible states and rewarding poorly managed ones, and also wielded national forces against the Whiskey Insurrection, a regional uprising that began in Pennsylvania. Adams ignored the attempts of the Kentucky and Virginia state legislatures when they tried to nullify the censorship and severity of the Alien and Sedition Acts. On the other hand, Madison and Monroe shifted power back to the side of the states. Madison sided with Pennsylvania against the Supreme Court ruling in *Olmstead v. the Executrices of the Late David Rittenhouse,* and both Madison and Monroe tried to keep internal improvements in the hands of the affected states and not the national government. As with the individual branches of the national government, the nation/state relationship wavered back and forth as each side sought a workable balance.

Domestic economics remained another recurring theme in the debates of the early presidents. No issue better underscores the fact that the presidents struggled with difficult issues—and the knowledge that their actions would set precedents for future generations—than that of the national bank. George Washington was so uncertain that he requested two drafts of a response, one for signing a bill and one for vetoing it, because he was not sure that the U.S. Constitution allowed the creation of a national bank. In the end, he decided it did. Yet in Madison's presidency, the executive vetoed a recharter of the same bank on the basis of its unconstitutionality. He later changed his interpretation of the phrase "necessary and proper" and supported the bank. Clearly, the presidents were visiting and revisiting key questions about economics and constitutionality, not always with the same answers.

Presidents also faced problems regarding civil liberties. John Adams, for example, came under heavy fire for his censorship of journalists under the Alien and Sedition Acts. Citizens believed he had mistaken free speech for treason. Thomas Jefferson, in the attempt to keep merchants safe, actually created a police state for some time under the Embargo Acts and kept citizens hostage in their own harbors. Both presidents were harshly criticized for their actions and lost some political credibility because of them.

Managing trade, too, was a learning experience for the early presidents. Though the Federalists such as Washington and Adams tended toward protectionism, and the Democratic-Republicans such as Jefferson, Madison, and Monroe tended toward laissez-faire policies, this general rule did not always apply. Jefferson's Embargo Acts provide an excellent example of this. The president supported free trade—in fact, he even fought with Tripoli to ensure safe passage in the Mediterranean for U.S. merchants—and yet, when the British began boarding U.S. ships in U.S. waters, Jefferson decided to cut off trade altogether for safety's sake. His policy made prisoners of the people and wrecked the domestic economy in the process. Learning when, if ever, to interfere in the market was a trial-and-error process for the early executives.

The questions of trade were exacerbated by mercurial international relations. Adams and Jefferson held office during periods of quasi war, and Madison held office during war. Early attempts by Washington and Adams at neutrality soon fell away, replaced by both negative military actions (Jefferson in Tripoli, Madison in Florida) and positive negotiations (the Louisiana Purchase with Jefferson, the Treaty of Ghent with Madison). The presidents wandered into gray areas during this time. How much information did they have to disclose about diplomacy? Adams kept quiet about the XYZ affair for some time after the fact; Jefferson hoped Congress would look the other way at his unauthorized actions with regard to the Louisiana Purchase. What should drive foreign relations: philosophy or practicality? Adams and Jefferson both failed to support the newly independent Santo Domingo and its revolutionary leader, Toussaint L'Overture, because such ideological action did not best serve U.S. interests. How much could the executive do militarily without declaring war, a power held by the legislature? Madison pushed the envelope in Florida, and General Andrew Jackson, under President Monroe, nearly did the same thing. How far should U.S. influence extend? The Monroe Doctrine proposed that Latin America was the business only of the United States and not of European powers. As the United States was alternately insulted, attacked, and appreciated on the world stage, the presidents positioned themselves to try to act in the interest of the nation.

International relations sparked old concerns about the military. One of the issues that predated and in many ways informed the War of Independence was a fear of standing armies. Washington's advance against the Whiskey Insurrection awoke this fear again. Adams felt he had to prepare for war, and created a department for the navy. Jefferson, though committed to balancing the national budget, faced an ongoing struggle over the size and funding of the navy and the army, as congressmen continued to worry about what a standing military meant for the freedom of the citizens. Adams also faced a different issue: partisanship in the armed forces. He saw military appointments as political tools, and planned for a geographically diverse, bipartisan staff for Lieutenant General George Washington. Washington, however, had other plans based on experience and affection. The two clashed about appointments, but the heart of the issue was the very nature of the military. Madison, a lifetime civilian, had to try to earn the respect of the soldiers who fought the War of 1812. Monroe faced his own problems with insubordination and unauthorized activity by General Andrew Jackson. The executives learned how to be (and not to be) military leaders as they went along, often under the scrutiny of an international audience.

Military questions also surrounded issues of expansion. The Jeffersonian ideal of an ever expanding republic began with the Louisiana Purchase, an act the president himself admitted was unconstitutional. From there, controversial occupations (Madison in West Florida, Jackson under Monroe in Pensacola) utilized military force in ways many legislators denounced. In the end, however, circumstances saved the United States from further quandaries; neither the French nor the Spanish had the resources readily available to strengthen their North American claims, so the United States eventually expanded to its natural borders through diplomacy. The general momentum behind manifest destiny made such expansion a natural, popular direction for executives to follow.

Native Americans, of course, did not benefit from the manifest destiny drive. Early policies such as Jefferson's "Indian Civilization Campaign"— which, though condescending and paternalistic on many levels, still respected the property rights of Amerindians—dissolved in the face of such laws as the Georgia Compact of 1802, which extinguished native land titles within Georgia state borders. By Monroe's presidency, many leaders discussed forced removal as a possible policy toward native Americans. Monroe held to the Jeffersonian ideal of rights protection, but even he had begun to think in terms of removal—voluntary, though, not coerced—as the best for Amerindians and their safety. The protests of American Indian leaders fell on deaf ears. The first presidential policy toward native Americans was arguably the best; each successive administration seemed to witness a devolving respect for Amerindian rights.

CONTRIBUTIONS

The Virginia Dynasty presidents debated issues such as the relationship among the branches of nation government, the relationship between national and state governments, the growth of the domestic economy, the protection of civil liberties, the nature of international trade, the nature of diplomacy, the size of the military, the expansion of territory, and the policy toward native Americans. Some of their positions prevailed and left lasting contributions to U.S. tradition. Jefferson's Louisiana Purchase became multiple states forming the heart of the nation, for example, and the Monroe Doctrine guided U.S. policy toward Latin America and the rest of the globe ever since its first articulation in 1823. The presidents also set lasting precedents for the way later executives conducted themselves. Washington started the tradition of voluntary retirement after serving two terms, which was followed until Franklin D. Roosevelt was elected to four terms in the early twentieth century. The two-term limit later became law. Despite Washington's dislike of parties, the other presidents also brought partisanship to the position. The informal process of naming advisors evolved into the cabinet system, which survives to the present day (though perhaps in a less vital form due to the expansion of the advice network surrounding the presidents).

Other contributions by the first five executives were not long-lived. The national bank died a natural death, though the current Federal Reserve system could be considered its institutional offspring. Reticence about building and maintaining a national army, a concern in the back of the presidents' minds even when they chose to expand the military, is no longer a widely debated sentiment. The Missouri Compromise, one in a series of stopgap measures to solve the slavery problem, did not halt the impending crisis of the Civil War. Slavery did not survive the century. Strong presidential support of states' rights seems like a moot point as the national government has gained control of the federal system. The election mechanisms of presidents and vice presidents also changed; the two positions detached from each other during the period with the passage of the Twelfth Amendment, and now states allow popular elections to determine their allocation of electoral college votes.

The founding fathers of the U.S. presidency faced perhaps the most challenging moments in the history of the institution as they made daily decisions that set long-term precedents for their position and their nation. The five men are remarkable for their presence of mind during this delicate time. They acted with an unusual unity of views and a dedication to consistency, actively building on their predecessors' administrations to form a coherent concept of executive power and responsibility. The Virginia Dynasty even retired itself, in a sense, when Monroe's chosen secretary of state, New Englander John Quincy Adams, followed him to office. The period began on a high note, a triumphant general's unanimous election, and ended on one as well, Monroe's successful Era of Good Feelings. The very different individuals who served as the first presidents at different points served as allies and critics of each other; it is a credit to them and their sense of citizenship that they died as friends as well as statesmen.

1

GEORGE WASHINGTON

(1789–1797)

INTRODUCTION

Historians, political scientists, and public figures have tried for centuries to capture the essence of the first president of the United States and his precedent-setting administration. In the end, however, George Washington did perhaps the best job of such an overview himself as he ended his days as chief executive. On September 17, 1796, President Washington offered the nation his Farewell Address, a summation of his two terms in office and a statement of his hopes for the young United States. The address revisited the major themes of Washington's presidency: his appreciation for public symbolism; his realism about his own political shortcomings; his wariness of power abuses; his desire for national unity; his emphasis on international neutrality; and his concern about internal factionalism. These themes provide a useful window through which each of the key policy questions during Washington's administration can be understood.

The Farewell Address opens with Washington's announcement that he would neither seek nor accept another term as the chief executive of the United States. Beyond his own personal desire to return to his home at Mount Vernon, Washington was also motivated by a concern for the pattern his tenure in office would set. He worried that popular leaders in the future might retain the position for multiple terms until the presidency came to resemble a monarchy. He knew that if he limited his own terms to two, he would set a precedent for others to follow. This he did. Presidents voluntarily followed the two-term limit until 1940 and 1944, when Franklin D. Roosevelt ran for and won his third and fourth terms, respectively. On February 27, 1951, the Twenty-Second Amendment made Washington's two-term precedent law.

The act of willingly relinquishing power in a free society—for the purpose, in fact, of preserving that freedom—meant a great deal to Washington. Leaving executive office while still popular was one means of doing this. Throughout his life, in the many leadership roles he played, he showed a keen appreciation and ability for these kinds of symbolic actions. He recognized that an elected official could say much and sway many simply by acting or, perhaps more importantly, declining to act. An excellent example of this sensitivity to symbolism is the president's position on the issue of titles. When his vice president elect, John Adams, led an initiative to require both houses of Congress to refer to the president as "His Highness the President of the United States of America, and Protector of their Liberties," Washington disapproved. He believed that elected officials should err on the side of republican simplicity. The president, to his mind, should be called simply "Mr. President."

He also realized that denying this title, and the power it suggested, did not need to be a public affair. He remained silent and let others make the arguments for him. When it became clear that the Adams proposal would not prevail, Washington let it die a quiet death. By doing so, he refrained from accepting unwanted titles and yet preserved harmony and spared Adams a public battle with his executive. Both Washington's position against the title and his action against it, or lack thereof, exemplifies the president's concern with symbolic behavior. He did not, however, assume that symbolic actions could take the place of policy initiatives.

Following the theme of symbolic action in the Farewell Address, the second topic of Washington's speech is one of humility. The president reminded the citizens that he had only offered the nation "exertions of which a very fallible judgment was capable."[1] From others, such modesty might seem insincere. But George Washington was an unusually self-aware man, one who appreciated that he was often less suited to be the captain of a ship of state than to be its figurehead.

Scholars since have agreed that Washington's historical importance rested primarily in who he was, not what he did. As commander in chief of the Continental army, Washington was a competent but unspectacular tactician. He provided great physical presence but little substantive contribution to the Constitutional Convention as that body's presiding officer. As president of the United States, Washington's gift was bearing, demeanor, and dignity. As historian Forrest McDonald once admitted, "He was cool and aloof, and tall, broad-shouldered, and narrow-hipped; and in a country populated mainly by people who were hot-tempered and overly confidential, and short and fat, such attributes were not to be taken lightly."[2] In short, Washington looked like a national leader, both in symbolic action and simple physical appearance. And he knew it.

When the time came to determine policy, though, President Washington recognized his own limitations. He therefore gathered around himself the leading and opposing minds of the day to advise him. Among these were John Adams, his vice president, Henry Knox, the superintendent of war, and Edmund Randolph, Washington's attorney general. The key members of Washington's inner circle, however, were Alexander Hamilton, secretary of the treasury, Thomas Jefferson, secretary of state, and James Madison, Virginia congressman. When Washington faced a decision on issues of state, he would listen to the arguments of these men and choose among their competing positions. Then, due to the superior abilities of his advisors and his own sense of presidential decorum and disinterestedness, Washington often allowed the "winner" of these debates to spearhead the initiative in question with the president's discreet blessing and support.

As far as policy was concerned, the most influential man in the Washington administration was undoubtedly Alexander Hamilton. Hamilton had literally grown to adulthood at Washington's side, first as the general's aide-de-camp during the War of Independence and later as the youngest member of the Constitutional Convention. Unlike the native Virginia planter he served, the West Indies-born Hamilton made New York his home and commercial enterprise his passion. Hamilton nonetheless shared with his mentor a concern for the unity and power of the United States internally and internationally.

Pro-British at heart, Hamilton admired the English system from its monarchy to its banking scheme, and his sympathies invariably leaned to the side of consolidating national power and expanding governmental authority. Washington appointed him secretary of the treasury and gave him the freedom to propose policy and, with Washington's consent, actively promote it. Hamilton's efforts prevailed not only with economic issues such as the public credit and the national bank, but also with questions of foreign policy such as neutrality. For all intents and purposes, when Hamilton spoke with the voice of the secretary of the treasury, on matters economic or otherwise, he also spoke with the support of the president of the United States. No other advisor could claim such power.

Alexander Hamilton's ideal citizen for the young United States was the banker/businessman, anxious to invest in native industries and stimulate the growing economy with the help of the national government. Conversely, Thomas Jefferson's ideal citizen was the yeoman farmer, the self-sufficient man of the soil who guarded his liberties from the encroachment of the government with constant vigilance. Like Washington, Jefferson also came from a family of Virginia planters. Comparable backgrounds did not always breed similar views, however. Just as Washington feared factionalism, Jefferson feared nationalism. His concern about the concentration of power and the tyranny of the government made him more sympathetic to France and its revolution than to Britain and its monarchy. Because he worried about the government's abuse of authority, he called for a strict reading of the Constitution. Without following its letters and exercising only the powers it enumerated, he argued, the United States had no effective means of protecting the people against those in power. His positions placed him in opposition to most of Alexander Hamilton's ideas and thus to most of Washington's policies. As Washington's secretary of state, Jefferson spent much of his time in the cabinet playing the devil's advocate.

In a way, the four most prominent figures in the Washington era formed two pairs, each consisting of a teacher and a student. Just as George Washington mentored Alexander Hamilton, the former the consummate public figure and the latter the classic man behind the throne, Thomas Jefferson, the elegant politician, mentored James Madison, the dedicated theorist. Both Washington and Jefferson often found themselves following the lead of the younger men they had helped to train. James Madison, like Thomas Jefferson, often criticized the policies proposed by Hamilton and supported by Washington. The two together led an impressive, but frequently unsuccessful, opposition to the president's position.

As the architect of the Constitution, Madison's concerns rested heavily with the federal system. He understood how the United States balanced national and state governments in order to protect citizens from both levels of government and from each other. Many of Washington's positions drew power to the national government in general and to the executive in particular, destabilizing the balance for which Madison had fought. Like Jefferson, Madison also believed that Washington allowed himself too much latitude when interpreting the Constitution. Madison accepted invitations to voice his opinion to the president, and he also seized opportunities in Congress and popular publications to offer policy proposals counter to the president's. His recurrent opposition to Washington helped to form the basis of the political party system. Nonetheless, Washington considered him a key advisor and personal friend.

It was James Madison, in fact, who put the president's ideas to paper and wrote Washington's Farewell Address. Based on Washington's request, the third theme Madison wove into the speech after symbolic action and personal humility was that of vigilance. Citizens should be prepared, the president warned, to stop any abuse of power and "correct a degeneracy."[3] Washington delivered the advice in the form of a prayer, but his message remained clear: citizens should stay active in the life of the United States and, by their activity, dissuade those who would collect and abuse authority. This idea again remembers the question of presidential title, when Washington failed to be seduced by the trappings of royalty. It also anticipates the following theme, that of national unity.

If Washington held one goal above others for his administration, he wanted to encourage citizens from the disparate states to see themselves as members of one united nation. In the Farewell Address, he reminded the people that they were "Children of one common Country."[4] The unifying experience of the War of Independence, coupled with the disintegration of such unity under the Articles of Confederation, impressed upon Washington the need to make a country out of a group of states. His policy initiatives reflected this goal.

First, Washington agreed with Alexander Hamilton's proposal for the national government to assume the debts of the individual states. This measure created controversy in two ways, first by punishing the responsible states and rewarding the indebted ones, and second by loosely interpreting the Constitution and its "necessary and proper" clause. Despite the opposition, Washington moved forward in the effort to set aside state consciousness, respond to problems on a nationwide level, and create a viable national economy. Washington proved willing to consolidate power in the national government in order to foster greater unity.

If Washington's public credit policy followed from his national unity concern, then the national bank initiative followed from the public credit policy. Again, Hamilton provided Washington with a plan that promised increased economic opportunity for the nation. Critics' concerns about a national bank's unfairness to individuals and regions, not to mention the unconstitutionality of exploiting implied powers to incorporate such a bank, fell before Washington's desire to make one people, and one economy, of many. Once more, Washington's position prevailed.

National unity remained a primary interest for George Washington, but it was not the only one. His concern for peace, too, is reflected in his departure speech. After discussing national unity, the president's Farewell Address continues with comments regarding neutrality. The president hoped "That we may avoid connecting ourselves with the Politics of any Nation," and that "we may be always prepared for War, but never unsheath the sword except in self defence."[5] Indeed, he intended his policies regarding the public credit and the national bank, in part, to encourage international commerce and friendly economic relations between nations. Washington saw other nations as potential trading associates and investors, business partners interacting with mutual respect for mutual benefit. He feared, however, that relations with other countries would lure the United States into political and military matters in which it had no interest or business.[6] Not only would such alliances be costly and complex, but they could also be dangerous. Nations such as

France or Britain possessed larger and more experienced armies and navies than the fledgling United States. Washington worried that the United States at best would overextend itself, at worst would lose itself, in the battles of Europe. Whenever possible, he stressed his belief that the United States must hold itself apart.

This came into high relief when events changed in Europe with France's Revolution and declaration of war against Britain. President Washington did not want to believe that the preexisting Franco-American treaty required the United States to involve itself in the fighting. Critics, on the other hand, argued that it did. They protested against breaking the treaty, abandoning a past ally, and allowing the president, who had no constitutional authority to decide the matter, to set foreign policy. The opposition could not trump Washington's—and the United States citizenry's—desire for peace, however. Washington's Proclamation of Neutrality kept the nation out of war and set precedents for future presidents and their role in international affairs.

If George Washington feared alliances and international intrigues as the gravest danger to the United States from abroad, then he also feared internal factionalization as the greatest threat to the United States from within its borders. He stressed this concern in the Farewell Address, warning citizens of the forces "tending to divide us into parties, and ultimately productive of all those evils and horrors which proceed from faction."[7] He saw the root of faction in his own cabinet, growing between Alexander Hamilton and Thomas Jefferson, becoming more organized and popularly supported with each year. What he dreaded the most took place in Pennsylvania with the uprising known as the Whiskey Insurrection.

Washington's call for order did not settle the people's violent protest of the excise tax on distilled spirits, and his use of militias did not weaken the citizens' interest in self-created political societies. Though the western counties of Pennsylvania eventually quieted, Washington had no victory. The precedents he set regarding standing armies and law enforcement were unintentional, and the message he meant to send about political parties went unheard. His short-term policy success was also his long-term policy failure. He still tasted the bitterness of that defeat when he presented his Farewell Address and warned that internal divisions could tear apart the nation.

After reviewing the themes of symbolism, humility, unity, neutrality, and solidarity, Washington ended his departure speech on a personal note. He said that he left the executive office "with undefiled hands" and "an uncorrupted heart."[8] In the final analysis, the Virginia planter was justified in the pride he felt about his two presidential terms. The nation had suffered an uncertain period under the Articles of Confederation, and Washington had led the country into a new era of internal stability and international recognition under the Constitution of the United States. He had chosen a path between egalitarian simplicity and royal majesty to create a chief executive position with honor, respect, and authority. His actions had set the standard on many aspects of the office, from when to accept dinner invitations to how to correspond with foreign heads of state.

Yet his tenure in office also contained contradictions. He attacked the abuse of authority, yet he expanded the blueprint for presidential power by calling the militias, declaring neutrality, and, in the case of the Jay Treaty in 1794, even invoking executive privilege, all without constitutional authority. He took the protection of the law of the land very seriously, but his actions pushed the envelope for loose constructionism and implied powers, weakening the letter of the Constitution and opening it for a variety of creative interpretations.

He did, however, meet his goal of creating a national consciousness from regional and local interests, and this remains one of his greatest accomplishments. Perhaps his greatest achievement, though, was delegating responsibility to a brilliant cabinet that became the birthplace of the modern party system and the training ground for two other noteworthy presidents, Thomas Jefferson and James Madison.

NOTES

1. George Washington. 17 September 1796. Farewell Address. The George Washington Papers at the Library of Congress. <http://memory.loc.gov/ammem/gwhtml/gwhome.html>.

2. Forrest McDonald, *The Presidency of George Washington* (Lawrence: University Press of Kansas, 1974), p. x.

3. George Washington. 17 September 1796. Farewell Address. The George Washington Papers at the Library of Congress. <http://memory.loc.gov/ammem/gwhtml/gwhome.html>.

4. Ibid.

5. Ibid.

6. Washington emphasized his aversion to alliances that could entangle the young nation in his Farewell Address: "The nation which indulges towards another a habitual hatred or a habitual fondness is in some degree a slave." Ibid.

7. Ibid.

8. Ibid.

THE PRESIDENT'S TITLE

As the first president of the United States, George Washington set the precedent for many aspects of the office, from how to deliver the State of the Union Address to when to attend tea parties. One of the very first challenges Washington faced involved the question of presidential title.

Lawmakers in the Senate and House of Representatives were uncertain how to address the chief executive. Although at first blush the issue seems rather trivial, both sides appreciated that it reflected a deeper argument between competing visions of the new nation.

Washington's personal view of presidential leadership drew partly from Roman inspiration. He modeled himself on the character of Cincinnatus, the ancient general who left his farm in 458 BCE to successfully command Rome's army and then, although he had the means to make himself emperor, instead returned to his plow and humble status as citizen. Washington himself intended to once again assume the mantle of gentleman farmer after his period of public service ended. Like Cincinnatus, he did not intend to abuse his popularity and seek personal power. He served only when the people called on him to do so.

Yet the Roman republican model of citizen-leader did not wholly fit the historical situation of the fledgling United States. Citizens had gone from the experience of a king as leader under British rule to an almost nonexistent executive authority under the Articles of Confederation. Washington believed that he had to strike a balance between overemphasizing his role with royal trappings and underemphasizing his duties by quiet modesty. The "patriot king" model of a leader above faction and without corruption, best reflected at the time by the writings of Henry St. John, Lord Bolingbroke, appealed to Washington as a more modern and celebratory version of Cincinnatus. But "patriot" and "king" were two very different concepts. On which side should he err?

Washington's vice president, John Adams, forced the president's hand on the issue almost immediately. Then just vice president elect, Adams arrived at the Senate on April 21, 1789, and two days later opened the debate on presidential title. Adams argued that republican simplicity— in this case, referring to the highest elected official simply as "Mr. President"—did not do the appropriate honor to the chief executive. In the process, Adams continued, such a title did not show proper respect to the electoral procedure, and the electors themselves, that determined who became president.

Adams' concerns went deeper than paying proper homage to Washington and his position, however. As his letter to Nathaniel Sargent reflects, Adams worried about the quality of individuals who would be drawn to public office in general and the highest national offices in particular. He feared that, as under the Articles of Confederation, people would see national office only as a stepping-stone for greater power in their home states. Only the less ambitious and less able would remain to seek election to the national government as the pinnacle of their careers in public service. Adams hoped that titles would be one way of enticing the best and brightest to seek higher office. At the same time, the best and brightest would be sure to maintain the strength of the national government against the vigorous states.

Just as he worried about the internal health of the nation, Adams also considered the future role of the United States on the world stage. As his letter to Jabez Brown explains, Adams saw the president's lack of title as a dangerous obstacle to assuming his rightful place among the leaders of the world. Would monarchies such as England conduct business and diplomacy with a chief executive who was simply known as "Mr. President" to his people? Adams thought not. He imagined that economic and diplomatic disasters would afflict the nation unless U.S. citizens gave their head of state all of the equipment, including titles, that would place him on a level playing field with the leaders of the world. To this end, Adams urged the legislature to agree to a title for the president such as "His Highness the President of the United States of America, and Protector of their Liberties."

Staunch republicans followed the Roman example far more stringently than even Washington. They saw Adams's suggestion as a betrayal of the very founding of the new nation. Why did the states rebel against England's rule, they asked, if the citizens intended to set up another monarchy? Thomas Jefferson and James Madison, for example, viewed titles as unwarranted pretension. They even feared that a new aristocracy, like the gentry of Britain, might evolve on American soil. Unlike Adams, who feared that the national government would lose ground to the state governments, Jefferson and Madison worried that too much power could naturally consolidate in the hands of the chief executive. Adding special titles to the president's position might only hasten such consolidation and, ultimately, tyranny. They argued for the simplicity and modesty of "Mr. President," and they prevailed.

In his years in office, Washington many times walked a delicate tightrope between grand gestures and Spartan simplicity. In this case, however, he was not conflicted. Like Jefferson and Madison, Washington did not see any additional titles as necessary for his position. The situation was nonetheless a delicate one, since Washington was, in effect, opposed to his new vice president trying to honor him. True to form, Washington remained rather quiet on the issue in public and agreed with the republicans in private.

As it turned out, public statements from Washington were not necessary. Before the Senate had resolved the issue, the House of Representatives officially addressed Washington as "Mr. President" in a communication and effectively set the precedent. Adams' prophecy of disaster did not come true; in fact, Jefferson and Madison's prediction about an ever stronger executive conform more closely to reality. With the issue of titles decided, though, the presidency has never developed into a royal role.

THE PRESIDENT'S POSITION: AGAINST TITLES

Journal of the Senate of the United States of America, 1789–1873
Thursday, May 14, 1789

... The committee, appointed the 9th instant, "to consider and report under what title it will be proper for the Senate to address the President of the United States of America," reported, that, in the opinion of the committee, it will be proper thus to address the President: His Highness the President of the United States of America, and Protector of their Liberties.

Which report was postponed;

And the following resolve was agreed to, to wit:

From a decent respect for the opinion and practice of civilized nations, whether under monarchical or republican forms of government, whose custom is to annex titles of respectability to the office of their Chief Magistrate; and that, on intercourse with foreign nations, a due respect for the majesty of the people of the United States may not be hazarded by an appearance of singularity, the Senate have been induced to be of opinion, that it would be proper to annex a respectable title to the office of President of the United States; but the Senate, desirious of preserving harmony with the House of Representatives, where the practice lately observed in presenting an address to the President was without the addition of titles, think it proper, for the present, to act in conformity with the practice of the House:

Therefore, Resolved, That the present address be "To the President of the United States," without addition of title.

A motion was made to strike out the preamble as far as the words "But the Senate;" which passed in the negative:

And, on the motion for the main question, it passed in the affirmative. ...

See *Annuals of Congress*, Library of Congress. <http://memory.loc.gov/ammem/amlaw/lwac.html>.

James Madison to Thomas Jefferson
New York, 23 May 1789

... My last inclosed copies of the President's inauguration Speech and the answer of the House of Representatives. I now add the answer of the Senate. It will not have escaped you that the former was addressed with a truly republican simplicity to G.W. Presidt. of the U.S. The latter follows the example, with the omission of the personal name, but without any other than the constitutional title. The proceeding on this point was in the House of Representatives spontaneous. The imitation by the Senate was exhorted. The question became a serious one between the two houses. J. Adams espoused the cause of titles with great earnestness. His friend R.H. Lee altho elected as a republican enemy to an aristocratic constitution was a most zealous second. The projected title was—His Highness the President of the U.S. and protector of their liberties. Had the project succeeded it would have subjected the President to a severe dilemma and given a deep wound to our infant government . . .

See *The Papers of Thomas Jefferson*, vol. 15, *27 March 1789 to 30 November 1789*, ed. Julian P. Boyd (Princeton: Princeton University Press, 1958), pp. 147–148.

Thomas Jefferson to James Madison
Paris, 29 July 1789

Dear Sir

I wrote to you on the 22nd. Since that I have received yours of the 23d. of May. The president's title as proposed by the senate was the most superlatively ridiculous thing I ever heard of. It is a proof the more of the justice of the character given by Doctr. Franklin of my friend: "Always an honest man, often a great one, but sometimes absolutely mad." I wish he could have been here during the late scenes. If he could then have had one fibre of aristocracy left in his frame he would have been a project subject for bedlam. . . .

See *The Papers of Thomas Jefferson*, vol. 15, *27 March 1789 to 30 November 1789*, ed. Julian P. Boyd (Princeton: Princeton University Press, 1958), pp. 315–316.

JOHN ADAMS: FOR TITLES

John Adams to Nathaniel Sargent
New York, 22 May 1789

Dear Sir

I received with pleasure your friendly letter of the 25th of April. . . . You call to my recollection an idea suggested to you in conversation "that we are in great danger." I wish I was quite delivered at this hour from such an apprehension. It would require a long letter to explain all the reasons I have for such thoughts, but I may say one thing that will go a great way. The Superiority, the Sovereignty of the national gov't if it is in words ascertained it is not in fact secured. The state governments have so much Power still, as to make the whole a Composition of thirteen Omnipotences against one Omnipotence. And to my Mortification, I find my general expectations too much unified in a general aversion, timidity, or something to assume a tone which might supply some aspects—I do not see a resolution nor an Inclination in Gentlemen to make seats in the new Gov't objects of Ambition or Desire. Seats in the new Governments are considered still as steps toward promotion at home. . . . Despondency is not one of my Characteristics: on the contrary the world in general suppose me too much inclined to be Sanguine. . . . Can there be a greater danger than that which arises from Sovereignty. . . . If the Sovereignty is uncertain and unknown then the Law must be uncertain and unknown. Who can tell where the Sovereignty of this Country is! Is it in the National Government or the State Govts. By the Constitution. . . . it is in the National Government!. . . . Is there not danger from another quarter hinted at before? Is there Pleasure, Proffit or honour in any Station in the new Govt sufficient to make it an object to the greatest best Men? If not will they not all leave it as they did the old Congress, for more agreeable, more profitable, and more honorable Places at home among their Friends, Families and Estates? And whereas these Men are there will the Honor, the Power, the Sovereignty really be—are these dangers real or imaginary? . . .

See *The Adams Papers*, microfilm, The Adams Manuscript Trust, Boston, Massachusetts Historical Society, reel 115.

John Adams to Jabez Brown
Richmond/New York, June 26, 1789

. . . It is in vain to talk of oversights . . . the actors are inexperienced. Much light has been obtained and diffused by the dissensions which have . . . [caused] delay—and there is no remedy but patience. Why will you afflict the modesty of any gentleman by expecting that they will give themselves Titles. They expect that you their creator will do Them honor. They are no quakers I warrant you and will not be offended if you assert your own majesty; by giving your own representatives in the executive authority the title of majesty. Many of these quakers think Highness not high enough, among whom I own I am one. In my opinion the American President will soon be introduced . . . in half the theatres of Europe and be held up to ridicule. It would not be extravagant the prophesy that the want of titles may cost this Country fifty thousand lives and twenty millions of money within twenty years. . . .

See *The Adams Papers*, microfilm, The Adams Manuscript Trust, Boston, Massachusetts Historical Society, reel 115.

PUBLIC CREDIT

The Washington administration inherited a new country deep in debt at the international, national, and state levels. Of these three, the issue of state debts became the most controversial. However the nation government chose to handle the question, it would open a new chapter in national-state government relations.

The War of Independence had cost a great deal, and the national government under the Articles of Confederation had lacked the authority to levy and collect taxes to pay for it. In 1780, the confederation was all but bankrupt. Superintendent of Finance Robert Morris therefore called on the individual states to fund the army directly. When the states did so, and tried to supply back pay to the soldiers as well, they accumulated debts rivaling those owed by Congress.

By the time of the Washington presidency, the states had attacked their debt problems in different ways. Some had all but paid their debts while others had nearly crippled their state economies in the effort to do so, and still others had allowed interest to accrue without taking action. In a way, the inequality of state debts was the crux of the issue. Could the national government—far from debt-free itself—find a way to treat each state justly, rewarding those that had practiced sound financial planning and punishing those that had behaved irresponsibly? Or should all states be treated equally, regardless of the economic strides individual states had made?

Either answer presupposed that it was, indeed, the national government's role to solve the problem. Of course the bankruptcy of the confederation had caused much of the debt in the first place. But the new United States of America also suffered as a whole from individual states' debts. In order for national and international commerce to blossom, the states and their citizens had to inspire confidence and encourage investment. Moreover, the governments at all levels could hardly enforce contracts among its citizens when they could not meet the obligations of contracts themselves. The debt problem required solution before a healthy economy could develop.

President Washington turned to his secretary of the treasury, Alexander Hamilton, for insight in how to handle the state debt question. Hamilton responded with his 1790 "Report on Public Credit," which outlined a plan for the national government to assume all state debts. The report included a strong nationalistic theme, reminding readers that the debt incurred in the war was "the price of liberty," and discouraging them from judging individual states' debts and fiscal policies. Hamilton suggested that the national government exercise its powers of taxation to raise duties on luxuries. The nation would pay the state debts with the income from these taxes. Seeing this as an opportunity to bolster confidence in the American name and economy both at home and overseas, Washington supported Hamilton's proposal.

Hamilton's plan was not without controversy, however. Though few believed that the state debt issue could be ignored, others thought Hamilton's plan unfair in principle and unworkable in practice. James Madison, for example, immediately thought of his native state Virginia when he considered the report. Unlike Massachusetts and South Carolina, states that had allowed their debts to run rampant with little control, Virginia had taken pains to try to solve its problem on its own. Rather than reward Virginia for its responsible management, Madison lamented that Hamilton's plan would punish Virginians for their foresight and plunder them to pay for their less considerate neighbors. Madison feared not only the immediate economic repercussions of such a plan, but also the larger moral the story would teach the states.

Madison and his colleagues such as Thomas Jefferson and Henry Lee worried about more than simple fairness, however. First, they wondered if the nation's emphasis on state debts overshadowed the question of international debts. They believed that other nations would have to find the United States to be a solvent and stable business partner before the nation could take its place on the world stage, and the most direct route to that solvency and stability rested in first paying off debts to international creditors. Since much of the states' debts were owed to U.S. citizens, they thought that state debts should be handled after international ones.

Second, and perhaps more importantly, Madison and friends doubted whether Hamilton's plan, once instituted, would even work. They found Hamilton's suggestion of taxing multiple, particularly foreign, luxury items, combining the revenue, and then apportioning it to pay the debts of different states to be overly complicated, especially when the records concerning what each state owed to whom were murky at best. The disorganized record keeping conducted by the states, and the swelling bureaucracy needed by the national government to untangle it, not to mention the added confusion created by speculators who had bought and sold in the market and divorced original holders from their certificates, promised to challenge the merits of any plan. Madison and his colleagues feared that Hamilton's proposal would not meet the challenge.

Opponents of the plan did not, however, deny that the nation needed to take some action to solve the problem. After two more reports from the secretary of the treasury, the national government instituted the plan and assumed the state debts. Hamilton oversaw the process with the continued blessing—or, to use his word, "aegis," or shield—provided by George Washington. The plan, complicated though it was, eventually met its goals. In doing so, the national government also consolidated more power and subtly shifted the federal balance away from state authority and toward its own. By helping the states, the national government brought them more squarely under its control.

THE PRESIDENT'S POSITION: FOR THE ASSUMPTION OF STATE DEBTS

Alexander Hamilton, "Report on Public Credit" January 1790

... In the opinion of the Secretary, the wisdom of the House, in giving their explicit sanction to the proposition which has been stated, cannot but be applauded by all, who will seriously consider, and trace through their obvious consequences, these plain and undeniable truths.

That exigencies are to be expected to occur, in the affairs of nations, in which there will be a necessity for borrowing.

That loans in times of public danger, especially from foreign war, are found an indispensible resource, even to the wealthiest of them.

And that in a country, which, like this, is possessed of little active wealth, or in other words, little monied capital, the necessity for the resource, must, in such emergencies, be proportionably urgent.

And as on the one hand, the necessity for borrowing in particular emergencies cannot be doubted, so on the other, it is equally evident, that to be able to borrow upon *good terms*, it is essential that the credit of a nation should be well established....

If the maintenance of public credit, then, be truly so important, the next enquiry which suggests itself is, by what means it is to be effected? The ready answer to which question is, by good faith, by punctual performance of contracts. States, like individuals, who observe their engagements, are respected and trusted....

This reflection derives additional strength from the nature of the debt of the United States. It was the price of liberty. The faith of America has been repeatedly pledged for it, and with solemnities, that give peculiar force to the obligation. There is indeed reason to regret that it has not hitherto been kept; that the necessities of the war, conspiring with inexperience in the subjects of finance, produced direct infractions; and that the subsequent period has been a continued scene of negative violation, or non-compliance. But a diminution of this regret arises from the reflection, that the last seven years have exhibited an earnest and uniform effort, on the part of the government of the union, to retrieve the national credit, by doing justice to the creditors of the nation; and that the embarrassments of a defective constitution, which defeated this laudable effort, have ceased. . . .

It cannot but merit particular attention, that among ourselves the most enlightened friends of good government are those, whose expectations are the highest.

To justify and preserve their confidence; to promote the increasing respectability of the American name; to answer the calls of justice; to restore landed property to its due value; to furnish new resources both to agriculture and commerce; to cement more closely the union of the states; to add to their security against foreign attack; to establish public order on the basis of an upright and liberal policy. These are the great and invaluable ends to be secured, by a proper and adequate provision, at the present period, for the support of public credit. . . .

The Secretary, after mature reflection on this point, entertains a full conviction, that an assumption of the debts of the particular states by the union, and a like provision for them, as for those of the union, will be a measure of sound policy and substantial justice.

It would, in the opinion of the Secretary, contribute, in an eminent degree, to an orderly, stable and satisfactory arrangement of the national finances. . . .

The sum may, in the opinion of the Secretary, be obtained from the present duties on imports and tonnage, with the additions, which without any possible disadvantages either to trade, or agriculture, may be made on wines, spirits, including those distilled within the United States, and tea and coffee. . . .

That the articles which have been enumerated, will, better than most others, bear high duties, can hardly be a question. They are all of them in reality—luxuries—the greatest part of them foreign luxuries; some of them, in the excess in which they are used, pernicious luxuries. . . .

Deeply impressed, as the Secretary is, with a full and deliberate conviction, that the establishment of public credit, upon the basis of a satisfactory provision, for the public debt is, under the present circumstances of this country, the true desideratum towards relief from individual and national embarrassments will be likely to press still more severely upon the community—He cannot but indulge an anxious wish, that an effectual plan for that purpose may, during the present session, be the result of the united wisdom of the legislature.

See Kenneth M. Dolbeare, ed., *American Political Thought*, 2d ed. (Chatham, N.J.: Chatham House Publishers, 1989), pp. 157–162.

JAMES MADISON: AGAINST THE ASSUMPTION
OF STATE DEBTS

James Madison to Thomas Jefferson
New York, 8 March 1790

Dear Sir,

The newspapers will have shewn you the late proceedings of the House of Representatives. The present subject of deliberation is the proposed assumption of the State debts. Opinions are nearly balanced on it. My own is no otherwise favorable to the measure than as it may tend to secure a final settlement and *payment* of balances among the States. An assumption even under such circumstances is liable to powerful objections. In the form proposed that object would be impeded by the measure, because it interests South Carolina and Massachusetts, who are to be chiefly relieved, against such a settlement and payment. The immediate operation of the plan would be peculiarly hard on Virginia. I think, also, that an increase of the federal debt will not only prolong the evil, but be further objectionable as augmenting a trust already sufficiently great for the virtue and number of the federal Legislature.

See *The Papers of James Madison*, vol. 13, *20 January 1790–31 March 1791*, ed. Charles F. Hobson and Robert A. Rutland (Charlottesville: University Press of Virginia, 1981), pp. 94–95.

James Madison to Henry Lee
New York, 13 April 1790

Dear Sir

Your favor of the 4th. ult. by Col. Lee was received from his hands on Sunday last. I have since recd. that of the 3d Instant. The antecedent one from Alexandria, though long on the way was recd. some time before. In all these, I discover strong marks of the dissatisfaction with which you behold our public prospects. Though in several respects they do not comport with my wishes—yet I cannot feel all the despondency which you seem to give way to. I do not mean that I entertain much hope of the Potomac, that seems pretty much out of sight—but that other Measures in view, however improper, will be less fatal than you imagine.

The plan of discrimination has met with the reception in Virginia on which I calculated. The towns would for obvious reasons disrelish it, and for a time they always set public opinion. The country in this region of America, in general, if I am not misinformed, has not been in unison with the Cities—nor has any of the latter except this, being unanimous against the Measure. Here the sentiment was in its full vigor, and produced every exertion that could influence the result.

I think with you that the Report of the Secretary of the Treasury is faulty in many respects—it departs particularly from that simplicity which ought to be preserved in finance, more than any thing else. The novelty and difficulty of the Task he had to execute form no small apology for his errors, and I am in hopes that in some instances they will be dimi[ni]shed, if not remedied.

The proposed assumption of the state debts has undergone repeated discussions, and contradictory decisions. The last vote was taken yesterday in a Committee of the whole and passed in the negative 31 vs. 29. The minority do not abandon however their object, and 'tis impossible to foretell the final destiny of the measure. It has some good aspects, and under some modifications would be favorable to the pecuniary interests of Virginia—and not inconsistent with the general principle of justice. In any attainable form it would have neither of these recommendations and is moreover liable to strong objections of a general nature. It would certainly be wrong to force an affirmative decision on so important and controvertible a point—by a bare majority, yet I have little hope of forbearance from that scruple.

Mass. & S. Carolina with their allies of Connecticut & N. York are too zealous to be arrested in their pursuit, unless by the force of an adverse majority.

I have recd. your reflections on the subject of a public debt with pleasure—in general they are in my opinion just and important. Perhaps it is not possible to shun some of the evils you point out, without abandoning too much the reestablishment of public debt. I hold that a Public Debt is a Public curse and in a Rep. Govt. a greater than in any other . . .

See *The Papers of James Madison*, vol. 13, *20 January 1790–31 March 1791*, ed. Charles F. Hobson and Robert A. Rutland (Charlottesville: University Press of Virginia, 1981), pp. 147–148.

THE NATIONAL BANK

The national bank plan formed phase two of the economic policy designed by Alexander Hamilton and backed by George Washington. Unlike the public credit issue, which affected the relationship of the national government to the state governments, the national bank issue brought up questions of constitutionality. Most leaders had agreed that something needed to be done about the states' debts; they disagreed on decisions about what, how, and when. In the bank debate, however, the opposition altogether disagreed that a bank was needed. They also countered that the national government had no right under the Constitution to create one. The arguments were fierce and persuasive, so much so that President Washington considered changing his position more than once.

Hamilton's proposal to create a national bank followed directly from his plan for the assumption of state debts. The bank, he noted, would aid the national government by helping to collect taxes, transfer and disburse funds, and offer short-term credit when needed. All of these functions supported the public credit policy. Hamilton also imagined that a national bank would fuel private commercial development by providing a concentrated pool of liquid capital available for investment. Modeling his plan on, among other things, the charter for the Bank of England, Hamilton accepted Washington's blessing and published his report on the national bank.

Reaction came swiftly. James Madison, Thomas Jefferson, and others responded that the Constitution did not provide the government the authority to incorporate an institution such as a national bank. What was the point, they asked, in expressly describing every power of government in the Constitution, if officials would simply assume that they had the justification to do whatever they wished? How could the compact protect citizens from the expansion of government, they continued, if leaders ignored the letter of the law and refused to strictly construct its provisions?

Had they been satisfied that the national government possessed the constitutional authority to incorporate the bank, though, Madison and others would still have opposed the institution. They worried that such a bank would give the national government, already more powerful than individuals, greater opportunity to favor some and abandon others. Citizens should all be treated equally by the government, they argued, and this could not happen when it made funds and opportunities accessible to some and unavailable to others. In short, they said that the national government was not in the banking business, and its pursuit of such a goal could only help the cause of tyranny.

The secretary of the treasury dismissed his opponents' fears of unfairness and reminded them that other banks in other places would continue to exist. Every citizen would surely have an opportunity to share in the services a bank could provide. A national bank would only be one of many banks available for customers.

But the objections about the bank's unconstitutionality proved harder for Hamilton to answer. Eventually Hamilton's formal response, "Opinion on the Constitutionality of an Act to Establish A National Bank," drew a distinction between express powers, which the Constitution enumerated, and implied powers, which dwelled, Hamilton argued, in vague clauses such as "necessary and proper." According to Hamilton's loose constructionist thought, the Congress needed no overt constitutional provision for incorporating institutions such as a national bank. The Constitution gave Congress the authority to "make all needful rules and regulations concerning the property of the United States," and the creation of the bank reasonably fit under this description.

The debate over the bank had escalated into a debate over how to interpret the Constitution. Should leaders strictly or loosely construct the document? Should they follow only express powers, so as not to allow for governmental abuses of authority against the people, or should they uncover and exercise implied powers for the benefit of U.S. citizens? What did the phrase "necessary and proper" really mean? President Washington found himself faced with a decision that would set serious precedents for the way power could be wielded and/or limited in the national government. And so, despite the fact that he had supported Hamilton's proposal, he opted to leave himself room to change his mind in the eleventh hour.

Washington appreciated the fact that he was himself not policy-minded. His greatest strength, and perhaps his ultimate frustration, was the fact that he surrounded himself with some of the ablest, and opposing, minds of his generation. In the case of the bank, he had read the proposal of the secretary of the treasury. Then he had requested and received written arguments from his secretary of state and attorney general, Thomas Jefferson and Edmund Randolph, against it. Hamilton's answer responded to many of their combined criticisms, but not all. For further rebuttal, Washington contacted James Madison. He asked the Virginia congressman to write a veto of the bank bill for him, in the event that he should decide to oppose its passage. Madison responded with a draft that attacked the bill on the grounds of blatant unconstitutionality and ultimate inefficacy.

The president did not use the veto. Washington remained convinced of Hamilton's plan and continued to support the secretary of treasury. The bill passed and Congress created the Bank of the United States.

The fact that Washington requested Madison's opinion in the middle of the process, after the legislature had followed Hamilton's proposal and created the bank bill, after Jefferson and Randolph had opposed the report in writing and Hamilton had responded in kind, shows that the president appreciated the seriousness of the key issues undergirding the debate and labored over his decision. The final word came with *McCulloch v. Maryland* in 1819, when the Supreme Court ruled that the act incorporating the bank was, indeed, constitutional. The eventual success of the loose constructionist view opened the door for the national government to invoke more implied powers under the "necessary and proper" clause in the future.

THE PRESIDENT'S POSITION: FOR THE NATIONAL BANK

Alexander Hamilton, "Opinion on the Constitutionality of an Act to Establish A National Bank" February 23, 1791

The Secretary of the Treasury, having perused with attention the papers containing the opinion of the secretary of state and attorney general concerning the constitutionality of the bill for establishing a national bank, proceeds, according to the order of the President, to submit the reasons which have induced him to entertain a different opinion. . . .

In entering upon the argument, it ought to be premised that the objections of the secretary of state and attorney general are founded on a general denial of the authority of the United States to erect corporations. The latter, indeed expressly admits that if there be anything in the bill which is not warranted by the Constitution, it is the clause of incorporation.

Now it appears to the secretary of the treasury that this *general principle* is *inherent* in the very *definition* of *Government* and *essential* to every step of the progress to be made by that of the United States, namely: that every power vested in a government is in its nature *sovereign* and includes, by *force* of the *term*, a right to employ all the *means* requisite and fairly *applicable* to the attainment of the *ends* of such power, and which are not precluded by restrictions and exceptions specified in the Constitution, or not immoral, or contrary to the essential ends of political society. . . .

The circumstance that the powers of sovereignty are in this country divided between the national and state governments does not afford the distinction required. It does not follow from this that each of the *portion* of powers delegated to the one or to the other is not sovereign *with regard to its proper objects*. It will only *follow* from it that each has sovereign power as to *certain things* and not as to *other things*. To deny that the government of the United States has sovereign power as to its declared purposes and trusts, because its power does not extend to all cases, would be equally to deny that the state governments have sovereign power in any case, because their power does not extend to every case. The 10th section of the 1st Article of the Constitution exhibits a long list of very important things which they may not do. And thus the United States would furnish the singular spectacle of a political society without sovereignty, or of a people governed without government. . . .

This general and indisputable principle puts at once an end to the *abstract* question whether the United States have power to *erect a corporation?* that is to say, to give a *legal* or *artificial capacity* to one or more persons, distinct from the natural. For it is unquestionably incident to *sovereign power* to erect corporations, and consequently to *that* of the United States, in *relation to the objects* entrusted to the management of the government. The difference is this—where the authority of the government is general, it can create corporations in *all cases;* where it is confined to certain branches of legislation, it can create corporations only in those cases.

Here then, as far as concerns the reasonings of the secretary of state and the attorney general, the affirmative of the constitutionality of the bill might be permitted to rest. . . .

It now remains to shew that the incorporation of a bank is within the operation of the provision which authorizes Congress to make all needful rules and regulations concerning the property of the United States. But it is previously necessary to advert to a distinction which has been taken by the attorney general.

He admits that the word *property* may signify personal property, however acquired, and yet asserts that it cannot signify money arising from the sources of revenue pointed out in the Constitution, "because," says he, "the disposal and regulation of money is the final cause for raising it by taxes."

But it would be more accurate to say that the *object* to which money is intended to be applied is the *final cause* for raising it than that the disposal and regulation of it as *such.* The support of government the support of troops. for the common defense the payment of the public debt, are the true *final causes* for raising money. The disposition and regulation of it, when raised, are the steps by which it is applied to the *ends* for which it was raised, not the ends themselves. Hence, therefore, the money to be raised by taxes, as well as any other personal property, must be supposed to come within the meaning, as they certainly do within the letter, of authority to make all needful rules and regulations concerning property of the United States. . . .

A hope is entertained that it has, by this time, been made to appear, to the satisfaction of the President, that a bank has a natural relation to the power of collecting taxes—to that of regulating trade—to that of providing for the common defense—and that, as the bill under consideration contemplates the government in the light of a joint proprietor of the stock of the bank, it brings the case within the provision of the clause of the Constitution which immediately respects the property of the United States.

Under a conviction that such a relation subsists, the secretary of the treasury, with all defence, conceives that it will result as a necessary consequence from the position that all the specified powers of government are sovereign, as to the proper objects; that the incorporation of a bank is a constitutional measure; and that the objections taken to the bill, in this respect, are ill-founded. . . .

It has been stated as an auxiliary test of constitutional authority to try whether it abridges any preexisting right of any state, or any individual. The proposed investigation will stand the most severe examination on this point. Each state may still erect as many banks as it pleases; every individual may still carry on the banking business to any extent he pleases.

See *Selected Writings and Speeches of Alexander Hamilton,* ed. Morton J. Frisch (Washington, D.C.: American Enterprise Institute for Public Policy Research, 1985), pp. 248–276.

JAMES MADISON: AGAINST THE NATIONAL BANK

James Madison to Edmund Pendleton
Philada, 13 February 1791

Dear Sir

Since the receipt of your favor of the 15 Jany. I have had the further pleasure of seeing your valuable observations on the Bank, more at length, in your communications to Mr. White. The subject has been decided, contrary to your opinion as well as my own, by large majorities in both Houses, and is now before the President. The power of incorporating can not by any process of safe reasoning, be drawn within the meaning of the Constitution as an appurtenance of any express power, and it is not pretended that it is itself an express power. The arguments in favor of the measure, rather increased my dislike to it because they were founded on remote implications, which strike at the very essence of the Govt. as composed of limited & enumerated powers. The Plan is moreover liable to a variety of other objections which you have so judiciously developed. . . .

The inclosed paper I observe has a sketch of some of the argts. agst. the Bank. They are extremely mutilated, and in some instances perverted, but will give an idea of the turn which the question took.

See *The Papers of James Madison,* vol. 13, *20 January 1790–31 March 1791,* ed. Charles F. Hobson and Robert A. Rutland (Charlottesville: University Press of Virginia, 1981), pp. 390–391.

James Madison
Draft Veto of the Bank Bill
21 February 1791

Feby. 21. 1791. Copy of a paper made out & sent to the President at his request, to be ready in case his judgment should finally decide agst. the Bill for incorporating a National Bank, the Bill being then before him.

Gentlemen of the Senate

Having carefully examined and maturely considered the Bill ... I am compelled by the conviction of my judgment and the duty of my Station to return the Bill to the House in which it originated with the following objections

(if to the Constitutionality)

I object to the Bill because it is an essential principle of the Government that powers not delegated by the Constitution cannot be rightfully exercised; because the power proposed by the Bill to be exercised is not expressly delegated; and because I cannot satisfy myself that it results from any express power by fair and safe rules of implication.

(if to the merits alone or in addition)

I object to the Bill because it appears to be unequal between the public and the Institution in favor of the institution; imposing no conditions on the latter equivalent to the stipulations assumed by the former. (Quer. if this be within the intimation of the President.) I object to the Bill because it is in all cases the duty of the Government to dispense its benefits to individuals with as impartial a hand as the public interest will permit; and the Bill is in this respect unequal to individuals holding different denominations of public Stock and willing to become subscribers. This objection lies with particular force against the early day appointed for opening subscriptions, which if these should be filled as quickly as may happen, amounts to an exclusion of those remote from the Government, in favor of those near enough to take advantage of the opportunity.

See *The Papers of James Madison*, vol. 13, *20 January 1790–31 March 1791*, ed. Charles F. Hobson and Robert A. Rutland (Charlottesville: University Press of Virginia, 1981), p. 395.

NEUTRALITY

The French Revolution and the following war between France and Britain placed the United States in a delicate position with regard to foreign policy. George Washington found himself caught between advisors with sympathies toward Britain (Alexander Hamilton, Henry Knox, John Adams) and advisors with sympathies toward France (James

Madison, Thomas Jefferson, Edmund Randolph). Two situations complicated the problem.

First, the French Revolution in 1789 had toppled one government and created another. This dramatic and bloody change evoked different responses from Washington's cabinet. On the one hand, the secretary of state ordered the U.S. minister in Paris to recognize the French National Assembly as the official, legitimate government of France. On the other hand, the secretary of the treasury responded by ordering a halt to U.S. payments on the nation's debt to France because he considered the new French republic too unstable and illegitimate to trust. President Washington knew he had to create unified policy out of the schizophrenic actions of his appointees.

Second, France had declared war on Britain. This brought the 1778 treaty between the United States and France into the equation. Though the treaty only provided that the United States intervene on behalf of France in a defensive war, this begged the questions of what "defensive war" meant and who determined it.

Washington, increasingly frustrated both by the international situation and by the domestic challenge of handling Citizen Edmond Charles Genet, the colorful emissary from the Republic of France, summoned his cabinet. He asked each department head to answer the same thirteen questions about the international situation. Then he sat back and let them debate.

Once again, Alexander Hamilton convinced Washington to pursue the policy he proposed. Hamilton suggested that the president proclaim neutrality and preserve peace for the United States. On April 22, 1793, Washington did just that.

Critics such as James Madison and Thomas Jefferson attacked the president's Proclamation of Neutrality on several grounds. First and foremost, they said, the president had no constitutional authority to make the proclamation. Though the president represented the nation and could certainly initiate dialogues between countries, they continued, the Constitution clearly vested policy decisions with Congress. If Congress held the authority to declare war, then the president could not hold the authority to declare peace. If the president could only make treaties with the consent of the Senate, then how could the president make a policy decision such as neutrality on his own?

Opponents also argued against the proclamation on legal and moral grounds. Legally, they claimed, Washington's statement of neutrality broke the Franco-American treaty; therefore the proclamation was invalid. Morally, they said, turning the nation's back to France, the country that had been an ally for years and had now followed in the footsteps of the United States with its own revolutionary war, was simply ungrateful and cowardly.

A war of words developed between Alexander Hamilton and James Madison, or, in this case, "Pacificus" and "Helvidius," respectively. Hamilton defended the president's actions. He asserted that the proclamation did not make new law; instead, it simply confirmed the current state of the existing law. In other words, Washington's neutrality statement only offered the president's interpretation of the treaty of 1778. All Washington did in the proclamation, according to Hamilton, was confirm to the citizens that the treaty did not require the United States to become involved in the current war. Since the president is the executor of the laws, and to execute a law one must first understand and interpret it, Hamilton reasoned, then Washington fulfilled his duties as chief executive by issuing his interpretation of the treaty.

Despite the protests of its opponents, and the convoluted logic of its supporters, Washington's Proclamation of Neutrality prevailed. In many ways, this may be due to the fact that, although many U.S. citizens liked France, they loved peace far more. Those who disliked Britain seemed to hate the idea of fighting a war even more, as well. The popularity of neutrality trumped the arguments of its critics.

Washington's proclamation did more than simply keep the nation from fighting. First, the president set precedents in the way he tried to enforce his policy. The proclamation not only announced neutrality, but also prohibited U.S. citizens from aiding or abetting hostilities within U.S. jurisdiction. With no navy and a small army occupied in the West, Washington had to rely on state governors and militias to enforce this prohibition voluntarily.

This became complicated. For example, the Philadelphia authorities arrested two U.S. citizens who had joined the crew of a French privateer in Charleston. Attorney General Randolph could find no federal law against recruiting, and could not consider the presidential proclamation itself as a law, and thus could only bring the charge of disturbing the peace against the pair. After the resulting acquittal, one of the former defendants reenlisted with the French without incident.

Second, and perhaps more importantly, the proclamation set the precedent for executives to assert initiatives in foreign policy. This created a sphere of uncertainty between the president and Congress that has led to various power struggles throughout the years in questions of wars, police actions, strikes, and interventions.

THE PRESIDENT'S POSITION: FOR NEUTRALITY

"Pacificus No. I" (Alexander Hamilton in Defense of George Washington)
June 29, 1793

As attempts are making very dangerous to the peace, and it is to be feared not very friendly to the constitution of the UStates—it becomes the duty of those who wish well to both to endeavour to prevent their success.

The objections which have been raised against the Proclamation of Neutrality lately issued by the President have been urged in a spirit of acrimony and invective, which demonstrates, that more was in view than merely a free discussion of an important public measure; that the discussion covers a design of weakening the confidence of the People in the author of the measure; in order to remove or lessen a powerful obstacle to the success of an opposition to the Government, which however it may change its form, according to circumstances, seems still to be adhered to and pursued with persevering Industry.

This Reflection adds to the motives connected with the measure itself to recommend endeavours by proper explanations to place it in a just light. Such explanations at least cannot but be satisfactory to those who may not have leisure or opportunity for pursuing themselves an investigation of the subject, and who may wish to perceive that the policy of the Government is not inconsistent with its obligations or its honor.

The objections in question . . . —

1. That the Proclamation was without authority
2. That it was contrary to our treaties with France
3. That it was contrary to the gratitude, which is due from this to that country; for the succours rendered us in our own Revolution.
4. That it was out of time & unnecessary.

In order to judge of the solidity of the first of these objection[s], it is necessary to examine what is the nature and design of a proclamation of neutrality.

The true nature & design of such an act is—to *make known* to the powers at War and to the Citizens of the Country, whose Government does the Act that such country is in the condition of a Nation at Peace with the belligerent parties, and under no obligations of Treaty, to become an *associate in the war* with either of them; that this being its situation its intention is to observe a conduct conformable with it and to perform towards each the duties of neutrality; and as a consequence of this state of things, to give warning to all within its jurisdiction to abstain from acts that shall contravene those duties, under the penalties which the laws of the land (of which the law of Nations is a part) annexes to acts of contravention.

This, and no more, is conceived to be the true import of a Proclamation of Neutrality.

It does not imply, that the Nation which makes the declaration will forbear to perform to any of the warring powers any stipulations in Treaties which can be performed without rendering it an *associate* or *party* in the War. It therefore does not imply in our case, that the UStates will not make those distinctions, between the present belligerent powers, which are stipulated in the 17th and 22d articles of our Treaty with France; because these distinctions are not incompatible with a state of neutrality; they will in no shape render the UStates an *associate* or *party* in the War. . . .

It can as little be disputed, that a Proclamation of Neutrality, where a Nation is at liberty to keep out of a War in which other Nations are engaged and means to do so, as a *usual* and a *proper* measure. *Its main object and effect are to prevent the Nation being immediately responsible for acts done by its citizens, without the privity or connivance of the Government, in contravention of the principles of Neutrality.*

An object this of the greatest importance to a Country whose true interest lies in the preservation of peace. . . .

The President is the constitutional Executor of the laws. Our Treaties and the laws of Nations form a part of the law of the land. He who is to execute the laws must first judge for himself of their meaning. In order to the observance of that conduct, which the laws of nations combined with our treaties prescribed to this country, in reference to the present War in Europe, it was necessary for the President to judge for himself whether there was any thing in our treaties incompatible with an adherence to neutrality. Having judges that there was not, he had a right, and if in his opinion the interests of the Nation required it, it was his duty, as Executor of the laws, to proclaim the neutrality of the Nation, to exhort all persons to observe it, and to warn them of the penalties which would attend its non observation.

The Proclamation has been represented as enacting some new law. This is a view of it entirely erroneous. It only proclaims a *fact* with regard to the *existing state* of the Nation, informs the citizens of what the laws previously established require of them in that state, & warns them that these laws will be put in execution against the Infractors of them.

See *Selected Writings and Speeches of Alexander Hamilton*, ed. Morton J. Frisch (Washington, D.C.: American Enterprise Institute for Public Policy Research, 1985), pp. 396–404.

JAMES MADISON: AGAINST NEUTRALITY

James Madison to Thomas Jefferson
Orange, 8 May 1793

Dear Sir

Your last received was of the 28 Apl. The receipt of all the preceeding is verified by the uninterrupted dates of the Gazettes inclosed. I anxiously wish that the reception of Genest [Genet] may testify what I believe to be the real affections of the people. It is the more desireable as a seasonal plum after the bitter pills which it seems must be administered. Having neither the Treaty nor Law of Nations at hand I form no opinion as to the stipulations of the former, or the precise neutrality defined by the latter. I had always supposed that the terms of the Treaty made some sort of difference, at least as far as would consist with the Law of Nations, between France and Nations not in Treaty, particularly G. Britain. I should still doubt whether the term *impartial* in the Proclamation is not stronger than was necessary, if not than was proper. Peace is no doubt to be preserved at any price that honor and good faith will permit. But it is no less to be considered that the least departure from these will not only be most likely to end in the loss of peace, but is pregnant with every other evil that could happen to us. In explaining our own engagements under the Treaty with France, it would be honorable as well as just to adhere to the sense that would at the time have been put on them. The attempt to shuffle off the Treaty altogether by quibbling on [Emeric de] Vattel is equally contemptible for the meanness and folly of it. If a change of Government is an absolution from public engagements, why not from those of a domestic as well as of a foreign nature; and what then becomes of public debts &c &c. In fact, the doctrine would perpetuate every existing Despotism, by involving in a reform of the Government a destruction of the Social pact, an annihilation of property, and a compleat establishment of the State of Nature. What most surprises me is that such a proposition should have been discussed.

See *The Papers of Thomas Jefferson*, vol. 25, *1 January to 10 May 1793*, ed. John Catanzariti (Princeton: Princeton University Press, 1992), pp. 688–689.

"Helvidius" (James Madison) Number 1
24 August 1793

The substance of the first piece, sifted from its inconsistencies and its vague expressions, may be thrown into the following propositions:

That the powers of declaring war and making treaties are, in their nature, executive powers:

That being particularly vested by the constitution in other departments, they are to be considered as exceptions out of the general grant to the executive department:

That being, as exceptions, to be construed strictly, the powers not strictly within them, remain with the executive:

That the executive consequently, as the organ of intercourse with foreign nations, and the interpreter and executor of treaties, those involving questions of war and peace, as well as others; to judge of the obligations of the United States to make war or not, under any casus federis or eventual operation of the contract, relating to war; and to pronounce the state of things resulting from the obligations of the United States, as understood by the executive:

That in particular the executive had the authority to judge whether in the case of the mutual guaranty between the United States and France, the former were bound by it to engage in the war;

That the executive has, in pursuance of that authority, decided that the United States are not bound: And,

That its proclamation of the 22nd of April last, is to be taken as the effect and expression of that decision . . .

. . . it must be evident, that although the executive may be a convenient organ of preliminary communications with foreign governments, on the subjects of treaty or war; and the proper agent for carrying into execution the final determinations of the competent authority; yet it can have no pretensions from the nature of the powers in question compared with the nature of the executive trust, to that essential agency which gives validity to such determinations. . . .

In the general distribution of powers, we find that of declaring war expressly vested in the Congress, where every other legislative power is declared to be vested, and without any other qualification than what is common to every other legislative act. The constitutional idea of this power would seem then clearly to be, that it is of a legislative and not an executive nature.

This conclusion becomes irresistible, when it is recollected, that the constitution cannot be supposed to have placed either any power legislative in its nature, entirely among executive powers, or any power executive in its nature, entirely among legislative powers, without charging the constitution, with that kind of intermixture and consolidation of different powers, which would violate a fundamental principle in the organization of free governments. . . . it could be shewn, that the constitution was originally vindicated, and has been constantly expounded, with a disavowal of any such intermixture.

The power of treaties is vested jointly in the President and in the Senate, which is a branch of the legislature. From this arrangement merely, there can be no inference that would necessarily exclude the power from the executive class: since the senate is joined with the President in another power, that of appointing to offices, which as far as relate to executive offices at least, is considered as of an executive nature. Yet on the other hand, there are sufficient indications that the power of treaties is regarded by the constitution as materially different from mere executive power, and as having more affinity to the legislative than to the executive character. . . .

Thus it appears that by whatever standard we try this doctrine, it must be condemned as no less vicious in theory than it would be dangerous in practice. It is countenanced neither by the writers on law; nor by the nature of the powers themselves; nor by any general arrangements or particular expressions, or plausible analogies, to be found in the constitution.

James Madison. "Helvidius" Number 1. New York, 24 August 1793. See *The Papers of James Madison*, vol. 15, *24 March 1793–20 April 1795*, ed. Thomas A. Mason, Robert A. Rutland, and Jeanne K. Sisson (Charlottesville: University Press of Virginia, 1985), pp. 66–73.

THE WHISKEY INSURRECTION

The plan to fund the national debt had many unforeseen ripple effects. Hamilton had suggested, and Washington had agreed, that one means of raising revenue should be the taxation of luxury items. To that end, Congress had levied an excise tax on domestically distilled spirits in 1791. Three years later, this led to an aberrant and violent event known as the Whiskey Insurrection.

The backcountry of Pennsylvania, namely, the western counties of Westmoreland, Fayette, Washington, and Allegheny, produced a good deal of whiskey; in fact, some historians speculate that one-quarter of the entire nation's whiskey stills were located in this region at this time. The citizens there protested the excise tax and its provisions, which required that the accused be tried in district courts, that were often far distant from homes and communities. In time the tax became a symbol for all of the westerners' complaints. Frustration felt about national policy toward native Americans, failure to open the Mississippi to western trade, the concentration of wealth in the East, and other perceived failings of the new government seemed to converge on the tax question.

After three years of citizens' poor compliance with the tax, the situation erupted. When U.S. marshal David Lenox went to serve processes under the tax law in Westmoreland County on July 15, 1794, armed citizens opposed him. Rioters also attacked his house that day and burned it two days later. Colonel John Neville, inspector of the revenue for that area, appealed to the state militia for aid in containing the violence.

Some lawmakers had anticipated such a passionate response to the tax when the measure first came up for vote. Congressman Josiah Parker, for example, had warned that the measure might "convulse the Government; it will let loose a swarm of harpies, who, under the denomination of revenue officers, will range through the country, prying into every man's house and affairs . . . like a Macedonian phalanx."[1] Senator William Maclay called the tax "the most execrable system that ever was framed against the liberty of people" and feared that "war and bloodshed are the most likely consequence of all this."[2]

The violence in Pennsylvania shook George Washington, however. On August 2 he met with his cabinet, Pennsylvania governor Thomas Mifflin, and a number of Pennsylvania leaders. Despite the misgivings of the state officials, Washington decided to make an example of the protesters in Pennsylvania and send the militia to restore order. He used the 1792 Militia Act as his foundation for a call to arms in the states of Pennsylvania, New Jersey, Maryland, and Virginia.

As the multistate militia gathered, Washington warned the "insurgents" to return to their homes in peace. He also appointed three federal commissioners to talk to the representatives of the western Pennsylvania counties, but the talks failed and the violence escalated. By September, an outraged Washington rode with a combined militia of 12,950 men to Harrisburg, Pennsylvania.

The bang of "rebellion" ended with a whimper. By the time the militia arrived, they could find no insurrection. The authorities captured twenty men and paraded them through Philadelphia as traitors, but only two were eventually convicted and they were pardoned by the president, one due to insanity and the other due to mental defect. The violence was over.

The effects of the insurrection, however, lingered on. During the crisis, a bewildered George Washington searched for an explanation for the event. He came to blame the area's Democratic-Republican organization, the Mingo Creek Society, for providing the catalyst for the uprising. His ride with the militia became a march against such self-created societies. Yet what Washington saw as a strike for law and order, others saw as danger to liberty.

James Madison, among others, worried about the president's militia campaign against the protesters. First, Madison feared that the quick federal use of the military—especially over the reservations of the state's leaders—would lead to the assumption that the nation needed a standing army in order to enforce its laws. The standing army issue remained a sore one for those who remembered the British army and its use against citizens. With such power, they argued, the national government could easily overpower any state or group of people, and thus the balance between the national government and the state governments, the balance on which federalism rested, would be lost.

Madison also disliked Washington's attack on self-created societies. The Mingo Creek Society, for instance, was a perfectly legal political organization. The Democratic-Republican societies of which it was an example reflected the first stage of the development of political parties—in this case, the Democratic-Republican Party, which would oppose the Federalist Party—at the grass-roots level. Madison saw Washington's campaign against the societies as a campaign against the freedom of speech and the freedom of assembly. He also believed that Washington overlooked the inherent problems with the excise tax and its provisions by making the societies a scapegoat for the insurrection.

In the end, Washington's reliance on the Militia Act and his use of the armed forces did pave the way for a standing U.S. army. Madison proved correct in recognizing the importance of, and inevitability of, the political societies. Although Washington loathed political division, he could not prevent the establishment of political parties in the United States. His own secretaries of the treasury and of state, in fact, would soon openly lead the first political parties in the nation, with the support of many "self-created societies."

NOTES

1. *The Annals of Congress: The Debates and Proceedings in the Congress of the United States*, vol. 2, ed. Joseph Gales (Washington, D.C., 1834–1856), pp. 1891–1892.

2. William Maclay, *The Journal of William Maclay: United States Senator from Pennsylvania, 1789–1791*, introduction by Charles A. Beard (New York: F. Unger 1965), pp. 375–376, 377.

THE PRESIDENT'S POSITION: FOR MILITARY ACTION

Statement of George Washington
As published in the *Gazette of the United States*
[Philadelphia], 25 Sept. 1794

I thought it sufficient, in the first instance, rather to take measures for calling for the militia, than immediately to embody them; but the moment is now come, when the overtures of forgiveness, with no other condition, than a submission to Law, have been only partially accepted—

when every form of conciliation not inconsistent with the being of Government, has been adopted without effect . . . when, therefore, Government is set at defiance, the contest being whether a small portion of the United States shall dictate to the whole union, and at the expence of those, who desire peace, indulge a desperate ambition; Now therefore I, George Washington, President of the United States, in obedience to that high and irresistible duty, consigned to me by the Constitution, "to take care that the laws be faithfully executed;" deploring that the American name should be sullied by the outrages of citizens on their own Government; . . . but resolved . . . to reduce the refractory to a due subordination to the law; Do Hereby declare and make known, that with a satisfaction, which can be equalled only by the merits of the Militia summoned into service from the States of New-Jersey, Pennsylvania, Maryland, and Virginia, I have received intelligence of their patriotic alacrity, in obeying the call of the present, tho' painful, yet commanding necessity; that a force, which, according to every reasonable expectation, is adequate to the exigency, is already in motion to the scene of disaffection; . . . And I do, moreover, exhort all individuals, officers, and bodies of men, to contemplate with abhorrence the measures leading directly or indirectly to those crimes, which produce this resort to military coercion. . . . And lastly, I again warn all persons, whomsoever and wheresoever, not to abet, aid, or comfort the Insurgents aforesaid, as they will answer the contrary at their peril.

Gazette of the United States (Philadelphia), 25 September 1794.

The Diary of George Washington
October 9, 1794

The substance of Mr. [William] Findleys communications were as follows—viz.—That the People in the parts where he was best acquainted, had seen there folly; and he believed were disposed to submit to the Laws; that he thought, but could not undertake to be responsible, for the re-establishment of the public Offices for the Collection of the Taxes on distilled spirits, & Stills—intimating however, that it might be best for the present, & until the peoples minds were a little more tranquilized, to hold the Office of Inspection at Pitsburgh under the protection—or at least under the influence of the Garrison. . . . That it was not merely the excise law their opposition was aimed at, but to all law, & Government; and to the Officers of Government; and that the situation in which he had been, & the life he had led for sometime, was such, that rather than go through it again, he would prefer quitting this scene altogether.

Mr. [David] Redicks information was similar to the above. . . . the situation of those who were not in the opposition to government whilst the frenzy was at its height, were obliged to sleep with their Arms by their bed Sides every night; not knowing but that before Morning they might have occasion to use them in defence of their persons, or their properties.

He added, that for a long time after the riots commenced, and until lately, the distrust of one another was such, that even friends were afraid to communicate their sentiments to each other; That by whispers this was brought about; and growing bolder as they became more communicative they found their strength, and that there was a general disposition not only to acquiesce under, but to support the Laws—and he gave some instances also of Magistrates enforcing them.

He said the People of those Counties believed that the opposition to the Excise law—or at least that their dereliction to it, in every other part of the U. States was similar to their own, and that no Troops could be got to March against them for the purpose of coercion; that every acct. until very lately, of Troops marching against them was disbelieved; & supposed to be the fabricated tales of governmental men; That now they had got alarmed . . .

After hearing what both had to say, I briefly told them—That it had been the earnest wish of governmt. to bring the people of those counties to a sense of their duty, by mild, & lenient means; That for the purpose of representing to their sober reflection the fatal consequences of such conduct Commissioners had been sent amongst them that they might be warned, in time, of what must follow, if they persevered in their opposition to the laws; but that coercion wou'd not be resorted to except in the dernier resort: but, that the season of the year made it indispensible that preparation for it should keep pace with the propositions that had been made; That it was unnecessary for me to enumerate the transactions of those people (as they related to the proceedings of government) forasmuch as they knew them as well as I did; That the measure which they were not witness to the adoption of was not less painful than expensive—Was inconvenient, & distressing—in every point of view; but as I considered the support of the Laws as an object of the first magnitude, and the greatest part of the expense had already been incurred, that nothing Short of the most unequivocal proofs of absolute Submission should retard the March of the army into the Western counties, in order to convince them that the government could, & would enforce obedience to the laws—not suffering them to be insulted with impunity. Being asked again what proofs would be required, I answered, they knew as well as I did, what was due to justice & example. They understood my meaning—and asked if they might have another interview. I appointed five oclock in the After noon for it.

See *The Diaries of George Washington*, vol. 1, ed. Donald Jackson and Dorothy Twohig (Charlottesville: University Press of Virginia, 1976), pp. 170–198.

JAMES MADISON: AGAINST MILITARY ACTION

James Madison to James Monroe
Philada., 4 December 1794

... You will learn from the Newspapers and official communications the unfortunate scene in the Western parts of Penna. which unfolded itself during the recess. The history of its remote & immediate causes, the measures produced by it, and the manner in which it has been closed, does not fall within the compass of a letter. It is probable also that many explanatory circumstances are yet but imperfectly known. I can only refer to the printed accounts which you will receive from the Department of State, and the comments which your memory will assist you in making on them. The event was in several respects a critical one for the cause of liberty, and the real authors of it, if not in the service, were in the most effectual manner, doing the business of Despotism. You well know the general tendency of insurrections to increase the momentum of power. You will recollect the particular effect, of what happened some years ago in Massachts. Precisely the same calamity was to be dreaded on a larger scale in this Case. There were eno' as you may well suppose ready to give the same turn to the crisis, and to propagate the same impressions from it. It happened most auspiciously however that with a spirit truly republican, the people every where and of every description condemned the resistance to the will of the Majority, and obeyed with alacrity the call to vindicate the authority of the laws. You will see in the answer of the House of Reps. to the P's speech, that the most was made of this circumstance as an antidote to the poisonous influence to which Republicanism was exposed. If the insurrection had not been crushed in the manner it was I have no doubt that a formidable attempt would have been made to establish the principle that a standing army was necessary for *enforcing the laws*. When I first came to this City about the middle of October, this was the fashionable language. Nor am I sure that the attempt would not have been made, if the P. could have been embarked in it, and particularly if the temper of N. England had not been dreaded on this point. I hope we are over that danger for the present. You will readily understand the business detailed in the Newspapers, relating to the denunciation of the "Self created Societies." The introduction of it by the President was perhaps the greatest error of his political life.

See *The Papers of James Madison*, vol. 15, *24 March 1793–20 April 1795*, ed. Thomas A. Mason, Robert A. Rutland, and Jeanne K. Sisson (Charlottesville: University Press of Virginia, 1985), pp. 405–408.

James Madison to Thomas Jefferson
Philada., 21 December 1794

... The phenomenon you wish to have explained is as little understood here as with you; but it would be here quite unfashionable to suppose it needed explanation. It is impossible to give you an idea of the force with which the tide has set in a particular direction. It has been too violent not to be soon followed by a change. In fact I think a change has begun already. The danger will then be of as violent a reflux to the opposite extreme.

The attack made on the essential & constitutional right of the Citizen, in the blow levelled at the "self-created Societies" does not appear to have had the effect intended. It is and must be felt by every man who values liberty, whatever opinion he may have of the use or abuse of it by those institutions. You will see that the appeal is begun to the public sentiment, by the injured parties. The Republican Society of Baltimore set the example. That of Newark has advertised a meeting of its members. It is said that if Edwd. Livingston, as is generally believed, has outvoted Watts, for the H. of Reps. he is indebted for it to the invigorated exertions of the Democratic Society of that place, of which he is himself a member. In Boston the subject is well understood, and handled in the Newspaper on the republican side, with industry and address ...

See *The Papers of James Madison*, vol. 15, *24 March 1793–20 April 1795*, ed. Thomas A. Mason, Robert A. Rutland, and Jeanne K. Sisson (Charlottesville: University Press of Virginia, 1985), pp. 419–420.

RECOMMENDED READINGS

Bradley, Harold W. "The Political Thinking of George Washington." *Journal of Southern History* 9 (1945): 469–486.

Brookhiser, Richard. *Founding Father: Rediscovering George Washington*. New York: Free Press, 1996.

Callahan, North. *Thanks, Mr. President: The Trail-Blazing Second Term of George Washington*. New York: Cornwall Books, 1991.

DeConde, Alexander. *Entangling Alliance: Politics and Diplomacy Under George Washington*. Durham, N.C.: Duke University Press, 1958.

Elkins, Stanley, and Eric McKitrick. *The Age of Federalism*. New York: Oxford University Press, 1993.

Flexner, James Thomas. *Washington: The Indispensable Man*. New York: Signet, 1969.

Gregg, Gary L., II, and Matthew Spalding, eds. *Patriot Sage: George Washington and the American Political Tradition*. Wilmington, Del.: ISI Books, 1999.

Hutson, James H. "John Adams' Title Campaign." *The New England Quarterly: A Historical Review of New England Life and Letters* (March 1968): 30–39.

Ketcham, Ralph. *Presidents Above Party: The First American Presidency, 1789–1829*. Chapel Hill: University of North Carolina Press, 1984.

McDonald, Forrest. *The Presidency of George Washington*. Lawrence: University Press of Kansas, 1974.

Phelps, Glenn A. *George Washington and American Constitutionalism*. Lawrence: University Press of Kansas, 1993.

Randall, Willard Sterne. *George Washington: A Life*. New York: Henry Holt, 1997.

Rasmussen, William M.S., and Robert S. Tilton. *George Washington: The Man behind the Myths*. Charlottesville: University Press of Virginia, 1999.

Rozell, Mark J., William D. Pederson, and Frank J. Williams, eds. *George Washington and the Origins of the American Presidency*. Westport, Conn.: Praeger, 2000.

Smith, Richard Norton. *Patriarch: George Washington and the New American Nation*. Boston: Houghton Mifflin, 1993.

Spalding, Matthew, and Patrick J. Garrity. *A Sacred Union of Citizens: George Washington's Farewell Address and the American Character*. Lanham, Md.: Rowan and Littlefield, 1996.

Washington, George. *The Papers of George Washington: Presidential Series*. 9 vols. Edited by Dorothy Twohig. Charlottesville: University Press of Virginia, 1987.

2

JOHN ADAMS

(1797–1801)

INTRODUCTION

John Adams faced the difficult challenge of following a president who was successful, beloved, and, most importantly, first to hold his position. In many ways, even before it began, the Adams administration was doomed to fail in living up to the Washingtonian legacy. The election of the second president of the United States serves as a telling metaphor for his entire term in office as chief executive.

By the time of the election, the factions Washington had feared had developed into full-fledged political parties. Federalists such as the Anglophilic John Adams and Alexander Hamilton supported a strong, centralized national government, protectionism, commercialism, and a loose construction of the U.S. Constitution. Democratic-Republicans such as the Francophilic Thomas Jefferson and James Madison supported states rights, decentralization, laissez-faire economics, agriculturalism, and a narrow construction of the U.S. Constitution. Partisanship among Federalists and Democratic-Republicans alike influenced the election and most everything that followed after it. Factions within the parties added complexity—and potential danger—to every decision.

Unlike George Washington, who was elected to his position unanimously by the Electoral College, John Adams won his presidency by only a three-vote margin, seventy-one to sixty-eight. If the former vice president barely won a majority for himself, then he also lost the opportunity to serve with the man he hoped would be his vice president, Thomas Pinckney. Fellow Federalist Alexander Hamilton supported Pinckney over Adams for the presidency. Hamilton's quiet campaign behind the scenes ended up being self-defeating, however. Since candidates for president and vice president ran separately at the time, instead of on tickets together by party, the Democratic-Republican vote firmly behind Thomas Jefferson gave him the second-highest number of votes and made him Adams' vice president. Adams therefore began his term with a vice president from a rival political party and split allegiance within his own.

The contentious election process set the tone for the new presidential administration. As the new president wrote to his wife, Abigail Adams, about his inauguration, "A solemn scene it was indeed, and it was made more affecting to me by the presence of the General [Washington], whose countenance was as serene and unclouded as the day. He seemed to me to enjoy a triumph over me. Methought I heard him say, 'Ay! I am fairly out and you fairly in! See which of us will be happiest.' "[1] Indeed, the next four years were not especially happy ones for Adams.

Though Adams had been active in politics for most of his adult life, he seemed something of an outsider on the presidential stage. In personal terms, Adams could not compete with the precedent set by the handsome, elegant George Washington. Adams presented a shorter, heavier figure than his predecessor. He was quicker to laugh and to anger than the aloof general. Adams' hair was thinning. His teeth were bad; despite the fact that he had once been known as a remarkable orator, his dental problems now threatened to make his speech difficult to understand. He also lacked Washington's cool before a crowd. Adams feared, in fact, that he would faint at his own inauguration.

He served as Washington's vice president, and yet Adams never enjoyed the intimacy and trust with Washington that Hamilton and even Jefferson and Madison experienced. He remained at odds with Hamilton, though the former secretary of the treasury continued to be a key power broker among Federalists. Adams' relationship with Jefferson was quite strained and often combative until years after both men had left the White House, when the two aging statesmen finally embraced retirement and friendship.

Adams exacerbated his outsider status during his administration by remaining quite literally outside the capital much of the time. Washington was away a total of 181 days during his eight years in office; in contrast, Adams was absent from the capital a total of 385 days in only four years.[2] Most of this time he spent in his home in Quincy, Massachusetts. Part of the time he spent at home he devoted to his wife, who was often ill. His close relationship with the intelligent and outspoken Abigail paved the way for other important First Ladies to assume key roles in administrations, including the influential Dolley Madison. Unfortunately for her husband, Abigail Adams was often at Quincy instead of the nation's capital, and her love of the place made it all the harder for Adams to return to the U.S. capital in Philadelphia.

Though Adams worked diligently to remain in contact with his cabinet and other officials from his house, many citizens attributed his long absences to a lack of interest and effort. He defended himself to close colleagues—pointing out, for example, that he could await word from Paris concerning international affairs as easily at Quincy as he could at Philadelphia—but he proved unable to answer his opposition in the press. The trips to Quincy reinvigorated Adams and gave him more energy to devote to his office, but this mattered little to his critics. Adams' frequent time away cost him precious standing in the court of public opinion.

While he was absent from the capital, Adams relied on members of his cabinet to keep him informed and advised. Here, as in other areas, Adams suffered from being the first president to succeed another. Precedents regarding transitions between administrations did not exist. Adams valued stability as a great virtue and sought to instill it in the national government; therefore, he retained many officials from Washington's cabinet rather than seeking advisors of his own. He never developed the working relationship with his officials that Washington had fostered. Charles Lee, the attorney general, and Benjamin Stoddert, who led the Department of the Navy after its creation, remained loyal to Adams. Secretary of State Timothy Pickering, Secretary of War James McHenry, and Secretary of the Treasury Oliver Wolcott Jr., however, looked to Alexander Hamilton for leadership before John Adams. Often, the question for the president was not whom he could agree with, but rather which official he could even trust. He had to remain braced for attacks from within his circle as well as from the populace at large. In order to do his job, Adams faced struggles on every possible front.

And his struggles were many. First, he inherited an already tense relationship with France from Washington. His concern over French privateers' attacks on U.S. merchant ships, added to his frustration over the rumored dismissal of U.S. diplomat Charles Pinckney by French leaders in Paris, led him to call for a reorganization of the army. He also focused on building U.S. naval forces, since the sea formed the backdrop for many of the violent confrontations between nations. Not only did his Democratic-Republican critics favor peace, but they also continued to nurse strong pro-France sentiments. They were willing to give the former ally of the colonies during the American War of Independence every benefit of the doubt. Opponents labeled Adams a warmonger in the press. Talk of fighting brought further criticism, as some claimed Adams was all but declaring war, a power reserved by the U.S. Constitution for Congress, not the president. Allegations that Adams was willing to step over constitutional boundaries to take more power fed the tide of resentment against him.

Adam's brief respite from public protest came at the cost of increased troubles abroad. National opinion turned en masse against France after news came that three of French minister Talleyrand's officials solicited bribes from the U.S. delegation sent to France to negotiate peace. The so-called XYZ affair introduced a unique moment of U.S. solidarity, yet it also marked increasing hostilities with France. The public rallied around Adams, yet the cost was the waging of a quasi war.

As Adams prepared the nation's forces to meet the French threat, he faced another struggle, this time with his predecessor, George Washington. This case underscored the difficulties caused by ever growing partisanship across the nation. It also proved that Adams' cabinet members used their positions of trust to further their own goals, even if they conflicted with the president's own agenda.

Adams looked to George Washington to return from retirement and lead the U.S. Army. Adams knew that Washington's name and reputation would be a coup for the administration and mean solid, long-term support from the U.S. citizenry. Adams also planned to create a bipartisan leadership group under Washington to unify public sentiment and bridge the gap of factionalism.

The president acted quickly to finalize Washington's appointment as lieutenant general and commander in chief—so quickly, in fact, that Washington had not yet even agreed to accept Adams' nomination. As Adams sought Washington's acceptance, Secretary of State Timothy Pickering worked behind Adams' back to try to convince Washington to give Hamilton the highest position possible: if not actual leadership, then the role of second in command. Washington needed little coaxing, however. When he accepted leadership of the army, he sent a list of appointments for his general staff to Adams. Each name represented an arch-Federalist, and the first name was Alexander Hamilton.

Adams' plan for bipartisan army leadership failed, as Washington threatened to resign if he could not work with the appointees (Alexander Hamilton, Charles Pinckney, and Henry Knox) he knew and trusted. Adams yielded to Washington. In the process, he allowed an experienced but highly partisan army corps to form, loyal first to Washington and second to Hamilton, with the president's authority running a distant third.

As Adams' popularity plummeted again, critics in the newspapers (such as the ever vocal *Aurora General Advertiser*) attacked the president and called for his resignation. When the Federalist majority in the legislature passed the Alien and Sedition Acts in 1798, then, Adams did not veto them; in fact, he used them on occasion. The Alien Act reflected the xenophobia of a young nation on the brink of war by blocking immigrants attempting to obtain U.S. citizenship. The Sedition Act was perhaps even more troublesome to Adams' opposition. This law allowed the administration to censor critics in the press through fines and jail sentences. If the unpopular president could not win the affection of his opposition, the Sedition Act allowed him to quiet his detractors by force.

The Alien and Sedition Acts drew fire from many directions, including Democratic-Republican leaders Thomas Jefferson and James Madison. Together the two penned state resolutions against the acts for adoption by the state legislatures of Kentucky and Virginia, respectively. These resolves argued that the acts were unconstitutional; furthermore, both documents proposed that a state could nullify unconstitutional acts and consider them void. In short, Jefferson and Madison suggested that states did not owe obedience to laws that contradicted the ultimate law of the land, the U.S. Constitution. Eventually, the provisions of the acts either expired or were overturned under the Jefferson presidency.

One of the last challenges facing Adams came from the Caribbean, namely the island of Santo Domingo. A self-educated freed slave named Toussaint L'Overture led a successful revolt against the French and invited the United States to establish trade with the independent island. Though Adams wanted the French out of the Caribbean and was pleased at Toussaint's accomplishment, his first concern remained the United States and its best interest. Adams did not wish to provoke potential enemies by establishing flamboyant trade and diplomatic relations with Santo Domingo; neither did he desire to frustrate Great Britain, Spain, Holland, or any other European nation that might press claims to the Caribbean islands. Adams' prudence all but paralyzed him. He left office after quietly establishing trade with Santo Domingo, but without ever taking decisive action with regard to Toussaint.

Jefferson disagreed with Adams' policy of inaction and changed the direction of relations with the island when he became president. Under Jefferson, the United States established trade with Toussaint and recognized him as the leader of an independent Santo Domingo, but it also opened covert talks with officials from the island's former colonizer, France. The United States reaped the benefits of being one of the sole suppliers of merchandise to Santo Domingo, all the while Jefferson determined to support a French bid to reestablish control of the island. Toussaint's experiment with freedom ended harshly when he was captured and taken to France, where he died in 1803.

In several cases such as the Alien and Sedition Acts and U.S. policy toward Santo Domingo, Adams' positions were reversed or changed by Jefferson. The lives and careers of the two statesmen remained intertwined until their deaths (on the same day, July 4, 1826). In many senses, Adams' administration proved to be an aberration in a cycle otherwise considered to be "the Virginia Dynasty" of presidents. Before him, Washington was a Virginia planter, agrarian though largely apartisan and moved by ties of experience and affection (Hamilton, Jefferson, Madison) over ideology. After Adams, the successive double terms of Thomas Jefferson, James Madison, and James Monroe created an almost seamless tradition of Democratic-Republican, southern leadership. Only Adams represented northern, Federalist views. Only Adams failed to win reelection to a second term in office. (Adams, however, raised a son to become president of the United States: John Quincy Adams.)

Adams and Charles Pinckney, once again his Federalist preference for vice president, lost the opportunity for a second administration in an election later termed the Revolution of 1800. Although Adams and Pinckney ran they received less support than they had enjoyed previously. A tie in the Electoral College between Democratic-Republicans Thomas Jefferson and Aaron Burr threw the election into the U.S. House of Representatives. In the end, Hamilton moved his influential support to Jefferson and the former vice president became the chief executive. The end of Adams' presidency, followed by the death of Alexander Hamilton (at the hands of Vice President Burr, in fact), signaled the end of the Federalist era and the triumph of the Democratic-Republicans.

In significant ways, however, the Democratic-Republican presidents who followed Adams achieved success based in part on his contributions. Adams saw the nation through a time of quasi-war from abroad and unrest to the point of potential civil war at home. He organized the army, built the navy, and preserved neutrality in a dangerous and trying time. Though not as popular as Washington, Adams was as strong as his predecessor, and he passed on to Jefferson an executive with undiminished power and potential. His emphasis on stability, balance, and continuity seemed lackluster to some witnesses, but provided a solid foundation for the new nation, especially in the face of domestic and international upheaval. He moved into the White House in Washington, D.C., thus preparing the way for successive presidents in the new capital of the United States. He also set a precedent for the peaceful transfer of power from one party to another—from defeat instead of retirement—with dignity and respect.

NOTES

1. John Adams, *Letters of John Adams, Addressed to His Wife*, ed. Charles Francis Adams, vol. 2 (Boston: C. Little and James Brown, 1841), pp. 244–245.

2. Ralph Adams Brown, *The Presidency of John Adams* (Lawrence: University Press of Kansas, 1975), p. 134.

INTERNATIONAL NEUTRALITY

The presidency of John Adams marked a further widening of the political gulf between Democratic-Republicans such as Thomas Jefferson and James Madison and Federalists such as Alexander Hamilton and

Adams himself. One of the litmus-test issues of this division was international relations—in particular, the relationship of the United States with France. The French Revolution certainly had changed the landscape of French-American affairs, but the nation was unsure exactly how this change would translate in terms of diplomacy. Unlike the Democratic-Republicans, who saw the French Revolution as the intellectual heir of the American War of Independence, and the French people as allies in deed as well as spirit, Federalists such as Adams were wary of the newly formed French Directorate and preoccupied with concerns of how U.S. relations with France might impact relations with that nation's traditional enemy, Great Britain.

Early in the Adams administration, the issue erupted when French officials were rumored to have protested the withdrawal of U.S. minister James Monroe from Paris and dismissed his replacement, Adams-appointed general Charles Pinckney. At the same time, U.S. merchants reported that French privateers were capturing their ships and cargo. Adams responded with a call for a strengthening of the navy and a reorganization of the militia. What seemed to be practical defensive measures to Adams, however, sounded like a declaration of war to Democratic-Republicans.

This brought up two distinct questions regarding U.S. foreign policy. First, what, if anything, did the United States owe France for its past assistance and friendship? The Washington administration already had set a precedent of reading U.S. treaties with France narrowly in order to avoid the entangling alliances that the first president feared could be the undoing of the young nation. Democratic-Republicans were less quick to forget that France had befriended the states as they fought for independence from Great Britain, however, and that the European power had followed the lead of the United States and fought a revolution of its own soon afterwards in the effort to bring liberty and equality to its people. Adams' opponents seemed willing to give France every benefit of the doubt and wait through its postrevolutionary growing pains without offensive or defensive moves against it.

The second, more crucial, issue was a question of constitutional powers. Adams' call for military reorganization and buildup sounded to many Democratic-Republicans like a *de facto* declaration of war, despite the fact that the Congress, not the president, possessed the constitutional power to declare war. This apparently unauthorized action, Adam's opponents argued, showed a disregard for constitutional limitations and a dangerous tendency to acquire and wield inappropriate power. Some voices, such as that of the Democratic-Republican newspaper *Aurora General Advertiser*, even called for John Adams to resign as president.

On the other side of the political spectrum, Adams not only saw France's actions as warranting response, but also saw this situation as a test case for U.S. actions on the international stage. In some sense, Adams was looking ahead to the potential the United States enjoyed to be a power broker, if not a leader, among nations. How the United States chose to respond to current slights and abuses, Adams believed, would determine whether or not the United States could meet its future destiny as a nation "forming a weight in that balance of power in Europe which never can be forgotten or neglected." Reticence now, he argued, would bring more troubles later. Strength now would purchase the United States respect and power from the nations of Europe.

The divisive nature of the French question was relatively short-lived, however, thanks to an event that unified the U.S. population, both Democratic-Republican and Federalist, known as the XYZ affair. In a last effort to persuade French officials to restrain their citizens from harassing U.S. merchant ships, Adams sent a three-man delegation to Paris in 1798. Once there, the U.S. ministers received insulting and illegal treatment. Three subordinates of the French minister Talleyrand even solicited bribes from the members of the U.S. delegation, who in turn adamantly refused to pay for the diplomatic reception to which they were entitled as envoys of a foreign nation. The U.S. ministers' report (which referred to the three French officials only as X, Y, and Z, hence the name of the affair) created outrage across the United States. Those who had supported the interests of France could not stomach such poor treatment from the recent ally. By April, 1798, the catchphrase "millions for defense, but not one cent for tribute" was repeated by even the staunchest Democratic-Republicans.

Though Adams had gained national unity, at least for the moment, the XYZ affair was not a good omen for the new president. His administration would face hostilities from France and England both, quasi wars that drained U.S. resources and patience, and his hopes for the United States as a powerful actor on the world stage would seem dim at best. Allegations of unconstitutional actions and unwarranted use of power also would plague him throughout his term and would thwart his attempt to win another four years in office. The unity created by the XYZ affair would vanish in an atmosphere of partisanship that would cement factions across the nation for years to come. His own political party, however, would not survive the following years, and would face extinction along with the hopes of Adams' reelection. In short, the challenges of international relations, played out at home among fellow citizens as well as abroad, would be the chief preoccupation and greatest downfall of the Adams administration.

THE PRESIDENT'S POSITION: PREPARATION FOR WAR
(ANTI-FRENCH)

John Adams to Elbridge Gerry
Philadelphia, 13 February 1797

. . . You are apprehensive "that France will view the discussion of gratitude in its full extent, as trespassing the line of defence." But Adet had laid his demands of gratitude so high, and all his partisans were in the habit of deafening our people with such rude, extravagant, and arrogant pretensions to it, that it seems to have become necessary to be explicit upon the subject. I may say to a friend of your discretion, what I believe you will agree in, that there is quite as modest a demand of gratitude due from them to us, as from us to them. I think I can demonstrate that the French nation derived more advantage from the connection than we did—that she owes her independence as much to us as we do ours to her. Whether she has thrown away her advantages by her revolution or not, is for her to consider. We had nothing to do with that by treaty or in practice. We have imprudently gone too far in our approbation of it, and adopted, by sympathy, too much of her enthusiasm in it; for we were, and still are, incapable of judging whether it was wise or not, useful or not, destructive or not. Our treaty obliged us to no approbation of it, or concern in it, and our weak ideas and sensations of gratitude have led us into the fundamental error of taking too large a share of interest and sympathy in it.

The people of this country must not lose their conscious integrity, their sense of honor, nor their sentiment of their own power and force, so far as to be upbraided in the most opprobrious and contumelious language, and be wholly silent and passive under it, and that in the face of mankind . . .

See *The Works of John Adams, Second President of the United States: With A Life of the Author, Notes and Illustrations, by His Grandson Charles Francis Adams*, vol. 8 (Boston: Little, Brown and Company, 1853), pp. 522–523.

John Adams,
Special Session Message
United States, May 16, 1797

Gentlemen of the Senate and Gentlemen of the House of Representatives:

. . . It would have afforded me the highest satisfaction to have been able to congratulate you on a restoration of peace to the nations of Europe whose animosities have endangered our tranquility; but we have still abundant cause of gratitude to the Supreme Dispenser of National Blessings. . . .

. . . It is my sincere desire, and in this I presume I concur with you and with our constituents, to preserve peace and friendship with all nations; and believing that neither the honor nor the interest of the United States absolutely forbid the repetition of advances for securing these desirable objects with France, I shall institute a fresh attempt at negotiation, and shall not fail to promote and accelerate an accommodation on terms compatible with the rights, duties, interests, and honor of the nation.

. . . As the sufferings of our mercantile and seafaring citizens can not be ascribed to the omission of duties demandable, considering the neutral situation of our country, they are to be attributed to the hope of impunity arising from a supposed inability on our part to afford protection. To resist the consequences of such impressions on the minds of foreign nations and to guard against the degradation and servility which they must finally stamp on the American character is an important duty of Government.

. . . And as our country is vulnerable in other interests besides those of its commerce, you will seriously deliberate whether the means of general defense ought not to be increased by an addition to the regular artillery and cavalry, and by arrangements for forming a provisional army.

. . . Although it is very true that we ought not to involve ourselves in the political system of Europe, but to keep ourselves always distinct and separate from it if we can, yet to effect this separation, early, punctual, and continual information of the current chain of events and of the political projects in contemplation is no less necessary than if we were directly concerned in them. However we may consider ourselves, the maritime and commercial powers of the world will consider the United States of America as forming a weight in that balance of power in Europe which never can be forgotten or neglected.

See *A Compilation of the Messages and Papers of the Presidents, 1789–1902,* ed. James D. Richardson, vol. 1 (Washington, D.C.: Bureau of National Literature and Art, 1904), pp. 233, 236, 238.

AURORA GENERAL ADVERTISER: FOR PEACE
(PRO-FRENCH)

Aurora General Advertiser
Tuesday, March 20, 1798

"Remarks on the President's Message"

The time is then come which (*in the opinion of the Executive*) calls on Americans to draw the sword. If our legislative councils are to be actuated by the impressions made on his mind, then the United States are to join in the European War on the side of the tottering *government* of Britain and against the French Republic. . . . From the . . . President's address, it would appear that, however he may acknowledge a right in the Legislature to *declare* war, he conceives he has that of *making* it. . . . If our merchantmen may now arm . . . we are at war. . . . [I]f our legislature does not interpose and prevent the arming, we shall be dragged into a war. Indeed the whole tenor of the president's message bears an aspect extremely threatening to our peace. . . . [D]oes not the crisis call upon the PEOPLE to step forward . . . [?]

Reprinted in Richard N. Rosenfeld, *American Aurora: A Democratic-Republican Returns, The Suppressed History of Our Nation's Beginnings and the Heroic Newspaper That Tried to Report It* (New York: St. Martin's Press, 1997), p. 46.

Aurora General Advertiser
Wednesday, March 21, 1798

The message . . . from the President of the United States to Congress is fatal and destructive to the peace of the United States. . . . Are the people of the United States prepared to draw the sword . . . against the French Republic at this presidential call without knowing either the necessity or the object to be obtained[?] . . . His harpies say it is not a declaration of war, although they know it amounts to the same thing. . . .

Mr. Adams has it now in his power to do a most acceptable service to his country by retiring from . . . public life. . . . He must be sensible himself that at this time he is unfit to be trusted with the interests of a peaceful nation. His personal pride has been wounded . . . and this leads him to do what it can never be the interests of his country to suffer. Let him manage his own passions on the occasion, and, without him, our councils will manage our differences with France.

Reprinted in Richard N. Rosenfeld, *American Aurora: A Democratic Republican Returns, The Suppressed History of Our Nation's Beginnings and the Heroic Newspaper That Tried to Report It* (New York: St. Martin's Press, 1997), pp. 47–48.

Aurora General Advertiser
Saturday, March 24, 1798

Let me ask for what cause does the President desire war with France? Is It to protect British trade and commerce with the United States. . . . ? Or is it to produce an alliance offensive and defensive between Great Britain and the United States, the more effectually to defeat and destroy republicanism In France and reestablish monarchy and thereby maintain that favorite government which Mr. Adams . . . declared "is the most stupendous fabric of human invention?"

Reprinted in Richard N. Rosenfeld, *American Aurora: A Democratic-Republican Returns, The Suppressed History of Our Nation's Beginnings and the Heroic Newspaper That Tried to Report It* (New York: St. Martin's Press, 1997), p. 50.

Aurora General Advertiser
Monday, March 26, 1798

[Reprint] FROM THE MIDDLESEX GAZETTE
[A Connecticut Paper]

Friends and fellow citizens:

You engaged in a long and bloody war with Great Britain—for what? To secure the fruits of your labours to yourselves with equal rights. . . . At the close of the revolution, the image of liberty was enstamped on every heart; we looked with a kind of horror on the British plans of oppression. . . . [Our government] have taught the people *that the President can do no wrong*; and that all are Jacobins, democrats, disorganizers, and enemies to their country who dare to doubt this doctrine. . . . [They] detach our government from France; and join it in close league with Great Britain. . . . Have not all the governmental papers abused and villified the French? Has not our [revolutionary war] treaty with them been so construed as to deprive them of almost all the advantages . . . meant to be secured to them by it? . . . We are now about entering on a war; not with a natural, not with an ordinary enemy; but with a nation which saved us from the rapacious jaws of Britain, now become a republic like our own . . .
A fellow citizen who does not believe in executive infallibility.

Reprinted in Richard N. Rosenfeld, *American Aurora: A Democratic-Republican Returns, The Suppressed History of Our Nation's Beginnings and the Heroic Newspaper That Tried to Report It* (New York: St. Martin's Press, 1997), pp. 51–52.

Aurora General Advertiser
Tuesday, March 27, 1798

John Fenno [in the *Gazette of the United States*] is very angry at the *Aurora* for having yesterday copied an article from a Connecticut newspaper hinting that the old soldiers were not fond of a French war. He affirms, on the contrary, that there is not one officer whose conduct in the late war will bear scrutiny, who is to be found among the "base hireling crew of calumniating Jacobins."

Looking into Congress, we find many respectable military characters opposed to the present plan for war, such as General Smith of Baltimore, Colonel Parker of Virginia, Gen. M'Dowell and Col. Gillespie, of North Carolina. It is needless to multiply further examples.

Reprinted in Richard N. Rosenfeld, *American Aurora: A Democratic-Republican Returns, The Suppressed History of Our Nation's Beginnings and the Heroic Newspaper That Tried to Report It* (New York: St. Martin's Press, 1997), p. 53

THE NATION'S ARMY

As the XYZ affair brought unity to the people of the United States, at least temporarily, President Adams looked to provide for the nation's defense by reorganizing the army and building the navy. He began in his efforts with little faith in himself and less confidence from the U.S. citizenry, however, as he tried to fill the shoes of the former commander in chief. More than once, Adams lamented that George Washington could not simply return from retirement and take over the reins of statecraft through this difficult period. In the end, Adams opted for the next best thing: placing the U.S. Army in Washington's experienced hands.

What should have been a simple issue of presidential appointment became a complex and frustrating tangle of egos and alliances, couched in terms of partisan concerns. In short, the routine questions of experience and ability in determining military appointments in the new army evolved into questions of party preference and political popularity. What Adams expected to be an end to his problems with the army—namely, appointing Washington as commander of the forces—actually spawned a whole new series of problems for Adams behind the scenes as he tried to steer Washington into choices with the best possible political, as well as military, outcomes.

Before Adams even approached Washington on the issue of the military, Hamilton and Washington were corresponding about the likelihood of war and the fate of the army. Washington admitted to Hamilton that he would feel obliged to serve if the worst came to pass, and Hamilton expressed his desire to serve under Washington once again, as he had during the War of Independence. Washington's affection and respect for Hamilton, in turn, was common knowledge, and it seemed clear that any plan to include Washington would automatically accept Hamilton as second in command.

By May 1798, Secretary of State Timothy Pickering was sending multiple letters to Washington on the issue of army leadership. His pro-Federalist queries asked Washington to serve or, if he declined, to name Hamilton as his preferred replacement. At the same time, Adams wrote Washington, inviting him to be lieutenant general and commander in chief of the army. In order to cinch the nomination—and, most probably, to abort support for Hamilton by arch-Federalists such as Pickering—Adams secured the appointment by unanimous vote by the Senate before even receiving a reply from Washington.

Washington at this time was writing to Secretary of War James Mc-Henry in order to be certain that, if he accepted the invitation (as yet he did not know he had already been appointed), he would have the freedom to make his own appointments, especially for his general staff. By the time he discovered the Senate had approved his nomination, a number of problems had emerged. Washington wanted Hamilton to serve beneath him as second in command. Yet any French land attack would probably come in the southern states, and southern Democratic-Republicans hated Hamilton and his policies. South Carolina's Charles Pinckney, however, had southern support and knowledge of the region. Pinckney would never serve under Hamilton, and the opposite seemed equally true. Who had the greater experience? The greater support? On what should the decision be based?

Adams hoped to build a decidedly bipartisan command in order to strengthen support for himself and his approach to the international crises. He sent a list of potential appointees to Washington after the former president accepted his new position at the head of the army. Washington, however, looked more to questions of military experience and personal knowledge while considering his general staff, and returned to Adams his own list of appointees, all of whom were staunch Federalists. This played directly into Pickering's own partisan plans, but threatened Adams' own bid for popularity.

Fighting Washington's preferences, Adams asked that the order, at least, of the top three appointees be switched so that Hamilton did not receive the first position; Adams favored Henry Knox, Charles Pinckney, and Alexander Hamilton appointed in that order. If Adams could not have a bipartisan staff, then at least he could bury the most politically charged appointment, Hamilton's, behind a few less contentious ones. Adams' political maneuverings backfired, however.

Washington was furious. He pointed out that Adams had arranged the original appointment before Washington could accept or decline.

Once he was thrust into the public eye again, Washington asked to be able to control the appointments of those directly beneath him. He was tired of Adams' politicization of the process. If he did not have his own choice of officers, Washington threatened, he simply would resign and toss the entire problem back into the lap of the president.

Adams had little choice. Accepting Hamilton as second in command would be difficult politically, but not as difficult as losing George Washington as commander in chief. The president was nothing if not a realist. Although he maintained the president's supremacy to the end—the final decision, he argued, should have fallen to the chief executive—he accepted Washington's appointees in the same order in which Washington specified them. Washington's preferences trumped Adams' political plans.

At first blush, Adams' reticence to support members of his own party seems unusual. But Adams appreciated that the nation's partisanship was a threat to its internal fabric—and certainly to his own administration. His efforts to find common ground with the opposing party were nonetheless short-lived. In the future, Adams would prove unwilling to make the effort at bipartisanship. By the end of his term, he would wield the power of his position against those who disagreed with him and his policies. In retrospect, it seems that Adams learned the wrong lessons from the military appointment debate.

THE PRESIDENT'S POSITION: POLITICS IN THE ARMED FORCES

John Adams to J. McHenry, Secretary of War
Quincy, 29 August 1798

. . . General Knox is gone to the eastward, as I understand, to return in ten or fifteen days. But if he were in Boston, I could not send him either your official or private letter, as neither contains sentiments that I can approve. My opinion is and has always been clear, that as the law now stands, the order of nomination or of recording has no weight or effect, but that officers appointed on the same day, in whatever order, have a right to rank according to antecedent services. I made the nomination according to the list presented to me by you, from General Washington, in hopes that rank might be settled among them by agreement or acquiescence, believing at the time, and expressing to you that belief, that the nomination and appointment would give Hamilton no command at all, nor any rank before any Major-General. This is my opinion still. I am willing to settle all decisively at present (and have no fear of the consequences), by dating the commissions, Knox on the first day, Pinckney on the second, and Hamilton on the third. If this course is not taken, and the commissions are all made out on the same day, I tell you my opinion is clear that Hamilton will legally rank after Hand, and, I fear, even after Lee.

You speak to me of the expediency of attempting an alteration in the rank of the gentlemen in question. You know, Sir, that no rank has ever been settled by me. You know my opinion has always been, as it is now, that the order of names in the nomination and record was of no consequence.

. . . The power and authority are in the President. I am willing to exert this authority at this moment, and to be responsible for the exercise of it. All difficulties will in this way be avoided. But if it is to be referred to General Washington, or to mutual and amicable accommodation among the gentlemen themselves, I foresee it will come to me at last after much altercation and exasperation of passions, and I shall then determine it exactly as I should now,—Knox, Pinckney, and Hamilton.

There has been too much intrigue in this business with General Washington and me; if I shall ultimately be the dupe of it, I am much mistaken in myself. . . .

See *The Works of John Adams, Second President of the United States: With A Life of the Author, Notes and Illustrations, by His Grandson Charles Francis Adams*, vol. 8 (Boston: Little, Brown and Company, 1853), pp. 587–588.

John Adams to J. McHenry, Secretary of War
Quincy, 13 September 1798

Sir,—I have received your favor of the 6th, and approve of your determination to make out the commissions in the order of Knox on the first day, Pinckney on the second, and Hamilton on the third. This being done, you may call Generals Knox and Hamilton into service as soon as you please.

Your request, to be informed whether I attach any portion of the intrigues, which I alluded to, if any have been employed, to you, is reasonable; and I have no scruple to acknowledge that your conduct through the whole towards me has been candid. I have suspected, however, that extraordinary pains were taken with you to impress upon your mind that the public opinion and the unanimous wish of the federalists was, that General Hamilton might be first, and even Commander-in-chief; that you might express this opinion to General Washington more forcibly than I should have done; and that this determined him to make the arrangement as he did. If this suspicion was well founded, I doubt not you made the representation with integrity. I am not and never was of the opinion that the public opinion demanded General Hamilton for the first, and I am now clear that it never expected nor desired any such thing.

The question being now settled, the responsibility for which I take upon myself, I have no hard thoughts concerning your conduct in this business, and I hope you will make your mind easy concerning it.

See *The Works of John Adams, Second President of the United States: With a Life of the Author, Notes and Illustrations, by His Grandson Charles Francis Adams*, vol. 8 (Boston: Little, Brown and Company, 1853), pp. 593–594.

GEORGE WASHINGTON ON EXPERIENCE IN THE ARMED FORCES

George Washington to John Adams
Mount Vernon, 25th Septr 1798

Sir,

With all the respect which is due to your public station, and with the regard I entertain for your private character, the following representation is presented to your consideration. If in the course of it, any expression should escape me which may appear to be incompatible with either, let the purity of my intentions; the candour of my declarations; and a due respect for my own character, be received as an apology.

The subject on which I am about to address you, is not less delicate in its nature, than it is interesting to my feelings. It is the change which you have directed to be made in the relative rank of the Major Generals, which I had the honor of presenting to you, by the Secretary of War; the appointment of an Adjutant General *after* the first nomination was rejected; and the *prepared* state you are in to appoint a third, if the second should decline, without the least intimation of the matter to me.

It would not have been unavailing, *after* the nomination and appointment of me to the Chief command of the Armies of the United States, (without any previous consultation of my sentiments) to have observed to you the delicate situation in which I was placed by that act. It was still less expedient, to have dwelt more than I did, on my sorrow at being drawn from my retirement; where I had fondly hoped to have spent the few remaining years which might be dispensed to me, if not in profound tranquility, at least without public responsibility. But if you had been pleased, previously to the nomination, to have enquired into the train of my thoughts upon the occasion, I would have told you with the frankness & candour which I hope will ever mark my character, on what terms

I would have consented to the nomination; you would then have been enabled to decide whether they were admissible, or not.

This opportunity was not afforded *before* I was brought to public view. To declare them *afterwards*, was all I could do; and this I did, in explicit language, to the Secretary of War, when he honoured me with your letter of the 7th of July; shewed me his powers; and presented the Commission. They were, that the General Officers, and General staff of the Army should not be appointed without my concurrence. I extended my stipulations no farther, but offered to give every information, and render every service in my power in selecting good officers for the Regiments. . . .

This, Sir, is a true, candid & impartial statement of facts. It was the ground on which I *accepted* and *retained* the Commission; and was the authority on which I proceeded to the arrangement that was presented to you by the Secretary of War.

Having *no idea* that the General Officers for the Provisional army would be nominated at that time they were, I had not even contemplated characters for those appointments.

I will now, respectfully ask, in what manner these stipulations on my part, have been complied with?

In the arrangements made by me, with the Secretary of War, the three Major Generals stood—Hamilton, Pinckney, Knox, and in this order I expected their Commissions would have been dated. This, I conceive, must have been the understanding of the Senate. And certainly was the expectation of all those with whom I have conversed. But you have been pleased to order the last to be first, and the first to be last. If four Brigadiers for the Provisional army, one I never heard of as a Military character, has been nominated and appointed; and another is so well known to all those who served with him, in the Revolution, as (for the appointment) to have given the greatest disgust, and will be the means of preventing many valuable Officers of that army from coming forward. . . .

Taking all these circumstances into view, you will not be surprised at my solicitude to intrench myself as I did; nor is it to be supposed that I made the arrangement of the three Major Generals without an eye to possible consequences. I wished for time, it is true, to have effected it, hoping that an amicable adjustment might have taken place, & offered, at a very short summons, (inconvenient as it would have been) to proceed to Philadelphia for that purpose; but as no subsequent notice was taken thereof, I presumed there were operative reasons against that measure, and did not repeat it.

It is proper too I should add, that, from the information I received from various quarters, & through different channels, I had no doubt in my mind that the current sentiment among the members of Congress, and particularly among those from New England, was in favor of Colonel Hamilton's being second in command—and this impression has been since confirmed in the most unequivocal manner by some respectable members of that body, whom I have myself seen & conversed with, on the subject. . . .

See *The Papers of George Washington: Retirement Series,* vol. 3, *September 1798–April 1799* (Charlottesville: University Press of Virginia, 1999), pp. 36–38, 40.

ALIEN AND SEDITION ACTS

Perhaps no single event is more linked with the Adams administration, and its ultimate failure, than the passage of the Alien and Sedition Acts. President Adams was not, obviously, a member of the legislature that passed these laws, but as president he tacitly supported them and proved willing to use them against individuals on more than one occasion. His acceptance of the acts overshadows his accomplishments during his tenure in office, according to many contemporary historians.

Adams found himself president during a time of unparalleled difficulty in the new nation. Violent international conflicts and bitter domestic partisanship threatened the union from many sides. Frequent, vocal opposition from critics of the president fed discontent; fears of foreign spies and agitators did as well. In 1798, Federalist majorities in both houses of Congress moved to try to quell some of these problems by limiting foreign influences in the nation and silencing internal opposition. The Alien Act created obstacles for immigrants who tried to obtain U.S. citizenship. Many noncitizens, especially French émigrés, fled the country for fear that the provisions of the Alien Act would be used against them. In an already nationalistic time, the Alien Act exacerbated the people's and government's tendencies to fear and distrust non-U.S. citizens. Adams himself signed warrants for the deportation of several aliens only to find they had already fled the country. Although he expected that the law would "upon trial be found inadequate to the object intended," Adams was willing to give it a try.

More problematic, and ultimately unpopular, was the Sedition Act. Adams faced a great deal of opposition from Democratic-Republicans, and they made use of the newspapers and printing presses to disagree with his policies and actions, particularly with regard to international affairs. The *Aurora General Advertiser*, for example, ran almost daily critiques of the administration and directly called for Adams' resignation on several different occasions. Even the First Lady, Abigail Adams, felt the pressure of the press. She wrote to her sister, "Yet dairingly do the vile incendiaries keep up in Baches paper the most wicked and base, violent and calumniating abuse. . . . But nothing will have an Effect until congress pass a Sedition Bill."[1] And so it did. The momentum of the opposition, coupled with the delicacy of the near state of war in which the administration was operating, seemed to justify the action for Congress. The Sedition Act expanded the power of the Adams administration to use censorship to silence its newspaper critics. A number of editors faced jail and fines for printing critical editorials, and others remained quiet for fear of similar treatment.

To Adams' credit, the president did not use the acts as aggressively as some arch-Federalists might have liked. Timothy Pickering, for one, seemed enthusiastic about using the law to deport as many noncitizens as possible. As historian Alexander DeConde once admitted about the Alien and Sedition Acts, "with Secretary of State Pickering as their chief enforcement officer, and Hamilton a leading advocate of their enforcement, the spirit . . . became one of intolerant, oppressive, and, at times, hysterical native Americanism."[2]

As the Adams administration waged one quasi war on the international front and another at home against U.S. citizens who opposed the president, Democratic-Republicans responded to the Alien and Sedition Acts through the voices of the states. Thomas Jefferson and James Madison led the way by drafting resolutions for the state legislatures of Kentucky and Virginia, respectively, which they in turn adopted. These resolutions underscored the unconstitutionality of the Alien and Sedition Acts. They also employed political philosopher John Locke's compact theory of government to suggest that the states could nullify acts that were passed by the United States Congress but did not conform to the U.S. Constitution. If the acts violated the law of the land, they reasoned, then the states were not bound to obey these acts. (This argument would return again in the 1830s' nullification debate and the secession crisis of the 1860s.)

In the end, as with many of the accomplishments of the Adams administration, the Alien and Sedition Acts, or rather those that had not already expired, were undone quickly. A new Congress under President Thomas Jefferson overturned them. The Congress also repaid with interest fines that had been levied under the acts. Those convicted due to these laws received pardons from Jefferson. Though a certain brand of new nationalism remained, the public transferred its energy to the new West, opened through the Louisiana Purchase. The ever expanding United States seemed big enough to hold citizens and newcomers, and all their associated factions and opponents, without the need for legislation and censorship—at least for a while.

The impact of the Alien and Sedition Acts continued to be felt nonetheless. Certainly they played a factor in the defeat of Adams and his bid for reelection. They tarnished his reputation in the eyes of successive generations of citizens and scholars. They also raised issues of constitutionality and national law. Who should decide when a law is unconstitutional, and how the states should react to unconstitutional legislation, became questions that would change the face of the nineteenth-century United States.

NOTES

1. Abigail Adams. Letter to Mary Cranch, April 26, 1798. Quoted in Ralph Adams Brown, *The Presidency of John Adams* (Lawrence: University Press of Kansas, 1975), p. 125.

2. Alexander DeConde, *The Quasi-War: The Politics and Diplomacy of the Undeclared War with France, 1797–1801* (New York: Charles Scribner's Sons, 1966), p. 100.

THE PRESIDENT'S POSITION: CENSORSHIP

John Adams to T. Pickering, Secretary of State
Quincy, 13 August 1799

And now, Sir, what shall I say to you on the subject of "libels and satires? Lawless things, indeed!" I have received your private letter of the 1st of this month, and considered the subject of it as fully as the pressure of other business of more importance would allow me time to do. Of Priestley and Cooper I will say no more at present than to relate to you two facts.

Anecdote first. Dr. Priestley's old friend, and my old acquaintance, Mr. Benjamin Vaughan, the celebrated M.P., soon after his arrival in Boston, came up to Quincy with his lady on a visit to us, who had visited his family in London. I was absent. They dined with Mrs. Adams, and in the course of conversation Mr. Vaughan told her that Mr. Cooper was a rash man, and he feared would lead him into others in America.

Anecdote the second. At the time when we were inquiring for an agent to conduct the affairs of the United States before the commissioners at Philadelphia, Mr. Cooper wrote me a letter, strongly recommending him. Both made apologies for his reputation as a democrat, and gave intimation of a reformation. I wondered that either could think it possible that the people of the United States could be satisfied or contented to intrust interests of such magnitude to an Englishman, or any other foreigner. I wondered that either should think it compatible with my duty, to prefer a stranger to the great number of able natives, who wished for this trust. But so it was. As it has been, from the beginning, a rule not to answer letters of solicitation or recommendation for offices, I never answered either. Mr. Read was appointed, and the disappointed candidate is now, it seems, indulging his revenge. A meaner, a more artful, or a more malicious libel has not appeared. As far as it alludes to me, I despise it; but I have no doubt it is a libel against the whole government, and as such ought to be prosecuted. I do not think it wise to execute the alien law against poor Priestley at present. He is as weak as water, as unstable as Reuben, or the wind. His influence is not an atom in this world.

Having long possessed evidence the most satisfactory to my mind, that [the French National] Collot is a pernicious and malicious intriguer, I have been always ready and willing to execute the alien law upon him. We are now about to enter on a negotiation with France but this is no objection against expelling from this country such an alien as he is. On the contrary, it is more necessary to remove such an instrument of mischief from among our people for his whole time will be employed in exciting corrupt divisions whether he can succeed or not. As to [Joseph Philippe] Letombe, if you can prove "that he paid the bribes ordered by the French Minister Adet," or any thing like it, he ought to be sent away too. But perhaps it would be better to signify that it is expected that he go, than to order him out at first by proclamation. There is a respect due to public commissions, which I should wish to preserve as far as may be consistent with safety.

The alien law, I fear, will upon trial be found inadequate to the object intended, but I am willing to try it in the case of Collot.

See *The Works of John Adams, Second President of the United States: With A Life of the Author, Notes and Illustrations, by His Grandson Charles Francis Adams*, vol. 9 (Boston: Little, Brown and Company, 1854), pp. 13–14.

AGAINST CENSORSHIP

Virginia Resolution, 1798

RESOLVED, That the General Assembly of Virginia, doth unequivocably express a firm resolution to maintain and defend the Constitution of the United States, and the Constitution of this State, against every aggression either foreign or domestic, and that they will support the government of the United States in all measures warranted by the former.

That this assembly most solemnly declares a warm attachment to the Union of the States, to maintain which it pledges all its powers; and that for this end, it is their duty to watch over and oppose every infraction of those principles which constitute the only basis of that Union, because a faithful observance of them, can alone secure its existence and the public happiness.

That this Assembly doth explicitly and peremptorily declare, that it views the powers of the federal government, as resulting from the compact, to which the states are parties; as limited by the plain sense and intention of the instrument constituting the compact; as no further valid that they are authorized by the grants enumerated in that compact; and that in case of a deliberate, palpable, and dangerous exercise of other powers, not granted by the said compact, the states who are parties thereto, have the right, and are in duty bound, to interpose for arresting the progress of the evil, and for maintaining within their respective limits, the authorities, rights and liberties appertaining to them.

That the General Assembly doth also express its deep regret, that a spirit has in sundry instances, been manifested by the federal government, to enlarge its powers by forced constructions of the constitutional charter which defines them; and that implications have appeared of a design to expound certain general phrases (which having been copied from the very limited grant of power, in the former articles of confederation were the less liable to be misconstrued) so as to destroy the meaning and effect, of the particular enumeration which necessarily explains and limits the general phrases; and so as to consolidate the states by degrees, into one sovereignty, the obvious tendency and inevitable consequence of which would be, to transform the present republican system of the United States, into an absolute, or at best a mixed monarchy.

That the General Assembly doth particularly protest against the palpable and alarming infractions of the Constitution, in the two late cases of the "Alien and Sedition Acts" passed at the last session of Congress; the first of which exercises a power no where delegated to the federal government, and which by uniting legislative and judicial powers to those of executive, subverts the general principles of free government; as well as the particular organization, and positive provisions of the federal constitution; and the other of which acts, exercises in like manner, a power not delegated by the constitution, but on the contrary, expressly and positively forbidden by one of the amendments thereto; a power, which more than any other, ought to produce universal alarm, because it is levelled against that right of freely examining public characters and measures, and of free communication among the people thereon, which has ever been justly deemed, the only effectual guardian of every other right.

That this state having by its Convention, which ratified the federal Constitution, expressly declared, that among other essential rights, "the Liberty of Conscience and of the Press cannot be cancelled, abridged, restrained, or modified by any authority of the United States," and from its extreme anxiety to guard these rights from every possible attack of sophistry or ambition, having with other states, recommended an amendment for that purpose, which amendment was, in due time, annexed to the Constitution; it would mark a reproachable inconsistency, and criminal degeneracy, if an indifference were now shewn, to the most palpable violation of one of the Rights, thus declared and secured; and to the establishment of a precedent which may be fatal to the other.

That the good people of this commonwealth, having ever felt, and continuing to feel, the most sincere affection for their brethren of the other states; the truest anxiety for establishing and perpetuating the union of all; and the most scrupulous fidelity to that constitution, which is the pledge of mutual friendship, and the instrument of mutual happiness; the General Assembly doth solemnly appeal to the like dispositions of the other states, in confidence that they will concur with this commonwealth in declaring, as it does hereby declare, that the acts aforesaid, are unconstitutional; and that the necessary and proper measures will be taken by each, for cooperating with this state, in maintaining the Authorities, Rights, and Liberties, referred to the States respectively, or to the people.

That the Governor be desired, to transmit a copy of the foregoing Resolutions to the executive authority of each of the other states, with a request that the same may be communicated to the Legislature thereof; and that a copy be furnished to each of the Senators and Representatives representing this state in the Congress of the United States.

Agreed to by the Senate, December 24, 1798.

The Avalon Project at Yale Law School, 1997, William C. Fray and Lisa A. Spar, co-directors. <http://www.yale.edu/lawweb/avalon/virres.htm.>

SANTO DOMINGO

One of the final challenges John Adams faced in his administration was the question of Saint Domingue, or Santo Domingo, the richest of the French islands in the Caribbean. Traditionally, the island had served as a base for privateers who preyed upon U.S. merchant ships. This pirating past, combined with the 1798 Non-Intercourse Act, which made it illegal to trade with France or French lands, meant that U.S. ships were not buying or selling cargo on the island. A slave revolt, however, overturned the power structure on Santo Domingo and throughout the Caribbean (sending many French citizens to the United States, incidentally, who would remain pro-France, and therefore pro-Jefferson, in their new home). The leader of this revolt, and in turn of Santo Domingo, was a self-educated freed slave named Toussaint L'Overture. He promised that he could protect U.S. merchant ships and asked Adams to resume trade with the newly liberated population of Santo Domingo.

At first glance, the situation seemed like a grand opportunity for the United States. Toussaint L'Overture and his people appeared to embody the very spirit of the American War of Independence, overthrowing their owner/oppressors and establishing a free society. Moreover, trade would be of two-way benefit, as the Caribbean was a ready-made and eager market for U.S. goods and produce.

Adams, however, found reason to pause. First, the idea of slave revolts never failed to spark panic in the southern states of the United States, especially since such insurrections grew more frequent after 1790. Second, and perhaps more importantly, relations with Santo Domingo would strain already uneasy international affairs. The relationship of France to the island, not to mention Great Britain, Spain, and Holland, was unclear. As different interests battled for rights to the wealthy islands, the United States could easily fall into hostilities with one or more European nations simply by trading with Toussaint and his followers. Adams wanted no part in becoming allies or enemies with other nations over the Santo Domingo situation; most importantly, he did not want to interfere in the plans of Great Britain, if that country should wish to expand its power among the islands.

Adams eventually put practical U.S. interest ahead of support for the Caribbean revolutionaries. His policy was prudent almost to the point of invisibility. If the United States remained uninvolved, he reasoned, then it could not get hurt. Adams ended his days as president in relative nonaction regarding the Caribbean islands; trade was established quietly, but the United States did little to support Toussaint publicly.

Adams' successor, Thomas Jefferson, did not agree with his approach to the issue. Whereas Adams looked to Great Britain first and other European powers second, Jefferson turned his eyes to France. In Toussaint L'Overture he saw no kindred soul dedicated to freedom. As much as he had identified with the French Revolution as an intellectual heir to the U.S. break with Great Britain, Jefferson did not view the slave revolt on Santo Domingo as yet another product of an enlightened age. As a southerner, Jefferson found the idea of slave rebellion even more frightful than Adams had. Although Jefferson named an official envoy to Santo Domingo, in effect recognizing Toussaint as the legitimate ruler of the island, and continued talks about trade, he also communicated with the French about regaining their possessions in the Caribbean.

The difference between the two presidents' positions on the issue of Santo Domingo underscores the partisan manner in which the two men viewed the world. Adams supported Toussaint at heart, though did very little to help him. His support, however, was less ideological than it was practical. Adams did not want to see a French presence in the Caribbean, because it would threaten U.S. power and trade in the region. By revolting against the French, then, Toussaint and his followers were creating a situation far friendlier to U.S. and British interests, at least in Adams' eyes. In short, Adams liked Toussaint because he improved the position of the United States. His appreciation, however, had severe limits.

On the other hand, Jefferson emphasized the claims of France over the rights of Toussaint and his followers. In the event the island did remain independent, of course, Jefferson looked for ways to maximize the benefits to the United States. Yet even the lure of almost-captive markets did not keep him from taking his diplomatic lead from the French. Jefferson even agreed to help the French restore their rule on Santo Domingo if France would make peace with Great Britain, saying to French officials that "nothing would be easier than to furnish your army and fleet with everything, and to reduce Toussaint to starvation."[1] In the end, Jefferson's Francophilism allowed him to look the other way as Toussaint was captured and taken to his death in France in 1803.

NOTE

1. Thomas Jefferson. Comment to Louis Pichon. Quoted in Charles Callan Tansill, *The United States and Santo Domingo, 1798–1873: A Chapter in Caribbean Diplomacy* (Gloucester, Mass.: Peter Smith, 1967), pp. 80–81.

THE PRESIDENT'S POSITION: NEUTRALITY/PRO-BRITISH

To T. Pickering, Secretary of State
Quincy, 17 April 1799

Sir,—I received yesterday your favor of the 8th . . .

These papers I have read with more than common interest and anxiety; and, however sanguine I may be in my disposition, or prone to determine my judgment on the first view of a subject, in this case I must own myself puzzled and in doubt. The whole affair leads to the independence of the West India Islands; and although I may be mistaken, it appears to me that independence is the worst and most dangerous condition they can be in, for the United States. They would be less dangerous under the government of England, France, Spain, or Holland all together, and least of all under the same powers in parcels or divisions, as they are now. This opinion, however, is liable to so much uncertainty, that not great dependence can be placed upon it.

Upon the projects proposed by the British ministry, a great number of questions arise. Will not the projected, partial, limited, and restrained independence of St. Domingo, excite and alarm jealousies in Spain and

Holland, such as will attach them entirely to France; and in Denmark and Sweden, so as to make them more timid, if not more complaisant to France? Will it not involve us in a more inveterate and durable hostility with France, Spain, and Holland, and subject us more to the policy of Britain than will be consistent with our interest or honor? These questions may all be useless, because the independence of St. Domingo, and consequently of all the other islands in the West Indies, and of the Spanish, Dutch, and Portuguese possessions on the continent, may be brought about without our interference, and indeed in opposition to all we can do to prevent it.

The project of a joint company is certainly liable to all the objections which occurred to Mr. King, and although the English government would meet with no difficulty, we should certainly find it very difficult to manage.

My own ideas are these. 1st. That it would be most prudent for us to have nothing to do in the business. 2d. That if we should meddle, we had better leave the independence of the island complete and total, in commerce as well as legislation. 3d. That if this is not the sense of the English, we had better leave the whole management of the affair to them. 4th. That if they think fit, they may stipulate that we shall have a right to accede to the treaty they make, when we can, within a certain period of one, two, or three years. 5th. That we should accede to it, provided the Senate advise and consent, as soon as it shall be determined that no negotiation with France is likely to take place with effect. 6th. That we remain faithful to our promise, to open our commerce with the island as soon as privateering shall cease. 7th. Although these are my prevailing opinions and inclinations, I am by no means fixed in them or bigoted in them. . . .

See *The Works of John Adams, Second President of the United States: With A Life of the Author, Notes and Illustrations, by His Grandson Charles Francis Adams*, vol. 8 (Boston: Little, Brown and Company, 1853), pp. 634–635.

To T. Pickering, Secretary of State
Quincy, 15 June 1799

. . . I am glad the heads of department did not form a definitive opinion on the very important question whether it will be expedient to renew the commerce, without a concurrence of the British. My judgment inclines the same way at present with theirs; but we had better wait for further information. I am afraid that the jealousy and avidity of the English will do an injury to themselves, as well as to us; but we cannot help it. My opinion is that, if the powers of St. Domingo will not admit British ships of war or commerce into their ports, the British government ought to be contented with sufficient assurances of the neutrality of that island, during the war between England and France, and not insist on defeating the connection between the United States and St. Domingo. It is my earnest desire, however, to do nothing without the consent, concert, and coöperation of the British government in this case. They are so deeply interested that they ought to be consulted, and the commerce of the island is not worth to us the risk of any dispute with them.

See *The Works of John Adams, Second President of the United States: With A Life of the Author, Notes and Illustrations, by His Grandson Charles Francis Adams*, vol. 8 (Boston: Little, Brown and Company, 1853), pp. 657–658.

PRO-INVOLVEMENT/PRO-FRENCH

Thomas Jefferson to James Madison
Philadelphia, February 5, 1799

The bill for continuing the suspension of intercourse with France & her dependencies, is still before the Senate, but will pass by a very great vote. An attack is made on what is called Toussaint's clause, the object of which, as is charged by the one party and *admitted* by the other, is to facilitate the separation of the island from France. The clause will pass however, by about 19. to 8., or perhaps 18. to 9. Rigaud, at the head of the people of color, maintains his allegiance. But they are only 25,000 souls, against 500,000, the number of the blacks. The treaty made with them by Maitland is (if they are to be separated from France) the best thing for us. They must get their provisions from us. It will indeed be in English bottoms, so that we shall lose the carriage. But the English will probably forbid them the ocean, confine them to their island, & thus prevent their becoming an American Algiers. It must be admitted too, that they may play them off on us when they please. Against this there is no remedy but timely measures on our part, to clear ourselves, by degrees, of the matter on which that lever can work.

The opposition . . . was not republican. I have however seen letters from New Hampshire from which it appears that the public sentiment there is no longer progressive in any direction, but that at present it is dead water. That during the whole of their late session not a word has been heard of Jacobinism, disorganization &c. No reproach of any kind cast on the republicans, that there has been a general complaint among the members that they could hear but one side of the question, and the great anxiety to obtain a paper or papers which would put them in possession of both sides. From Massachusetts & R.I. I have no information. Connecticut remains riveted in her political & religious bigotry.

See Thomas Jefferson Papers at the Library of Congress. <http://mem-ory.loc.gov/ammem/mtjhtml/mtjhome.html>.

Thomas Jefferson to James Madison
February 19, 1799

I wrote to you last on the 11th; yesterday the bill for the *eventual* army of 30 regiments (30.000) & 75.000 volunteers, passed the Senate. By an amendment, the P was authorized to use the volunteers for every pur-pose for which he can use militia, so that the militia are rendered com-pleatly useless. The friends of the bill acknoleged that the volunteers are a *militia*, & agreed that they might properly be called the Presidential militia. They are not to go out of their state without their own consent. Consequently, all service out of the state is thrown on the constitutional militia, the Presidential militia being exempted from doing duty with them. Leblanc, an agent from Desfourneaux of Guadaloupe, came in the *Retaliation*. You will see in the papers Desfourneaux's letter to the Pres-ident, which will correct some immaterial circumstances of the statement in my last. You will see the truth of the main fact, that the vessel & crew were liberated without condition. Notwithstanding this, they have obliged Leblanc to receive the French prisoners, & to admit, in the pa-pers, the terms, "in *exchange* for *prisoners* taken from us," he denying at the same time that they consider them as *prisoners*, or had any idea of *exchange*. The object of his mission was not at all relative to that; but they chuse to keep up the idea of a cartel, to prevent the transaction from being used as evidence of the sincerity of the French govent towards a reconciliation. He came to assure us of a discontinuance of all irregular-ities in French privateers from Guadaloupe. He has been received very cavalierly. In the meantime, a *consul general* is named to St. Domingo; who may be considered as our minister to Toussaint.

But the event of events was announced to the Senate yesterday. It is this: it seems that soon after [Elbridge] Gerry's departure, overtures must have been made by Pichon, French chargá d'affaires at the Hague, to [William Vans] Murray. They were so soon matured, that on the 28th of Sep, 98, Talleyrand writes to Pichon, approving what had been done, & particularly of his having assured Murray that *whatever* Plenipotentiary the govent of the U S should send to France to end our differences would undoubtedly be received with the respect due to the representative of a *free, indepndt & powerful nation*; declaring that the President's instructions to his envoys at Paris, if they contain the whole of the American gov-ernment's intentions, announce dispositions which have been always en-tertained by the Directory; & desiring him to communicate these expressions to Murray, in order to convince him of the sincerity of the French government, & to prevail on him to transmit them to his government. This is dated Sep 28. & may have been received by Pichon Oct 1; and nearly 5. months elapse before it is communicated. Yesterday, the P nominated to the Senate W V Murray Mr Pl to the French republic, & adds, that he shall be instructed not to go to France, without direct & unequivocal assurances from the Fr government that he shall be received in character, enjoy the due privileges, and a minister of equal rank, title & power, be appointed to discuss & conclude our controversies by a new treaty. This had evidently been kept secret from the Feds of both Houses, as appeared by their dismay. The Senate have passed over this day without taking it up. It is said they are graveled & divided; some are for opposing, others do not know what to do. But in the meantime, they have been permitted to go on with all the measures of war & patronage, & when the close of the session is at hand it is made known. However, it silences all arguments against the sincerity of France, and renders desperate every further effort towards war. I enclose you a paper with more particulars. Be so good as to keep it till you see me, & then return it, as it is the copy of one I sent to another person, & is the only copy I have. Since I began my letter I have received yours of Feb 7 and 8, with it's enclosures; that referred to my discretion is precious, and shall be used accordingly.

See Thomas Jefferson Papers at the Library of Congress. <http://memory.loc.gov/ammem/mtjhtml/mtjhome.html>.

RECOMMENDED READINGS

Adams, John. *Papers of John Adams*. Edited by Robert J. Taylor. 10 vols. Cambridge, Mass.: Belknap Press of Harvard University Press, 1977.

Brown, Ralph Allen. *The Presidency of John Adams*. Lawrence: University Press of Kansas, 1975.

Brown, Walt. *John Adams and the American Press: Politics and Journalism at the Birth of the Republic*. Jefferson, N.C.: McFarland & Company, 1995.

Cappon, Lester J., ed. *The Adams-Jefferson Letters: The Complete Correspondence*. Chapel Hill: University of North Carolina Press, 1988.

Elkins, Stanley, and Eric McKitrick. *The Age of Federalism*. New York: Oxford University Press, 1993.

Ellis, Joseph J. *Passionate Sage: The Character and Legacy of John Adams*. New York: Norton, 1993.

Ferling, John E. *John Adams: A Life*. New York: Holt, 1996.

———. *John Adams: A Bibliography*. Westport, Conn.: Greenwood, 1994.

Ketcham, Ralph. *Presidents Above Party: The First American Presidency, 1789–1829*. Chapel Hill: University of North Carolina Press, 1984.

Kurtz, Stephen G. *The Presidency of John Adams: The Collapse of Federalism, 1795–1800*. New York: A.S. Barnes and Company, 1961.

Miller, John C. *Crisis in Freedom: The Alien and Sedition Acts*. Boston: Little, Brown, and Company, 1951.

Smith, Page. *John Adams*. 2 vols. New York: Doubleday, 1962.

Tansill, Charles Callan. *The United States and Santo Domingo, 1798–1873: A Chapter in Caribbean Diplomacy*. Baltimore: Johns Hopkins Press, 1938.

Thompson, C. Bradley. *John Adams and the Spirit of Liberty*. Lawrence: University Press of Kansas, 1998.

3

THOMAS JEFFERSON

(1801–1809)

INTRODUCTION

When John Adams took the presidency by a three-vote margin in the Electoral College, he entered office as a successor. He inherited George Washington's cabinet and agenda in a position literally made to fit the general. Adams ultimately failed by not providing the nation with another four years of Washingtonian leadership: he was not beloved, he was not first, and thus he was not successful. Instead, he was uncomfortable in his own executive skin: wary of his colleagues and their treachery, unhappy at the press's constant criticism. He chose to act at inopportune moments and remained paralyzed in key times. Though he held to his ideas with surprising strength, he was plagued by self-doubt and paranoia when trying to communicate and employ them. Intellectually brighter than Washington, and certainly more politically experienced, Adams could not shine in the shadow of the former president's image. Adams' personality simply did not suit the role of second president.

Thomas Jefferson came to power by a less impressive margin—a tie vote in the Electoral College landed the election in the U.S. House of Representatives—but when he did, he came with the force of a revolution. (Indeed, he called his election the Revolution of 1800.) By sheer strength of will, Jefferson remade the presidency in his own unique and eccentric image. He was no Washingtonian citizen among citizens, humble and serving, wigged, powdered, and pressed as the shining symbol of the new republic. In homespun suits and bedroom slippers, disheveled and comfortable, Jefferson was the man in power. He wined and dined officials and praised and badgered legislators. He made and broke his own rules and then excused himself. He did everything he could during his time in office to make his vision for the nation reality. Jefferson was not Washington, and he did not even try to be; the citizenry soon learned that Jefferson could be Jefferson as impressively as Washington had been Washington.

Whereas Washington liked to foster and observe debates among his adversarial advisors, and Adams withdrew and tried to weather the disloyalty of his own, Jefferson surrounded himself with like-minded, trustworthy colleagues who could support his vision with their own specialized knowledge. He made politically savvy and personally amenable cabinet choices: Henry Dearborn as secretary of war, Robert Smith as secretary of the navy, and Levi Lincoln as attorney general. He kept outgoing Virginia governor James Monroe close at hand as well. He fostered a sense of camaraderie and maintained an open-door policy to those with whom he worked closely. The real strength of his presidency, however, rested with his inner circle, his right and left hands: Secretary of State James Madison and Secretary of the Treasury Albert Gallatin. The two chief advisors dedicated themselves to Jefferson and the three presented a united front to the rest of the nation.

Madison's political partnership with Jefferson predated the founding of the United States. They collaborated and supported each other on countless occasions; the Kentucky and Virginia Resolutions were only one example of their combined efforts. Neighbors and friends as well as co-fathers of the Democratic-Republican Party, Jefferson and Madison shared an almost legendary loyalty for most of their adult lives, moving deftly from the roles of mentor and student to intellectual equals. Jefferson surprised no one when he supported Madison as his successor to the White House.

Jefferson's link with Madison was as much personal as professional. Gallatin's role in the triumvirate was more cerebral. Gallatin complemented Jefferson's imaginative, ideological vision and Madison's thorough statecraft with a carefully logical, analytical mind. Jefferson and Madison instinctively believed the economic system created by Hamilton during the Washington years to be faulty; it was Gallatin who could systematically critique it on economic grounds. In short, often Jefferson supplied the what, Madison supplied the how, and Gallatin supplied the why. The three did not always agree, however. When Madison described his half-formed notion of embargo to solve Jefferson's problem of danger to U.S. merchant trade—a notion that would haunt Madison and eventually lead him to a brief breakdown—Jefferson adopted it wholesale against Gallatin's detailed, and ultimately justified, protests. Once the president determined policy, however, all three men were aboard for the duration.

Jefferson did not need the trappings of formality to impose his ideas—his personality, and the fierce loyalty of his inner circle, allowed him to be casual in the nation's highest office without losing authority. On the contrary, his lack of self-consciousness, so different from Washington's propriety and Adams' isolation, charmed even his opponents. Critics knew, however, that Jefferson differed from both former presidents in another way: he made no pretense toward bipartisanship. Washington despised factions and Adams, though partisan, at times tried for unity and at other times suffered from only partial support from fellow Federalists. Jefferson, on the other hand, unified Democratic-Republicans and helped to raise the party beyond majority status to the point where the Federalist faction all but disappeared.

Jefferson's political acumen was underscored by his relationship with his first vice president. Aaron Burr, who originally tied with Jefferson for the presidency before the election fell to the U.S. House of Representatives, presented a unique obstacle to the Jeffersonian administration. After becoming vice president, Burr shot and killed Federalist leader Alexander Hamilton in a duel. Indicted for murder in both New York and New Jersey, he fled to South Carolina but later returned to serve out his term as vice president. Jefferson simply ignored Burr. He distanced himself from his fellow party member and therefore suffered little for Burr's embarrassments. George Clinton became Jefferson's vice president for his second term. Again, Burr hurt Jefferson little when arrested and tried for treason for trying to establish his own country in the Southwest. Jefferson's great presence was felt when he wished it to be; his disinterest also translated to the public, and saved him from any guilt by association.

In some senses, though Washington was the father of the presidency, Jefferson was the father of the Virginia Dynasty of presidents. Washington was a Virginian, but not in the same political and ideological sense as those who followed him. For sixteen years after Jefferson's retirement, his handpicked successors, Madison and Monroe, practiced a distinctly Jeffersonian brand of Democratic-Republicanism. They acted as Jefferson's heirs and invoked his superior charisma in the process. From the sidelines, Jefferson remained involved and interested in both presidential administrations.

Jefferson's term in office cannot be considered an unmitigated success, however, especially by his own standards. Jefferson's political theory, which espoused limited government and individual liberty, did not always translate into practice. The president turned his back on revolutionaries who fought for their independence in Santo Domingo, for example, allying with France against Toussaint L'Overture and the former slaves who followed him. Rather than delivering limited government, Jefferson overstepped his constitutional boundaries in order to transact the Louisiana Purchase in 1803 and left the executive office far stronger because of his actions. In the waning days of his final term he also established a *de facto* police state to enforce an embargo, disabling both free trade and individual liberties. Even with his failures—most notably the embargo, which was extremely unpopular—Jefferson's legacy included two more presidencies, each with double terms. Jefferson at his worst still competed and triumphed over his opposition.

The eight years Jefferson served in office provided disparate challenges for the chief executive. He came to power just as the pasha of Tripoli demanded higher tributes from the United States in exchange for safe passage for merchant ships in the Mediterranean. The resulting war declared by Tripoli against the United States led Jefferson to call for an expanded navy and to wage a quasi war against the Barbary Coast states. This began an eight-year trend of resizing and reworking the military, often with concern from Congress and cabinet members over the cost and purpose of extra forces. Jefferson's goal of defense often was at odds with his Democratic-Republican goal of downsizing the armed forces, though he managed to achieve both. The Tripolitan situation eventually dissolved; hostilities with Great Britain would spill over violently into Madison's administration.

The Spanish decision to cede North American lands to the French meant that the port of New Orleans, a vital center for trade and transportation, could be closed to the United States. Federalists urged the president to take advantage of the transition time between the Spanish and the French and occupy New Orleans by force. Jefferson, on the other hand, believed a military response would not solve the situation. He opted for diplomacy and sent James Monroe to France to discuss the matter. As fate would have it, Napoleon faced multiple simultaneous setbacks that made the once-attractive New Orleans a sudden burden to him. Napoleon was eager to sell and Monroe was eager to buy. In the end, Jefferson's diplomacy secured not only New Orleans for the United States, but the whole of the Louisiana Purchase, thus nearly doubling the size of the nation.

The Louisiana Purchase raised difficult questions for Jefferson despite its overwhelming popularity. A minority criticized Jefferson for exceeding the limits of his office and acting unconstitutionally by authorizing the transaction; oddly enough, Jefferson agreed with his critics. The U.S. Constitution did not name the power to purchase land for the nation among the president's powers, or the Congress's, for that matter. Jefferson admitted this was the case. He disagreed with his critics about the importance of the problem. He believed that acquiring the lands in the Louisiana Purchase justified the unconstitutional means he used; moreover, he tried to rectify what he did by penning a constitutional amendment to address the issue for future presidents. The amendment fell to the wayside in the haste to get approval for the purchase, however, and Jefferson never repaired the damage he feared he did the Constitution. Critics aside, though, the Louisiana Purchase remained the political and popular success that defined his presidency.

Perhaps the most influential decision Jefferson's predecessor John Adams made as president was the appointment of John Marshall to the U.S. Supreme Court. Even as the Federalist Party withered during Jefferson's tenure in office, Chief Justice Marshall kept Federalist views alive from the highest bench in the judiciary. One of his decisions—*Marbury v. Madison*—became a sticking point for Thomas Jefferson. The case revolved around a last-minute judicial appointment made by John Adams and left for delivery by the Jefferson administration. Madison held the commission instead of delivering it, and the would-be recipient, William Marbury, sued. Rather than ruling on the issue of the delivery, the Court declared the act under which Marbury brought the suit to be unconstitutional. This established the precedent of judicial review, or the judiciary's power to scrutinize legislation and judge its constitutionality. This increased the potential power of the judicial branch of government considerably.

Even though he technically won the *Marbury* case, Jefferson protested Marshall's loose construction of the Constitution and his willingness to declare opinions on extraneous or moot points. He believed that Marshall expanded the power of the national judiciary, and himself in the process, with too much arrogance and too little appreciation for the law. He feared that the decision would take more authority from the hands of the people and concentrate it among a centralized elite. There was little Jefferson could do, however; Marshall's precedent of judicial review continues to stand today.

Jefferson also could do little about the changing tide of public opinion concerning native Americans. Since his time serving in George Washington's cabinet, Jefferson was committed to what he called the "Indian Civilization Campaign." He admired the native Americans, particularly for some of their political structures, and tried alternately to protect them and reshape their lifestyles by creating consistent trade procedures, encouraging American Indian education, stabilizing Amerindian economies, promoting indigenous stability versus mobility, and protecting native landholdings. The last effort formed the heart of his concern; he respected native American sovereignty and property rights. Much of his efforts revolved around assuring Amerindian nations that the land they claimed was theirs to sell or to keep.

As president, Jefferson continued to negotiate with American Indian leaders and to discuss the status of their lands with them. Though he made the promise that the United States would respect the property rights of the Amerindians, he could not keep that promise. The Georgia

Compact of 1802 was a harbinger of things to come. Among its provisions was a trade: Georgia would cede lands in the West if the United States would extinguish native American property titles within the boundaries of the states. At first, legislators expected that the land would be purchased from the Amerindians. This assumption begged the question of what would happen if some groups did not wish to sell. Talk of enforcing the Georgia Compact of 1802 eventually led to talk of forced removal of native American peoples from their land. In short, the compact paved the way for future bloody business such as the forced removal and relocation of Native Americans known as the Trail of Tears.

Jefferson began his administration in a position of near war with the Barbary Coast states and ended it in near war with Great Britain. When a British ship stopped a U.S. vessel along the U.S. coast and removed alleged British deserters, it was clear that international hostility threatened merchants in close waters as well as the high seas. Jefferson instituted an embargo; in effect, he treated U.S. citizens as prisoners in their own country without the right to assume risk and undertake trade. He hoped to keep U.S. vessels and their crews safe; he also hoped to force the international community to negotiate peace by depriving it of U.S. goods. In the end, however, the policy damaged only the domestic economy. If the Louisiana Purchase marked the peak of Jefferson's popularity, then the embargo marked its low point.

A frustrated Jefferson allowed himself to be taunted into ever increasingly severe policies to enforce the embargo. By the end of his second term, he had created something of a police state in the name of the people's own good. Forcing people to be safe, especially when their purses and bellies are empty, did not prove to be a wise move. It only postponed war with Great Britain for another president to fight. Even with the disastrous embargo in effect, Jefferson's political power retained currency. His chosen successor, James Madison, took the presidency (far more easily than Jefferson himself did in his first election) and carried on the Jeffersonian tradition. So would Madison's successor, James Monroe.

Jefferson left the presidency a different institution from the one he had inherited. Thanks to actions such as the Louisiana Purchase, it was a far more powerful office than it had ever been. The nature of the cabinet, the president's natural support system, seemed far clearer as well. The country, though embroiled in hostilities and economically suffering, was also almost twice the size it had been during the Adams presidency, making it and its leader more formidable. And the rivalry between the political parties that defined and plagued earlier presidencies had all but disappeared; Democratic-Republicanism was the new national consensus.

The presidency was also a more personal position. Gone were the rigorous formalities and symbolic walls Washington had erected and Adams had struggled to maintain. Jefferson infused the office with his own informality, humor, and taste, thus making it an ever changing institution capable of great growth and diversity across the years. He proved that a powerful personality could command respect in shabby clothes and slippers if he so wished. The style of the man could affect the style of the office. Jefferson illustrated that differences in individual presidents could be a source of strength for the position and the country.

A larger nation, a stronger office, an ideologically unified people: it might have been all that James Madison could have asked for, if it had not been for war.

DEFENSE

John Adams was not the only president to face a quasi war. Almost as soon as Jefferson took the Oath of Office, the pasha of Tripoli declared war on the United States. The pasha had stolen the throne of the African province, or satrapy, from his brother, and thereby inherited the debt of his brother, his brother's many wives, and the supporters of his coup, as well. The pasha hoped to gain wealth by demanding a large tribute from the United States in exchange for safe passage of U.S. merchant ships.

This plan made sense in a certain context. For years, the United States, aware of the limitations of its anemic naval forces, had paid bribes to several of the Barbary Coast states to ensure the safety of U.S. merchant vessels in the Mediterranean. The United States traditionally gave Tripoli less in tributes than it gave to Algiers or Morocco, though, and this angered the new pasha. When he tore down the U.S. flag—a customary statement of war—and declared open season on U.S. vessels, President Jefferson bristled. He had at his disposal the new U.S. Navy that Adams had built and he added to it himself. Jefferson decided the United States would pay no more tributes to Tripoli.

The fighting that followed was rather trivial in the military sense. Jefferson had far more to fear from the constant hostilities between England and France. It did not spawn a constitutional crisis, either, as the military technically provided only a "spirited defense" of trade, as opposed to a legitimate, official war. The years of the Tripolitan hostilities, however, did impact the administration insofar as they required more gunboats, more navy personnel, and more money. Even when Jefferson tried to cut back the expenditures, the bills multiplied. He remained dedicated to the Democratic-Republican goal of downsizing the armed forces, but reducing the number did not always mean reducing the cost. Change of any kind—different weapons, different emphases—was expensive.

The battles with Tripoli created strain on Jefferson's cabinet members.

Secretary of the Navy Robert Smith wanted to pursue events with enthusiasm; Secretary of the Treasury Albert Gallatin wanted to cut costs. Senior naval officer Commodore Thomas Truxtun resigned in frustration, and Secretary of State James Madison had no strong vision about the navy at all. Gallatin eventually all but crippled the Mediterranean forces and yet still faced spiraling costs. The fate of the young navy, and the purse of the young nation, seemed imperiled. After five years of fighting, neither side had a decisive victory. The Tripolitan War eventually ran out of momentum.

The problem of defense outlived the quasi war in Africa, however. Once the gunboats and ships were built, they had to be maintained. Once the officers were commissioned, they needed to be used. The armed forces, grown to new sizes to meet pressing events, seemed unlikely to shrink back to their original forms. And so, in 1809, years after the Tripolitan War had concluded, the legislature found itself staggered by the military budget, and wary of still more expansion.

Many during Jefferson's term questioned the growth of the military for more than economic reasons. The fear of a standing army remained prevalent in the nation, harkening back to the colonial experience with Great Britain, and even earlier to the classical Roman republic that in part inspired the U.S. system of government. Soldiers were ambitious, the thought went, and if idle, they could look to riding the tide of military support straight to the head of the government—legally or otherwise. Armies were restless; if not challenged by a foreign foe, they might easily turn their weapons against their own people. Jefferson's battles with Tripoli, and the following expansion of the U.S. territory via the Louisiana Purchase as well as other events, led Jefferson to ask for an expanded military throughout his two terms in office. His opponents, however, looked on the growing U.S. forces with frustration and even fear.

Toward the end of his second term, Jefferson had specific plans for an enlarged army. Talks with Great Britain, ongoing for years, broke down altogether after the British vessel *Leopard* stopped the U.S. ship *Chesapeake* in the waters off the Chesapeake Bay and removed four alleged English deserters in 1807. Jefferson expected war. He feared the militias would not be as reliable as needed, but he also realized that Congress would balk at requests for an even larger standing army. He eventually asked for a number of men for limited service only, a finite number of years, but still the legislators refused. They worried not only about funding the troops, but also if such service truly would prove "limited" once the men were employed. The expenses already incurred by the burgeoning navy and army, coupled with their concerns over larger standing forces, trumped Jefferson's requests.

Congress's refusal to expand the army at the rates Jefferson wanted kept the United States from entering a second war during Jefferson's term. Instead, Jefferson turned his strategy to embargo and sought to address the European problems by restricting travel and trade. This policy arguably proved even more unpopular and destructive than war might have been, and it added a bitterness to public opinion at the end of Jefferson's second term. War with Great Britain flared despite it all during James Madison's tenure in office.

Jefferson succeeded in building the navy but did not develop the army to the degree he wished. In return, the United States gained little in terms of rights in the Mediterranean or the Atlantic. The president watched one war dissolve and merely postponed the other. The military changes hit the United States in the purse nonetheless, much to Gallatin's despair, and remained a point of contention within the cabinet and between the executive and legislature throughout Jefferson's administration.

THE PRESIDENT'S POSITION: PRO-DEFENSE

First Annual Message
December 8, 1801

It is a circumstance of sincere gratification to me that on meeting the great council of our nation I am able to announce to them on grounds of reasonable certainty that the wars and troubles which have for so many years afflicted our sister nations have at length come to an end, and that the communications of peace and commerce are once again more opening among them.

... To this state of general peace with which we have been blessed, one only exception exists. Tripoli, the least considerable of the Barbary States, had come forward with demands unfounded either in right or in compact, and had permitted itself to denounce war on our failure to comply before a given day. The style of the demand admitted but one answer. I sent a small squadron of frigates into the Mediterranean, with assurances to that power of our sincere desire to remain in peace, but with orders to protect our commerce against the threatened attack. The measure was seasonable and salutary. The Bey had already declared war. His cruisers were out. Two had arrived at Gibralter. Our commerce in the Mediterranean was blockaded and that of the Atlantic in peril. The arrival of our squadron dispelled the danger. One of the Tripolitan cruisers having fallen in with and engaged the small schooner *Enterprise*, commanded by Lieutenant Sterret, which had gone as a tender to our larger vessels, was captured, after a heavy slaughter of her men, without the loss of a single one on our part. The bravery exhibited by our citizens on that element will, I trust, be a testimony to the world that it is not the want of that virtue which makes us seek their peace, but a conscientious desire to direct the energies of our nation to the multiplication of the human race, and not to its destruction. Unauthorized by the Constitution, without the sanction of Congress, to go beyond the line of defense, the vessel, being disabled from committing further hostilities, was liberated with its crew. The Legislature will doubtless consider whether, by authorizing measures of offense also, they will place our force on an equal footing with that of its adversaries. I communicate all material information on this subject, that in the exercise of this important function confided by the Constitution to the Legislature exclusively their judgment may form itself on a knowledge and consideration of every circumstance of weight.

I wish I could say that our situation with all the other Barbary States was entirely satisfactory. Discovering that some delays had taken place in the performance of certain articles stipulated by us, I thought it my duty, by immediate measures for fulfilling them, to vindicate to ourselves the right of considering the effect of departure from stipulation on their side. From the papers which will be laid before you you will be enabled to judge whether our treaties are regarded by them as fixing at all the measure of their demands or as guarding from the exercise of force our vessels within their power, and to consider how far it will be safe and expedient to leave our affairs with them in their present posture. . . .

. . . With respect to the extent to which our naval preparations should be carried, some difference of opinion may be expected to appear; but just attention to the circumstances of every part of the Union will doubtless reconcile all. A small force will probably continue to be wanted for actual service in the Mediterranean. Whatever annual sum beyond that you may think proper to appropriate to naval preparations, would perhaps be better employed in providing those articles which may be kept without waste or consumption, and be in readiness when any exigence calls them into use. . . .

See Thomas Jefferson Papers at the Library of Congress. <http://memory.loc.gov/ammem/mtjhtml/mtjhome.html>.

AGAINST BIG DEFENSE

House of Representatives, 10th Congress, 2nd Session
January 27, 1809

An engrossed bill providing an additional military force was read the third time, and the question being on its passage—

Mr. [Benjamin] Tallmadge [of Connecticut] moved the postponement of the bill indefinitely.

Mr. Tallmadge said it was a very unpleasant circumstance to rise and address a deliberative assembly, when the subject was an unpleasant one; but, after the observations which had fallen from some gentlemen in the majority, charging the minority with a systematic determination to oppose and retard all the measures of the Administration, it required some effort of the mind to undertake the task. Nothing but an imperious sense of duty, and regard for the rights of his constituents and country, which he could not sacrifice, induced him to trouble the House with his objections to the bill now under consideration. Sir, said Mr. T., in the discharge of this duty, while I confine myself within the rules of decorum in debate, I hold myself responsible only to my country, to my conscience, and to my God.

In relation to the subject now under consideration, I hope this honorable House will do me the justice to acknowledge that, on every question which has been brought forward since I have been honored with a seat on this floor, the object of which was to protect and defend our common country, my vote and exertions have been in favor of such measures. One solitary instance do I except from the general rule, which relates to gunboats; and of these I have long entertained such a contemptible opinion, that I have felt constrained to withhold my vote from giving to them such liberal support. This frank declaration, I hope, will shield me from the reproach of wishing to thwart the measures of the Administration, or to throw any obstacles in the way of its operation.

When we examine this bill, as predicated upon the recommendation of the Secretary of War, we must be at a loss to conjecture how it should assume its present shape. In the report of that officer, which was printed and laid upon our tables, it will be found that he recommends the plan of engaging fifty thousand volunteers; but this bill proposes raising an army of fifty thousand men. Yes, sir, I repeat it; if you pass this bill, you sanction the enlistment, organization, and equipment, of an army of fifty thousand men, all the officers of which are to be appointed and commissioned by the President of the United States. . . .

Are gentlemen aware of the immense expense which will be incurred by raising this body of troops? It may be objected, that this monstrous military force is to be under pay only while it is kept in actual service. But it ought to be remembered that, as soon as the officers are appointed and the troops are enlisted, it becomes a positive army, liable to do duty twelve months out of two years, wherever the President of the United States shall direct. Give me leave once more to call the attention of the House to the report of the Secretary of War, which, for some reason or other, he did not think proper to assign, but which I know he presented to the committee. In this report, the head of the War Department estimates the expense of fifty thousand volunteers, to be encamped only thirty days in the year, at two millions one hundred thousand dollars. I have made a calculation on this subject and, and am convinced that, to provide for this army only one year, we must pay fifteen millions of dollars. Sir, the history of our Revolutionary war exhibits no example of this sort. We have at this moment, probably, about ten thousand troops in the field. To these may be added one hundred thousand militia lately put in requisition by the President of the United States, and now we are called upon to add fifty thousand regularly enlisted troops to the number. . . .

. . . What is the use and destination of this army? Inasmuch as we have no information on this head from the Executive department, I inquire, with deep solicitude, of the majority of this House, (inasmuch as they hold the destinies of our country at this portentous day), where is this force to be directed? Against what enemy, visible or invisible, is this army of freemen to be prepared to act? Indeed, Mr. Speaker, this duty becomes so imperious upon this House, and so important to our constituents, that without some definite information on this point, I know not how we can proceed. Since the present session commenced, we have been passing laws and adopting measures of the most serious and important consequence to this country, and, I am constrained to say, with less consideration, I fear, than the solemnity and importance of their nature seemed to demand. We are now called upon to pass a bill, placing in the hands of the Executive one of the most tremendous weapons which Government can yield. For my own part, I can discover but two objects which can be in view, in framing this present bill. This force, when raised, must be directed against an enemy, or it must be pointed against ourselves. . . .

See Additional Military Force Discussion, January 27, 1809. House of Representatives, 10th Congress, 2nd Session. *Annals of Congress*, Library of Congress. <http://memory.loc.gov/ammem/amlaw/lawhome.html>.

NEW ORLEANS

If the Jefferson administration is remembered for one thing, it is the Louisiana Purchase: the near doubling of the U.S. territory through one single sales transaction with a potentially hostile France. What ended as an amicable business deal, however, could easily have been a war involving not only the United States and France, but Spain and Britain as well. Before U.S. officials considered the Louisiana Territory as a whole, they debated about policy concerning the port of New Orleans.

The fate of New Orleans affected the United States in many ways, for it served as the entrance point to the Mississippi River and allowed the transport of goods and information across many states and territories.

Any blockage of the river brought movement to a halt and harmed the nation financially, socially, and militarily. When Jefferson became president, the Spanish controlled New Orleans and therefore the Mississippi River. Jefferson, like most in his day, itched to secure the port under U.S. control. He went so far as to say, "there is on the globe one single spot, the possessor of which is our natural and habitual enemy. It is New Orleans, through which the produce of three-eighths of our territory must pass to market, and from its fertility it will ere long yield more than half of our whole produce and contain more than half our inhabitants."[1]

Even so, the Spanish were a weaker presence in North America than some other European powers might have been. Napoleon's France, for one, could have made U.S. access to New Orleans impossible. When Jefferson learned in 1802 that Spain had ceded New Orleans to France as a means of appeasing Napoleon he became very concerned. He wrote: "France placing herself in that door assumes to us the attitude of defiance."[2] The situation grew graver when, in the fall, the Spanish intendant at New Orleans, Juan Morales, announced that he closed New Orleans to foreign, or non-Spanish, trade and denied U.S. citizens the right to deposit in the port. Morales kept the authority behind his order a secret, and the mystery added fuel to the flames of discontent. The U.S. public assumed France was to blame. The French had not yet arrived, but they already seemed to be endangering U.S. interests.

Nonetheless, Jefferson bided his time. He appreciated that the departing Spaniards, the entering French, and agitated U.S. citizens could make a volatile mix. The same president who offered a "spirited defense" of trade against privateers on the high seas, and who expanded the naval and army forces of the nation throughout his time in office, proved unwilling to leap to battle against a former ally. Despite the persistence of Congress he banished thoughts of war and approached the situation through diplomacy.

Jefferson's Federalist opponents urged him to take stronger action with regard to the fate of New Orleans. As citizens with commercial interests, they appreciated that a French presence posed great danger to trade. As Anglophiles, the Federalists also never shied away from the prospect of hostilities with France and resulting alliances with Great Britain. Alexander Hamilton, writing under the pseudonym Pericles, proposed that the president "seize at once on the Floridas and New Orleans, and then negotiate."[3] Jefferson remained cautious. Federalists stepped up their efforts to motivate him. In the Senate, Federalists led by James Ross tried to prod Jefferson by proposing resolutions to give him $5 million and 50,000 troops to capture and occupy New Orleans by force. The measure did not pass, however, and Jefferson did not allow himself to be pressured into hasty military action. He named James Monroe minister extraordinary to France, gave him $2 million for "expenses," and sent him across the sea to learn what business opportunities awaited.

The president's lack of decisive military action upon hearing that New Orleans would pass from Spanish to French hands turned out to be fortuitous. Before Napoleon could dispatch his troops to the North American port, he faced a number of setbacks in different arenas. The leader of the French expedition bound for New Orleans, Claude Victor, became trapped in Holland when his entire fleet was frozen in for the winter. After Toussaint L'Overture's capture in Santo Domingo, Victor Leclerc's troops subdued the island only to fall victim to yellow fever and then guerilla warfare, losing 20,000 men before all was over. Napoleon's world seemed to be coming apart at the seams. His ambitious plans for a North American colony quite suddenly became impossible. Word then reached him that the U.S. Senate was calling for a military takeover of the port, and he knew he could not defend it if the United States pressed its advantage. Before he could even claim New Orleans, Napoleon found it to be a liability; its cost in money and men was simply too high.

Some Federalists would later complain that a military takeover of New Orleans would have cost the United States less funds than the Louisiana Purchase; moreover, the French were in no position to resist if the United States had established control of the port. This position benefited from hindsight, however. Much of Napoleon's problems—one fleet frozen, another decimated—were not common knowledge at the time. Such complaints also beg the question of the moral legitimacy of possession by pure might. At any rate, the detractors remained in the minority. Jefferson's actions won the loyalty and affection of the U.S. mainstream and secured his place in history.

NOTES

1. Thomas Jefferson. Letter to Robert R. Livingston, April 18, 1802. In the Thomas Jefferson Papers at the Library of Congress. <http://memory.loc.gov/ammem/mtjhtml/mtjhome.html>.

2. Ibid.

3. "Pericles" (Alexander Hamilton) in *New York Evening Post*, February 8, 1803. See Forrest McDonald, *The Presidency of Thomas Jefferson* (Lawrence: University Press of Kansas, 1976), p. 67.

THE PRESIDENT'S POSITION: NEGOTIATION

Thomas Jefferson to Dr. Hugh Williamson
Washington, April 30, 1803

Dear Sir,

For the present we have a respite on that subject, Spain having without delay restored our infracted right, and assured us it is expressly saved by her cession of Louisiana to France. . . . In the meantime we have obtained by a peaceable appeal to justice, in four months, what we should not have obtained under seven years of war, the loss of one hundred thousand lives, and hundred millions of additional debt, many hundred millions worth of produce and property lost for want of market, or in seeking it, and that demoralization which war superinduces on the human mind. To have seized New Orleans, as our federal maniacs wish, would only have changed the character and extend of the blockade of our western commerce. . . .

See Thomas Jefferson Papers at the Library of Congress. <http://memory.loc.gov/ammem/mtjhtml/mtjhome.html>.

Thomas Jefferson to General Horatio Gates
Washington, July 11, 1803

Dear General,—I accept with pleasure, and with pleasure reciprocate your congratulations on the acquisition of Louisiana: for it is a subject of mutual congratulations as it interests every man of the nation. The territory acquired, as it includes all the waters of the Missouri & Mississippi, has more than doubled the area of the U.S. and the new part is not inferior to the old in soft, climate, productions & important communications. If our legislature dispose of it with the wisdom we have a right to expect, they may make it the means of tempting all our Indians on the East side of the Mississippi to remove to the West, and of condensing instead of scattering our population. I find our opposition is very willing to pluck feathers from Monroe, although not fond of sticking them into Livingston's coat. The truth is both have a just portion of merit and were it necessary or proper it could be shewn that each has rendered peculiar service, & of important value. These grumblers too are very uneasy lest the administration should share some little credit for the acquisition, the whole of which they ascribe to the accident of war. They would be cruelly mortified could they see our files from April 1801, the first organization of the administration, but more especially from April 1802. They would see that tho' we could not say when war would arise, yet we said with energy what would take place when it should arise. We did not, by our intrigues, produce the war: but we availed ourselves of it when it happened. The other party saw the case now existing on which our representations were predicted, and the wisdom of timely sacrifice. But when these people make the war give us everything, they authorize us to ask what the war gave us in their day? They had a war. What did they make it bring us? Instead of making our neutrality the grounds of gain to their country, they were for plunging into the war. And if they were now in place, they would not be at war against the Alliests & disorganizers of France. They were for making their country an appendage to England. We are friendly, cordially and conscientiously friendly to England, but we are not hostile to France. We will be rigorously just and sincerely friendly to both. I do not believe we shall have as much to swallow from them as our predecessors had.

With respect to the territory acquired, I do not think it will be a separate government as you imagine. I presume the island of N. Orleans and the settled country on the opposite bank, will be annexed to the Mississippi territory. We shall certainly endeavor to introduce the American laws there & that cannot be done but by amalgamating the people with such a body of Americans as may take the lead in legislation & government. Of course they will be under the Governor of Mississippi. The rest of the territory will probably be locked up from American settlement, and under the self-government of the native occupants.

You know that every sentence from me is put on the rack by our opponents, to be tortured into something they can make use of. No caution therefore I am sure is necessary against letting my letter go out of your hands. I am always happy to hear from you, and to know that you preserve your health. Present me respectfully to Mrs. Gates, and accept yourself my affectionate salutations and assurances of great respect & esteem.

See Thomas Jefferson Papers at the Library of Congress. <http://memory.loc.gov/ammem/mtjhtml/mtjhome.html>.

IN FAVOR OF MILITARY POSSESSION

February 16, 1803
7th Congress, 2nd Session
Remarks of Mr. James Ross from Pennsylvania

Resolved, That the United States have an indisputable right to the free navigation of the river Mississippi, and to a convenient place of deposit for their produce and merchandise in the island of New Orleans.

That the late infraction of such, their unquestionable right, is an aggression hostile to their honor and interest.

That it does not consist with the dignity or safety of this Union to hold a right so important by a tenure so uncertain.

That it materially concerns such of the American citizens as dwell on the western waters, and is essential to the union, strength, and prosperity of these States, that they obtain complete security for the full and peaceable enjoyment of such their absolute right.

That the President be authorized to take immediate possession of such place or places, in said island, or the adjacent territories, as he may deem fit and convenient for the purposes aforesaid; and to adopt such other measures for obtaining complete security as to him in his wisdom shall seem meet.

That he be authorized to call into actual service any number of the militia of the States of South Carolina, Georgia, Ohio, Kentucky, Tennessee, or of the Mississippi Territory, which he may think proper, not exceeding fifty thousand, and to employ them, together with the military and naval forces of the Union, for effecting the objects above mentioned. . . .

See Fred L. Israel, ed., *Major Presidential Decisions* (New York: Chelsea House, 1980), p. 67.

February 23, 1803
7th Congress, 2nd Session
Remarks of Mr. Samuel White of Delaware

Mr. President, on this subject . . . I shall submit the few observations that I may make, in as concise a manner as I am capable of, for it is very far from my wish to occupy the time or attention of the Senate unnecessarily.

. . . We can never have peace on our Western waters, till we possess ourselves of New Orleans, and such other positions as may be necessary to give us the complete and absolute command of the navigation of the Mississippi. We have now such an opportunity of accomplishing this important object as may not be presented again in centuries, and every justification that could be wished for availing ourselves of the opportunity. Spain has dared us to the trial, and now bids us defiance; she is yet in possession of that country; it is at this moment within your reach and within your power; it offers a sure and easy conquest; we should have to encounter there now only a weak, inactive, and unenterprising people; but how may a few months vary this scene, and darken our prospects! Though not officially informed, we know that the Spanish provinces on the Mississippi have been ceded to the French, and that they will as soon as possible take possession of them. What may we then expect? When in the last extremity we shall be driven to arms in defence of our indisputable rights where now slumbers on his post with folded arms the sluggish Spaniard, we shall be hailed by the vigilant and alert French grenadier, and in the defenceless garrison that would now surrender at our approach, we shall see unfurled the standards that have waved triumphant in Italy, surrounded by impregnable ramparts, and defended by the disciplined veterans of Egypt.

I am willing, sir, to attribute to honorable gentlemen the best of motives; I am sure they do not wish to involve this country in a war, and God knows, I deprecate its horrors as much as any man; but this business can never be adjusted abroad; it will ultimately have to be settled upon the banks of the Mississippi; and the longer you delay, the more time you waste in tedious negotiations, the greater sacrifices you make to protract a temporary and hollow peace, the greater will be your embarrassments when the war comes on; and it is inevitable, unless honorable gentlemen, opposed to us, are prepared to yield up the best interest and honor of the nation. I believe the only question now in our power to decide, is whether it shall be the bloodless war of a few months, or the carnage of years.

See Fred L. Israel, ed., *Major Presidential Decisions* (New York: Chelsea House, 1980), pp. 68–69.

LOUISIANA PURCHASE

The Louisiana Purchase marked arguably the greatest triumph for Jefferson as president in the eyes of U.S. leaders and citizens alike. The new territory promised national expansion, terrific wealth, and personal independence for the yeoman farmers Jefferson so admired. Opportunity seemed limitless, and U.S. citizens soon said it was the nation's manifest destiny to harness the power and promise of the American West all the way to the Pacific Ocean.

Enthusiasm could not hide the fact that the Louisiana Purchase was a deal made quickly—perhaps by the right people at the right time, but with little information and even less authorization. As celebration gripped the country, Jefferson had to wrestle with the fact that he had maneuvered in political, economic, and, most importantly, constitutional gray areas to make the transaction happen. To Jefferson, the ends justified the means. Some others were not quite sure.

Politically, the sale was problematic due to the terms of Spain's cession to France. When Spain turned its North American lands over to France, part of the agreement provided that France would not sell it to a third party. Napoleon, in fact, reiterated this pledge to Spanish officials less than a year before he offered Louisiana to Jefferson. In short, the United States had no right to buy what France had no right to sell.

The purchase also introduced the question of finances. Paying for Louisiana—the total, including the assumption of U.S. claims against France, came to approximately $15 million—increased the U.S. public debt by almost twenty percent, which more than threatened Jefferson's dear personal mission to balance the national budget and retire the debt. Opponents questioned how much the nation might have saved if those involved had shown more patience; the bargain was struck, after all, the night James Monroe arrived in France. Taking the territory off the hands of a desperate Napoleon helped France as well as the United States. Some wondered how hard it would have been to negotiate a more favorable price for the lands.

Concerns about politics and finances paled in comparison to the chief complaint about the Louisiana Purchase, namely, its foundation in constitutional law. Jefferson admitted that he and his officials lacked the constitutional authority to make the purchase. He feared that the absence of legal grounds for the action would endanger the transaction—or, worse, the Constitution. His hope remained that Congress would approve the purchase and then add specific provisions to the Constitution for "holding foreign territory" and "incorporating foreign nations" into the Union. Paradoxically, he wanted approval for what he had done and he also wanted insurance that no other leader could take such liberties with the law of the land again.

At the time of the purchase, James Madison suggested to Jefferson that the power to make such a deal—to buy land for future inclusion in the Union—was inherent in the notion of nationhood. Nations expand their borders. Jefferson agreed with this vague argument in passing, but developed skepticism after the fact. In reality, the president only had one defense: the opportunity was simply too good to ignore. The ends, doubling the nation's size, justified the means, "an act beyond the Constitution." The opportunity required immediate action, and he took responsibility for making the decision to buy. Jefferson never argued that his behavior was constitutional; he proposed instead only that it was justified. As historian Forrest McDonald once said of the president's actions during the Louisiana Purchase, "With some effort, he managed to overcome his scruples."[1]

Some voices came out against the president's decision despite its overwhelming popularity. Jefferson asked Secretary of the Treasury Albert Gallatin to summarize some such arguments. Gallatin did his best to refute them, then admitted his own uncertainty: "I must, however, confess that after all I do not feel myself perfectly satisfied." Even in Jefferson's own cabinet, doubts lingered about the sale that seemed at the time too good to refuse.

In fact, the U.S. Constitution did not list the power to acquire territory among the enumerated powers. The chief executive, then, could not claim it. According to the Tenth Amendment, all unenumerated powers belonged to the states or the people. Jefferson pursued this line of thought after the purchase by drafting a constitutional amendment to legitimize the acceptance of new territories into the Union. Again, however, he was persuaded that time was of the essence; he needed to secure congressional votes to ratify the purchase treaty, and other details such as amendments could slow the process considerably. In the end, Congress turned a blind eye to the constitutional issues and sided with Jefferson.

Any hopes of cleaning up the constitutional uncertainties left by the Louisiana Purchase faded in the face of the challenges posed by the new territory. Jefferson never repaired the damage he feared he had done by acting outside of the law. Other issues commanded attention. The West needed exploration, mapping, and analysis. Soon Jefferson dispatched expeditions to study the territory. Mass excitement over the new land and its potential drowned the voices of critics, and soon few remembered that the purchase had inspired controversy at all.

NOTE

1. Forrest McDonald, *The Presidency of Thomas Jefferson* (Lawrence: University Press of Kansas, 1976), p. 71.

THE PRESIDENT'S POSITION: THE LOUISIANA PURCHASE IS JUSTIFIED

Thomas Jefferson to Senator John Breckinridge (of Kentucky)
August 12, 1803

... This treaty must of course be laid before both Houses, because both have important functions to exercise respecting it. They, I presume, will see their duty to their country in ratifying and paying for it, so as to secure a good which would otherwise probably be never again in their power. But I suppose they must then appeal to *the nation* for an additional article to the Constitution, approving and confirming an act which the nation had not previously authorized. The Constitution has made no provision for our holding foreign territory, still less for incorporating foreign nations into our Union. The executive in seizing the fugitive occurrence which so much advances the good of their country, have done an act beyond the Constitution. The Legislature in casting behind them metaphysical subtleties, and risking themselves like faithful servants, must ratify and pay for it, and throw themselves on their country for doing for them unauthorized, what we know they would have done for themselves had they been in a situation to do it. It is the case of a guardian investing the money of his ward in purchasing an important adjacent territory; and saying to him when of age, I did this for your good; I pretend to no right to bind you: you may disavow me, and I must get out of the scrape as I can: I thought it my duty to risk myself for you. But we shall not be disavowed by the nation, and their act of indemnity will confirm and not weaken the Constitution, by more strongly marking out its lines. . . .

See Fred L. Israel, ed., *Major Presidential Decisions* (New York: Chelsea House, 1980), p. 165.

Thomas Jefferson to Attorney General Levi Lincoln
August 30, 1803

. . . On further consideration as to the amendment to our Constitution respecting Louisiana, I have thought it better, instead of enumerating the powers which Congress may exercise, to give them the same powers they have as to other portions of the Union generally, and to enumerate the special exceptions, in some form as the following:

"Louisiana, as ceded by France to the United States, is made a part of the United States, its white inhabitants shall be citizens, and stand, as to their rights and obligations, on the same footing with other citizens of the United States in analogous situations. Save only that as to the portion thereof lying north of an east and west line drawn through the mouth of Arkansas river, no new State shall be established, nor any grants of land made, other than to Indians, in exchange for equivalent portions of land occupied by them, until an amendment of the Constitution shall be made for these purposes.

"Florida also, whensoever it may be rightfully obtained, shall become part of the United States, its white inhabitants shall thereupon be citizens, and shall stand, as to their rights and obligations, on the same footing with other citizens of the United States, in analogous situations."

I quote this for your consideration, observing that the less that is said about any constitutional difficulty, the better; and that it will be desirable for Congress to do what is necessary, *in silence*. I find but one opinion as to the necessity of shutting up the country for some time. We meet in Washington the 25th of September to prepare for Congress. Accept my affectionate salutations, and great esteem and respect.

See Fred L. Israel, ed., *Major Presidential Decisions* (New York: Chelsea House, 1980), pp. 167–168.

THE LOUISIANA PURCHASE VIEWED AS
UNCONSTITUTIONAL

Albert Gallatin to President Thomas Jefferson
Washington, Department of Treasury, January 13, 1803

I have read Mr. Lincoln's observations, and cannot distinguish the difference between a power to acquire territory for the United States and the power to extend by treaty the territory of the United States; yet he contends that the first is unconstitutional, supposes that we may acquire East Louisiana and West Florida by annexing them to the Mississippi Territory. Nor do I think his other idea, that of annexation to a State, that, for instance, of East Florida to Georgia, as proposed by him, to stand on a better foundation. If the acquisition of territory is not warranted by the Constitution, it is not more legal to acquire for one State than for the United States; if the Legislature and Executive established by the Constitution are not the proper organs for the acquirement of new territory for the use of the Union, still less can they be so for the acquirement of new territory for the use of one State; if they have no power to acquire territory, it is because the Constitution has confined its views to the then existing territory of the Union, and *that* excludes a possibility of enlargement of one State as well as that of territory common to the United States. As to the danger resulting from the exercise of such power, it is as great on his plan as on the other. What could, on his construction, prevent the President and the Senate by treaty annexing Cuba to Massachusetts, or Bengal to Rhode Island, if ever the acquirement of colonies shall become a favorite object with governments, and colonies shall be acquired?

But does any constitutional objection really exist?

The 3d Section of the 4th Article of the Constitution provides:

1st. That new States may be admitted by Congress into this Union.

2d. That Congress shall have power to dispose of and make all needful rules and regulations respecting the territory or other property belonging to the United States.

Mr. Lincoln, in order to support his objections, is compelled to suppose, 1st, that the new States therein alluded to must be carved either out of other States, or out of the territory belonging to the United States; and, 2d, that the power given to Congress of making regulations respecting the territory belonging to the United States is expressly confined to the territory *then* belonging to the Union.

A general and perhaps sufficient answer is that the whole rests on a supposition, there being no words in the section which confine the authority given to Congress to those specific objects; whilst, on the contrary, the existence of the United States as a nation presupposes the power enjoyed by every nation of extending their territory by treaties, and the general power given to the President and Senate of making treaties designates the organs through which the acquisition may be made, whilst this section provides the proper authority (viz., Congress) for either admitting in the Union or governing as subjects the territory thus acquired. . . .

. . . The only possible objection must be derived from the 12th [10th] Amendment, which declares that powers not delegated to the United

States, nor prohibited by it to the States, are reserved to the States or to the people. As the States are expressly prohibited from making treaties, it is evident that, if the power of acquiring territory by treaty is not considered within the meaning of the Amendment as delegated to the United States, it must be reserved to the people. . . .

I must, however, confess that after all I do not feel myself perfectly satisfied; the subject must be thoroughly examined. . . .

See Fred L. Israel, ed., *Major Presidential Decisions* (New York: Chelsea House, 1980), pp. 160–163.

JUDICIAL REVIEW

Though the Revolution of 1800 meant victory for the Democratic-Republicans, the Jefferson administration still faced Federalist challenges. One of the most important of these came from John Marshall, chief justice of the U.S. Supreme Court. By allowing Jefferson to win a battle in *Marbury v. Madison* 1803, Marshall managed to win a war against the Democratic-Republicans and forever change the role of the judiciary. His decision raised a crucial question for Jefferson: by reviewing the constitutionality of legislation, did the Court itself act unconstitutionally? Jefferson found no answers for his queries, and years after his terms in executive office he still argued against the precedents Marshall set.

The issue began on the last night of John Adams' presidency, when the outgoing executive used his powers one last time to fill a number of outstanding positions in the government. He left these so-called midnight appointments for Jefferson and his staff to deliver. The next day, when Thomas Jefferson assumed office, he saw no reason to mail the notices and fill the empty seats with Federalist appointees; he instructed his new secretary of state, James Madison, to sit on the appointments instead. William Marbury, a midnight appointee Adams intended to make justice of the peace in the District of Columbia, in turn sued Madison for not delivering his commission.

Marbury sued under Section 13 of the Judiciary Act of 1789, which gave the U.S. Supreme Court original jurisdiction in such a case, so arguments began before the highest court in the land. Jefferson and Madison expected the Federalist Marshall to issue a writ of mandamus requiring Madison to give Marbury his commission—thus a Federalist judge would allow a Federalist appointee to take office as a former Federalist president had intended. Marshall and the Court, however, did not do what Jefferson and Madison expected.

Instead, the Court ruled that Section 13 of the Judiciary Act of 1789 was unconstitutional. Giving the Supreme Court original jurisdiction, Marshall argued, directly violated the U.S. Constitution, which provided that the Court should hear only appeals except in very specific cases. By throwing out the act, then, Marshall gave Jefferson and Madison a small concession; according to the letter of the law, they did not have to deliver Marbury's commission or any other notices to Adams' midnight appointees. (Marshall scolded them for not doing so, nonetheless, and intimated that their failing in this situation was a question of morality. He also went on to instruct future Courts as to how they might handle a similar case, in effect issuing a warning to the Jefferson administration.)

Marshall emerged as the real winner from the *Marbury v. Madison* decision, however. Jefferson could have his way on the appointee issue, but only at the expense of admitting the Court's right to decide if acts of Congress were constitutional. This power of judicial review over legislation expanded the role of the Court tremendously and provided a unique check on the other two branches of government. Ironically, supporting the notion that the court could decide on questions of constitutionality required a loose reading of the Constitution. This Marshall proved willing to do; the concept of judicial review seemed only natural to him: "Why does a judge swear to discharge his duties agreeably to the constitution of the United States, if that constitution forms no rule for his government? If it is closed upon him, and cannot be inspected by him?"

Judicial review did not seem natural to Thomas Jefferson, however. He judged Marshall to be arrogant. He feared that Marshall meant to tip the scale of power within the judiciary to the Supreme Court, and not share the authority among the state governments as well. Like the parties they represented, Marshall thought in terms of national centralization and Jefferson in terms of federal decentralization. Marshall also displayed the tendency toward elitism associated with the Federalists, reserving decisions for the few; Jefferson, more egalitarian like his fellow Democratic-Republicans, preferred to let the people decide through the elected branches of government. When asked about judicial review and the resulting supremacy of the judiciary, Jefferson wrote: "The ultimate arbiter is the people of the Union, assembled by their deputies in convention, at the call of Congress, or of two-thirds of the States. Let them decide to which they mean to give an authority claimed by two of their organs."

Marshall's opinion stood and the precedent of judicial review remains today. Perhaps more than Adams or Hamilton, Marshall proved willing and able to leave the most substantial imprint of Federalist ideas upon the U.S. system. Years after Jefferson's retirement from public service, the former president still argued against the decisions Marshall had made. He believed Marshall had overstepped his bounds on many occasions and in a sense made law by offering opinions on hypothetical cases or moot issues. *Marbury v. Madison* served as one of his primary examples. He noted that "the Chief Justice says 'there must be an ultimate arbiter somewhere.' True, there must; but does that prove it is either party?" The case that began with acts of partisanship on the part of both Adams and Jefferson ended, arguably, with yet another one by the chief justice himself.

THE PRESIDENT'S POSITION: AGAINST JUDICIAL REVIEW

Thomas Jefferson to William Johnson
Monticello, June 1823

You request me confidentially, to examine the question, whether the Supreme Court has advanced beyond its constitutional limits, and trespassed on those of the State authorities? I do not undertake, my dear Sir, because I am unable. Age and the wane of mind consequent on it, had disqualified me from investigations so severe, and researches so laborious. . . .

. . . This practice of Judge Marshall, of traveling out of his case to prescribe what the law would be in a moot case not before the court, is very irregular and very censurable. I recollect another instance, and the more particularly, perhaps, because it in some measure bore on myself. Among the midnight appointments of Mr. Adams, were commissions to some federal justices of the peace for Alexandria. These were signed and sealed by him, but not delivered. I found them on the table of the department of State, on my entrance into office, and forbade their delivery. Marbury, named in one of them, applied to the Supreme Court for a mandamus to the Secretary of State (Mr. Madison) to deliver the commission intended for him. The court determined at once, that being an original process, they had no cognizance of it; and therefore the question before them was ended. But the Chief Justice went on to lay down what the law would be, had they jurisdiction of the case, to wit: that they should command the delivery. The object was clearly to instruct any other court having the jurisdiction, what they should do if Marbury should apply to them. Besides the impropriety of this gratuitous interference, could anything exceed the perversion of law? For if there is any principle of law never yet contradicted it is that delivery is one of the essentials to the validity of the deed. Although signed and dealed, yet as long as it remains in the hands of the party himself, it is in *fieri* only, it is not a deed, and can be made so only by its delivery. In the hands of a third person it may be made an escrow. But whatever is in the executive offices is certainly deemed to be in the hands of the President; and in this case, was actually in my hands, because, when I countermanded them, there was as yet no Secretary of State. Yet this case of Marbury and Madison is continually cited by bench and bar, as if it were settled law, without any animadversion on its being merely an *obiter* dissertation of the Chief Justice.

. . . But the Chief Justice says "there must be an ultimate arbiter somewhere." True, there must; but does that prove it is either party? The ultimate arbiter is the people of the Union, assembled by their deputies in convention, at the call of Congress, or of two-thirds of the States. Let them decide to which they mean to give an authority claimed by two of their organs. And it has been the peculiar wisdom and felicity of our constitution, to have provided this peaceable appeal, where that of other nations is at once to force.

See Kenneth M. Dolbeare, *American Political Thought*, 2d. (Chatham, N.J.: Chatham House Publishers, 1989), pp. 204–207.

SUPREME COURT DECISION ON JUDICIAL REVIEW

Marbury v. Madison (1803)

. . . If an act of the legislature, repugnant to the constitution, is void, does it, notwithstanding its invalidity, bind the courts, and oblige them to give it effect? Or, in other words, though it be not law, does it constitute a rule as operative as if it was a law? This would be to overthrow, in fact, what was established in theory; and would seem, at first view, an absurdity too gross to be insisted on. It shall, however, receive a more attentive consideration.

It is, emphatically, the province and the duty of the judicial department, to say what the law is. Those who apply the rule to particular cases, must of necessity expound and interpret that rule. If two laws conflict with each other, the courts must decide on the operation of each. So, if a law be in opposition to the constitution; if both the law and the constitution apply to a particular case, so that the court must either decide that case, conformably to the law, disregarding the constitution; or conformably to the constitution, disregarding the law; the court must determine which of these conflicting rules governs the case: this is of the very essence of judicial duty. If then, the courts are to regard the constitution, and the constitution is superior to any ordinary act of the legislature, the constitution, and not such ordinary act, must govern the case to which they both apply.

Those, then, who controvert the principles, that the constitution is to be considered, in court, as a paramount law, are reduced to the necessity of maintaining that courts must close their eyes on the constitution, and see only the law. This doctrine would subvert the very foundation of all written constitutions. It would declare that an act which, according to the principles and theory of our government, is entirely void, is yet, in practice, completely obligatory. . . .

. . . From these, and many other selections which might be made, it is apparent, that the framers of the constitution contemplated that instrument as a rule for the government of courts, as well as of legislature. Why otherwise does it direct the judges to take an oath to support it? This oath certainly applies, in an especial manner, to their conduct in their official character. How immoral to impose it on them, if they were to be used as the instruments, and the knowing instruments, for violating what they swear to support!

The oath of office, too, imposed by the legislature, is completely demonstrative of the legislative opinion on this subject. It is in these words: "I do solemnly swear, that I will administer justice, without respect to persons, and do equal right to the poor and to the rich; and that I will faithfully and impartially discharge all the duties incumbent on me as— ——according to the best of my abilities and understanding, agreeable to the constitution of the United States." Why does a judge swear to discharge his duties agreeably to the constitution of the United States, if that constitution forms no rule for his government? If it is closed upon him, and cannot be inspected by him? If such be the real state of things, this is worse than solemn mockery. To prescribe, or to take this oath, becomes equally a crime.

It is also not entirely unworthy of observation, that in declaring what shall be the supreme law of the land, the constitution itself is first mentioned; and not the laws of the United States, generally, but those only which shall be made in pursuance of the constitution, have that rank.

Thus, the particular phraseology of the constitution of the United States confirms and strengthens the principle, supposed to be essential to all written constitutions, that a law repugnant to the constitution is void; and that courts as well as other departments, are bound by that instrument.

The rule must be discharged.

John Marshall. *Marbury v. Madison.* Decision. 1803. In U.S. Supreme Court Collection. <http://supct.law.cornell.edu/supct/>.

AMERICAN INDIAN POLICY

After the ratification of the U.S. Constitution and the election of George Washington as the first president of the newly incarnated country, federal officials turned their attention to the issue of the American Indians. Of these men, Secretary of State Thomas Jefferson remained the most vocal and interested in indigenous American matters. In an idyllic way, as a philosopher and theorist more than as a policymaker, Jefferson admired the native Americans and even believed that they compared favorably when contrasted with their European counterparts. In 1787, for example, he argued: "I am convinced that those societies (as the Indians) which live without government, enjoy in their general mass an infinitely greater degree of happiness than those who live under the European governments. Among the former, public opinion is in the place of law, and restrains morals as powerfully as laws ever did anywhere. Among the latter, under pretense of governing, they have divided into two classes, the wolves and sheep. I do not exaggerate."[1]

With Jefferson's guidance and support, the United States adopted a series of measures collectively called the "Indian Civilization Campaign." A series of laws governing trade and intercourse with the Indians opened with the first act in 1790 and included amendments and renewals in 1793, 1796, 1802, and 1822. The United States recognized the Indians as the owners of the land on which they lived, with the rights to cede or sell these lands as well as to retain them.[2] Federal agents assigned to each native nation took up residence within these lands to act as liaisons with the U.S. federal government. The laws standardized trade and treaty negotiation procedures and provided funds for native American schools. On paper, if not always in practice, the United States constructed an aggressive and involved policy toward North America's natives.

Jefferson obviously idealized the indigenous Americans, using them to symbolize the noble savage in what he imagined as a pre-government state of nature. As a rhetorical device the archetypal Indian served the purposes of Jefferson's political theory. And, to be fair, Jefferson tended to reduce the Europeans to equally abstract symbols, as well. When contrasted with European "wolves" and "sheep," in fact, the noble aborigines appeared in a good light indeed. The "Civilization Campaign" he followed, however, was a concrete one devising consistent trade procedures, encouraging American Indian education, stabilizing Amerindian economies, promoting indigenous stability versus mobility, and protecting native landholdings.

As president, Jefferson took a particularly active interest in the different American Indian nations. He watched as the people of the Cherokee Nation, for example, made strides in English literacy, established a vibrant trade and agricultural economy, embraced western agricultural systems, including plantation slavery, and called for greater protection of their private property. Jefferson even presented Cherokee chief Doublehead with an official commendation in 1806 "in consideration of his active influence in forwarding the arts of civilization."[3]

At the heart of his hopes for native Americans—much like his hopes for the yeoman farmer U.S. citizens—rested an abiding emphasis on the civilizing role of private property. If they could hold their own lands securely, without fear, then landowners, be they white or Amerindian, could enjoy the industry and reward of self-reliant hard work. As an agriculturalist Jefferson believed in the transformative power of that kind of connection to the land. His policy as president maintained the vision of the Civilization Campaign and its commitment to respecting the property of indigenous Americans.

Not all U.S. leaders took the land claims of native Americans seriously, however. Even as Jefferson promised the heads of native nations "We, indeed, are always ready to buy land; but we will never ask but when you wish to sell," other U.S. officials agreed to extinguish the property rights of many Amerindian peoples through the Georgia Compact of 1802. This agreement between the state of Georgia and the U.S. national government offered both sides a winning scenario. It did not, however, take the Amerindian people or their rights into consideration at all.

The Georgia Compact of 1802 did two things. Georgia agreed to relinquish its western lands and turn them over to the U.S. national government. In return, U.S. officials promised to extinguish native American titles to all land within the borders of the state. These lands added up to be "a tract of about one million and a half acres." This included much of the land of Jefferson's prided Cherokee Nation as well as many other indigenous groups. At first, U.S. liaisons asked the native Americans to sell their lands in Georgia. Many did not want to, however, and government's position grew more difficult. Ultimately, the compact opened the door for military action against the native Americans. Two presidential administrations later, talk of lands sales had given way to serious plans for forced removal.

The Georgia Compact of 1802 marked the beginning of the end for Jefferson's Indian Civilization Campaign. Though Jefferson wanted in a sense to remake native Americans in his own image, he at least respected their claims of sovereignty and property. The new Indian policy that followed from the Compact of 1802 was not so generous.

NOTES

1. Thomas Jefferson, quoted in Saul K. Padover, ed., *Thomas Jefferson on Democracy* (New York: Mentor, 1939), pp. 92–93. Jefferson appreciated what he perceived as the limited political state of the natives. He wrote in 1787: "And we think ours a bad government. The only condition on earth to be compared to ours, in my opinion, is that of the Indian, where they have still less law than we. The European, are government of kites over pigeons." Ibid., p. 25.

2. Jefferson was careful to explain that the Indians retained the rights to their lands. When asked about this by an English minister in 1792, he responded:

We consider it as established by the usage of different nations into a kind of *Jus gentium* for America, that a white nation settling down and declaring that such and such are their limits, makes an invasion of those limits by any other white nation an act of war, but gives no right of soil against the native possessors.

Thomas Jefferson, quoted in Francis Paul Prucha, *The Great Father: The United States Government and the American Indians* (Lincoln: University of Nebraska Press, 1986), p. 22.
3. Henry Dearborn to R.J. Meigs, January 8, 1806, "Letters Sent by the Secretary of War Relating to Indian Affairs, 1800–1824" (M-15), Roll 2:153, Records of the Bureau of Indian Affairs, National Archives.

THE PRESIDENT'S POSITION: INDIAN CIVILIZATION CAMPAIGN

To Brother Handsome Lake
Washington, November 3, 1802

TO BROTHER HANDSOME LAKE:—
I have received the message in writing which you sent me through Captain Irvine, our confidential agent, placed near you for the purpose of communicating and transacting between us, whatever may be useful for both nations. I am happy to learn you have been so far favored by the Divine spirit as to be made sensible of those things which are for your good and that of your people, and of those which are hurtful to you; and particularly that you and they see the ruinous effects which the abuse of spirituous liquors have produced upon them. It has weakened their bodies, enervated their minds, exposed them to hunger, cold, nakedness, and poverty, kept them in perpetual broils, and reduced their population. I do not wonder then, brother, at your censures, not only on your own people, who have voluntarily gone into these fatal habits, but on all the nations of white people who have supplied their calls for this article. But these nations have done to you only what they do among themselves. They have sold what individuals wish to buy, leaving to every one to be the guardian of his own health and happiness. Spirituous liquors are not in themselves bad, they are often found to be an excellent medicine for the sick; it is the improper and intemperate use of them, by those in health, which makes them injurious. But as you find that your people cannot refrain from an ill use of them, I greatly applaud your resolution not to use them at all. We have too affectionate a concern for your happiness to place the paltry gain on the sale of these articles in competition with the injury they do you. And as it is the desire of your nation, that no spirits should be sent among them, I am authorized by the great council of the United States to prohibit them. I will sincerely

cooperate with your wise men in any proper measures for this purpose, which shall be agreeable to them.

You remind me, brother, of what I said to you, when you visited me the last winter, that the lands you then held would remain yours, and shall never go from you but when you should be disposed to sell. This I now repeat, and will ever abide by. We, indeed, are always ready to buy land; but we will never ask but when you wish to sell; and our laws, in order to protect you against imposition, have forbidden individuals to purchase lands from you; and have rendered it necessary, when you desire to sell, even to a State, that an agent from the United States should attend the sale, see that your consent is freely given, a satisfactory price paid, and report to us what has been done, for our approbation. This was done in the late case of which you complain. The deputies of your nation came forward, in all the forms which we have been used to consider as evidence of the will of your nation. They proposed to sell to the State of New York certain parcels of land, of small extent, and detached from the body of your other lands; the State of New York was desirous to buy. I sent an agent, in whom we could trust, to see that your consent was free, and the sale fair. All was reported to be free and fair. The lands were your property. The right to sell is one of the rights of property. To forbid you the exercise of that right would be a wrong to your nation. Nor do I think, brother, that the sale of lands is, under all circumstances, injurious to your people. While they depended on hunting, the more extensive the forest around them, the more game they would yield. But going into a state of agriculture, it may be as advantageous to a society, as it is to an individual, who has more land than he can improve, to sell a part, and lay out the money in stocks and implements of agriculture, for the better improvement of the residue. A little land well stocked and improved, will yield more than a great deal without stock or improvement. I hope, therefore, that on further reflection, you will see this transaction in a more favorable light, both as it concerns the interest of your nation, and the exercise of that superintending care which I am sincerely anxious to employ for their subsistence and happiness. Go on then, brother, in the great reformation you have undertaken. Persuade our red brethren then to be sober, and to cultivate their lands; and their women to spin and weave for their families. You will soon see your women and children well fed and clothed, your men living happily in peace and plenty, and your numbers increasing from year to year. It will be a great glory to you to have been the instrument of so happy a change, and your children's children, from generation to generation, will repeat your name with love and gratitude forever. In all your enterprises for the good of your people, you may count with confidence on the aid and protection of the United States, and on the sincerity and zeal with which I am myself animated in the furthering of this humane work. You are our brethren of the same land; we wish your prosperity as brethren should do. Farewell.

See Thomas Jefferson: Indian Addresses. <http://libertyonline.hypermall.com/Jefferson/Indian.html>.

CONGRESS EXTINGUISHES LAND TITLE

7th Congress, February 16, 1803
Georgia Land Claims Report

The Commissioners appointed in pursuance of the act, entitled, "An act for an amicable settlement of limits with the State of Georgia, and authorizing the establishment of a government in the Mississippi Territory," in obedience to the provisions of the act supplemental to the last mentioned act, respectfully submit the following report on the claims made by settlers and other persons to lands within the territory situate west of the river Chatahoochee, and south of the cession made to the United States by South Carolina:

The territory of the United States south of the State of Tennessee, extends in breadth 275 miles, from the 31st to the 35th degree of north latitude. From east to west, its greatest length, from the river Chatahoochee to the Mississippi, measures 380 miles along the northern boundary of West Florida; the length of its northern boundary along the State of Tennessee is not precisely ascertained, but it is believed that the average length of the whole, may, without material error, be estimated at 300 miles, and the contents of the territory at 52,000,000 acres.

The only portions of that vast extent to which the Indian title has been extinguished, are a tract of about one million and a half acres, extending along the Mississippi, from the mouth of the river Yazoo, southwardly to the Spanish line, and another tract at least equal in extent, and extending between the rivers Pascagoula and Mobile, or Tombigbee, more than fifty miles north of that line.

The settlements within those two tracts, which are separated from each other by a wilderness of 120 miles in breadth, form the whole population of the Mississippi Territory.

The claims to lands within these boundaries are derived either from the British Government of West Florida, from the Spanish Government, or from the State of Georgia.

The British Governors of West Florida, after the boundaries of that province had been extended as far north as the parallel of latitude which crosses the Mississippi at the mouth of the river Yazoo, granted lands south of that parallel until the year 1781, when the province was conquered by Spain.

A great portion of the lands granted in that manner, has since been regranted by the Spanish Government; several tracts have continued in the occupancy of the original grantees, or of their representatives; and several remain unoccupied, or are inhabited by persons who have no other claim but that of possession. . . .

On the 7th of February, 1785, the State of Georgia passed an act for the purpose of laying out that tract of country extending along the Mississippi from the 31st degree of north latitude to the mouth of the river Yazoo, to which the Indian title had been extinguished, into a county by the name of Bourbon, and declared that whenever a land office should be opened, there should be a right of preference reserved to the possessors of lands within that district, provided they actually lived on and cultivated the said lands. That act was repealed by the 1st day of February, 1788. . . .

See *Annals of Congress*, Library of Congress, <http://memory.loc.gov/ammem/ amlaw/lawhome.html>.

EMBARGO

Jefferson began his first term in office under the shadow of war with the pasha of Tripoli and the Barbary Coast states. His second term drew to an end before the backdrop of potential war with Great Britain. He proved unable to resolve either problem decisively. His response to the latter, however, contradicted the laissez-faire economic system he and his party espoused and became the most unpopular act of his presidency.

In 1807, uneasy relations between the United States and Great Britain reached a breaking point after the British vessel *Leopard* stopped the U.S. ship *Chesapeake* in the waters off the Chesapeake Bay and removed four alleged English deserters. For a time Jefferson seemed unsure of what to do. He forwarded diplomatic correspondence to Congress without recommendations and waited to see what consensus about action the members could reach. In the meantime, both Great Britain's King George III and France's Napoleon stepped up hostilities on the high seas and made it clear that U.S. ships sailed into the fray at their own peril.

Eventually someone had to move, and that someone was James Madison. He convinced Jefferson that the only way to protect U.S. ships and citizens was to forbid them—not just government crafts, but private ones as well—from sailing into danger. Domestic coastal trade was safe enough, but trips to foreign ports posed too great a risk, he argued. On December 18, 1807, the president sent Congress suggestions for enacting an embargo. In less than a week, the first of several successive embargo acts was law.

The embargo policy contradicted traditional Democratic-Republican values such as free trade. If private citizens wished to conduct business at home or abroad at their own risk, laissez-faire economics suggested that the government had no right to forbid them. By trying to protect U.S. citizens, Jefferson denied them the opportunity to choose safety or danger for themselves. Jefferson also invited financial problems by closing the usual conduits for commerce. In a sense, he was punishing his own people for the hostilities of other nations. Secretary of the Treasury Albert Gallatin warned Jefferson of these things. He noted that the embargo would bring unintended consequences, since "governmental prohibitions do always more mischief than had been calculated," and that Jefferson wounded national morale by making citizens prisoners in their own country. After tallying the potential cost in terms of "privations, sufferings, revenue, effect on the enemy, [and] politics at home," Gallatin believed even war was more desirable than embargo.[1]

In a moment when the citizenry embraced Democratic-Republican thought more dearly than the president, many people agreed with Gallatin. They used terms such as "oppression" and "repression" in the press to describe their plight. Federalist Timothy Pickering and his followers, in a last effort to revive their party and power, tried to goad Jefferson into more coercive use of the embargo in order to make the president even more unpopular. Pickering called for a nullification of the embargo by state legislatures, turning Jefferson's argument from the days of the Alien and Sedition Acts against him. Pickering also accused Jefferson, widely known to be sympathetic to the French, of enacting the embargo at the order of Napoleon. The public grew more outraged.

Jefferson took the bait and responded as Pickering had intended. His enforcement measures became more coercive and, when his own appointees overruled his policies, he authorized the use of the armed forces and created what amounted to a police state in the United States. He had hoped that cutting the international markets off from U.S. goods would force other nations to the bargaining table, but the only economy severely injured by the embargo was the U.S. market.

The public's anger and frustration about the embargo and the havoc it wreaked on their finances followed Jefferson into his final days in office. Despite Timothy Pickering's machinations, however, the Federalist Party was on its way to extinction. Pickering offered James Madison little competition in the presidential election. By the time Madison came to office, Congress had revised the embargo through the Non-Intercourse Act of 1809, which opened trade to all nations except Great Britain and France. The problems in foreign relations that preceded the embargo still remained, however. Hostilities with Great Britain blossomed. John Adams and Thomas Jefferson had only postponed the inevitable, it seemed;

Madison would see the nation through its first official war since the War of Independence.

NOTE

1. Albert Gallatin. Letter to Thomas Jefferson, December 18, 1807. In *The Writings of Albert Gallatin*, Vol. 1, Henry Adams, ed. (Philadelphia: Lippincott, 1879), p. 368.

THE PRESIDENT'S POSITION: IN FAVOR OF EMBARGO

Thomas Jefferson to Albert Gallatin
March 31, 1808

If, on considering the doubts I shall suggest, you shall still think your draught of a supplementary embargo law sufficient, in its present form, I shall be satisfied it is so, for I have but one hour in the morning in which I am capable of thinking, and that is too much crowded with business to give me time to think.

[The following is the draught by Jefferson alluded to above.]

March 30, 1808.
A bill supplementary to the several Acts for laying an embargo eyre vessels, &c.
For vessels coming down rivers, &c.—Be it enacted, &c., that it shall not be lawful for any vessel laden with provisions or lumber to pass by or depart from any port of entry of the United States without examination and a special license from the collector of the customs of such port; nor shall any vessel be so laden on any part of the coasts or shores of the United States without the limits of any port of entry until previously examined by some person authorized by the nearest collector of the customs, and a special license from the said collector to be so laden, and to depart according to her lawful destination, on pain of incurring the same penalties and forfeitures as if the said lading had been exported contrary to the tenor of the Acts for laying on embargo, &c. And it shall be lawful for all officers of the revenue and of the armed vessels of the United States to bring to and examine all vessels suspected to be laden with provisions or lumber, and to have departed, or to be about to depart, without having obtained such license and on examination and probable grounds to seize and place the same under a due course of legal inquiry.

For Passamaquoddy and St. Mary's, and the secret coves and inlets of the coast.—And be it further enacted, &c., that wheresoever, in any port or on the coasts or shores of the United States elsewhere, a collection of provisions or of lumber shall be made or making which is suspected to be intended for exportation contrary to the provisions of the said laws for laying an embargo, it shall be lawful for the collector of the same port, or of the nearest port, by any agent to be appointed by him, to have the same deposited, if provisions, in warehouses to be approved by him, and to be duly secured by lock, the key of which shall remain with such agent; or if lumber, then to be placed under a sufficient guard by day and night, the expense of which shall be paid by the owner of such lumber, or be levied by sale of sufficient part thereof; and not to permit the said provisions or lumber to be removed but to such other places, and on such conditions, as shall in his judgment sufficiently guard their being exported contrary to the provisions of the said Acts. And the said collectors and agents shall in all cases within the purview of this Act be governed by such regulations as shall be prescribed by the Secretary of the Treasury, with the approbation of the President of the United States, in all matters of detail necessary for preventing the evasion of this law and for carrying the same into effectual execution.

Thomas Jefferson to Albert Gallatin

The above is a very imperfect sketch (for I am not in a condition to think attentively) of what your better knowledge of the subject will enable you [to] prepare for preventing the evasions of the law at Passamaquoddy, St. Mary's, and everywhere else as to provisions and lumber. If you will prepare something on these or any other ideas you like better, Mr. Eppes will give them to Mr. Newton (or you can endorse them to him yourself), and he will push them through the House. Affectionate salutations.

April 2, 1808.

See Thomas Jefferson Papers at the Library of Congress. <http://memory.loc.gov/ammem/mtjhtml/mtjhome.html>.

Thomas Jefferson to Caesar A. Rodney
April 24, 1808

Th. Jefferson returns the endorsed to Mr. Rodney with thanks for the communication. It is very evident that our embargo, added to the exclusions from the continent will be most easily felt in England and Ireland. Liverpool is remonstrating & endeavoring to get the other ports into motion. Yet the bill confirming the orders of Council is ordered to a 3d reading, which shews it will pass. Congress has just passed an additional embargo law, on which if we act as boldly as I am disposed to do, we can make it effectual. I think the material parts of the enclosed should be published. It will show our people that while the embargo gives no double rations it is starving our enemies. This six months session has drawn me down to a state of almost total incapacity for business. Congress will certainly rise tomorrow night, and I shall leave this for Monticello on the 5th of May to be here again on the 8th of June.

See Thomas Jefferson Papers at the Library of Congress. <http://memory.loc.gov/ammem/mtjhtml/mtjhome.html>.

AGAINST EMBARGO

"The Embargo and the Farmer's Story"
Columbia Sentinel, 25 May 1808

A zealous Boston Democrat was lately in the country extolling the embargo to a plain farmer, as a wise as well as a strong measure, and urging the farmer to express his opinion upon it. The farmer, however, modestly declined, saying that he lived in the bush where he had not the means of information on which to ground an opinion on political measures; but if Boston folks, who knew more, said it was right, he supposed it was so; but, says he, I will tell you a story. Our minister one day sent his boy to the pasture after a horse. He was gone so long that the parson was afraid the horse had kicked his brains out; he went therefore with anxiety to look after him. In the field he found the boy standing still with his eyes steadily fixed upon the ground. His master inquired with severity what he was doing there. Why, sir, said he, I saw a woodchuck run into this hole, and so I thought I would stand and watch for him until he was starved out; but I declare I am almost starved to death myself.

See Debates on Government Neutrality. <http://www.hillsdale.edu/dept/History/Documents/War/America/1812/1807-Newspapers-Prelude.htm>.

"Hateful Measures for Enforcing the Embargo"
Boston Gazette, 2 February, 1809

Within a few days past Colonel Boyd, commanding at the Castle, received orders from the Secretary of War to interdict all vessels from passing Fort Independence; in consequence of this edict the acting Collector has been placed under the necessity of withholding clearances to every description of vessels.

This aggravated repression was not generally known until yesterday, when the vessels in the harbor bound their colors in black, and hoisted them half-mast. The circumstance has created some considerable agitation in the public mind, but to the honor of the town has been yet unattended with any serious consequences.

It is to be presumed that this new edict will at least continue to be enforced until Secretary Dearborn is at leisure to come on, to mark out his favorites, and take upon himself the office, so long reserved for him, of the Customs.

The spirit of our citizens is rising and may burst into a flame. Everything should therefore be done to calm them till the Legislature has had time to mature its plans of redress. It is feared that the caution necessary in such an assembly may protract our relief too long; but we must wait patiently the aid of our Constitutional Guardians, rather than stain the character of this metropolis by mobs and riots. If our government cannot do anything now that shall afford full and complete relief, they may at least do enough to calm the public mind and lead the citizens to wait for events, which must place the means for a radical cure completely in our hands.

The spirit of New England is slow in rising; but when once inflamed by oppression, it will never be repressed by anything short of complete justice.

See Debates on Government Neutrality. <http://www.hillsdale.edu/dept/History/Documents/War/America/1812/1807-Newspapers-Prelude.htm>.

Aurora General Advertiser
31 July 1809

The prints which, by their subserviency to the baleful oppression of Great Britain, have contributed so much to the disgrace of this nation, and encouraged, by their corruption, the insolence of the enemy, are now seeking to make a sett off by rumors from France, which, like their usual fabrications, are too clumsy and preposterous to merit regard.

. . . The crisis comes upon us now, when we must look to our own security, and the policy which is best adapted to ensure our rights and our prosperity.

France has fought our battles—had Britain triumphed, we should have been enslaved.

We can have no natural sympathies for a government which has tyrannised over us in every shape—which has murdered, torn from their homes, and plundered our citizens, insulted our flag, our territory, and our independence—and trampled upon the laws of civilized nations.

. . . We want no alliance—we look for none—we look for peace—we have a right to insist on free commerce and peace; and neither of the belligerents have a right to invade the one or the other.

In our policy we must detest the nation that insults or injures us. Our policy in regard to Europe has not been naturally wise.

We must stand upon that ground which asserts the rights of property alike, on the earth and the seas. Which assures neutral commerce, and which gives the high road of the ocean, as God has given it to man free, and without any other bounds to it than the creator has placed.

We have no need to league with the belligerents, we have only to defend ourselves from oppression.

See Debates on Government Neutrality. <http://www.hillsdale.edu/dept/History/Documents/War/America/1812/1807-Newspapers-Prelude.htm>.

RECOMMENDED READINGS

Brown, David S. *Thomas Jefferson: A Biographical Companion*. Santa Barbara, Calif.: ABC-CLIO, 1998.

Cappon, Lester J., ed. *The Adams-Jefferson Letters: The Complete Correspondence*. Chapel Hill: University of North Carolina Press, 1988.

Elkins, Stanley, and Eric McKitrick. *The Age of Federalism*. New York: Oxford University Press, 1993.

Ellis, Joseph J. *American Sphinx: The Character of Thomas Jefferson*. New York: Alfred A. Knopf, 1997.

———, ed. *Thomas Jefferson: Genius of Liberty*. New York: Viking Press, 2000.

Israel, Fred L., ed. *Major Presidential Decisions*. New York: Chelsea House, 1980.

Jefferson, Thomas. *Thomas Jefferson, Political Writings*. Edited by Joyce Appleby and Terence Ball. New York: Cambridge University Press, 1999.

Jefferson, Thomas, and James Madison. *The Republic of Letters: The Correspondence between Thomas Jefferson and James Madison, 1776–1826*. New York: Norton, 1995.

Kaplan, Lawrence S. *Thomas Jefferson: Westward the Course of Empire*. Wilmington, Del.: S Books, 1999.

Ketcham, Ralph. *Presidents Above Party: The First American Presidency, 1789–1829*. Chapel Hill: University of North Carolina Press, 1984.

Malone, Dumas. *Jefferson and His Time*. 6 vols. Boston: Little, Brown, 1948–1981.

Mayer, David N. *The Constitutional Thought of Thomas Jefferson*. Charlottesville: University Press of Virginia, 1994.

McDonald, Forrest. *The Presidency of Thomas Jefferson*. Lawrence: University Press of Kansas, 1976.

McLaughlin, Jack, ed. *To His Excellency Thomas Jefferson: Letters to a President*. New York: W.W. Norton & Company, 1991.

Onuf, Peter S., ed. *Jeffersonian Legacies*. Charlottesville: University Press of Virginia, 1993.

Peterson, Merrill D. *Thomas Jefferson and the New Nation: A Biography*. New York: Oxford University Press, 1970.

Risjord, Norman K. *Thomas Jefferson*. Madison, Wis.: Madison House, 1994.

Sheldon, Garrett Ward. *The Political Philosophy of Thomas Jefferson.* Baltimore: Johns Hopkins University Press, 1991.

Yarbrough, Jean M. *American Virtues: Thomas Jefferson on the Character of a Free People.* Lawrence: University Press of Kansas, 1998.

4

JAMES MADISON

(1809–1817)

INTRODUCTION

When John Adams followed George Washington as president of the United States, he had remarkable shoes to fill; the general's vision of the office shaped it to such a degree that Adams seemed like a poor fit. The precedent of personality even over policy fueled expectations from the citizens and leaders alike. Adams withdrew rather than reinterpret the position for himself, and this caused many of the problems and frustrations of his term in office. His achievements paled in comparison to his failure to be another Washington.

Thomas Jefferson's presidency was like another first. He reformed the office in his own image and reaped great disappointments and even greater successes. Paradoxically, Jefferson behaved less as monarch than as everyman, and yet he wielded more power in his administration than Washington even imagined. Jefferson's successor seemed doomed to the same cycle Adams had faced. James Madison could not be Thomas Jefferson.

The second and fourth presidents did share similarities. Both highly admired the men they replaced as chief executive. Both were smaller men in stature and force of personality than the presidents they followed. Both had perhaps intellectually meatier, though certainly less glamorous, lives in public service than the men who preceded them. Both inherited cabinet members and agendas from their predecessors. Unlike Adams, however, Madison had never been called a fiery orator or a rousing leader. The diminutive, scholarly Madison rose to the foreground when forced, but preferred to contribute from behind the scenes through writings rather than speeches. And unlike the family men before him, the long-term bachelor and eventual husband to Dolley Madison seemed a loner, with no children and few affectionate attachments. His health troubled him as well. In short, Madison faced many of the same challenges Adams had experienced, only with less stamina and charisma. At first look, it did not seem like a recipe for success.

There was one telling difference between the two, however. Whereas Adams admired Washington, the two could not be said to be close. Madison, though, had studied Jefferson from all angles for most of his adult life, first as a student and then as a political partner. The two collaborated professionally and personally in almost all of the undertakings that mattered to either man. As secretary of state and primary advisor and confidant to the president, Madison in part had created the Jefferson presidency; he inherited an office, then, of which he had already been a part. And as he had been there for Jefferson, Jefferson in turn stood behind Madison throughout his eight-year tenure. For the first term, Madison also had Jefferson's vice president, George Clinton, at his side. For the second term, Elbridge Gerry served as vice president until his death.

Madison chose officials from across the nation to create a cabinet of breadth rather than depth. Dr. William Eustis became secretary of war. Paul Hamilton became secretary of the navy. What the gentlemen lacked in experience they made up for in political currency. Madison moved Jefferson's secretary of the navy, Robert Smith, to the position of secretary of state, but later dismissed him. Madison maintained Caesar Rodney as attorney general and Gideon Granger as postmaster general, both Jefferson appointees. With the exception of Smith, who proved incompetent in work and intolerant of colleagues, Madison had amicable relations with his advisors. In some ways, the cabinet members meant less to Madison than to past presidents because, along with former president Jefferson, Madison relied on one close confidant for his advice and counsel: Albert Gallatin. Gallatin maintained his role as secretary of the treasury for the two terms of Madison's presidency and served as the executive's second-in-command in every sense. The eight years the two had worked together under Jefferson had cemented a close camaraderie and trust on which Madison relied. Conferences between the two could substitute for full cabinet meetings. Gallatin's personal life included a solid marriage and behavior beyond reproach and gave critics little foothold for criticism. When Robert Smith, already troubled by a series of incompetent actions, developed antagonism for the president's closest advisor, Madison dismissed Smith outright.

The secretary of state position had already gained the reputation of being the training ground for future presidents. Jefferson and Madison had served in this position in the Washington and Jefferson administrations, respectively. When Madison looked for a replacement for Robert Smith, then, he made a conscious choice to propose a successor to his office. James Monroe accepted the appointment and became secretary of state, as well as acting secretary of war during key moments of the War of 1812. Madison and Monroe, though both dear friends of Thomas Jefferson, had harbored disagreements in the past that made their relationship difficult. Nevertheless, Madison made the first move to mend the past and Monroe accepted the gesture. The two worked well together and Monroe indeed followed Madison as president of the United States.

Aside from Jefferson's encouragement from his retirement, Gallatin's constant support and friendship, and the late addition of Monroe's presence in the cabinet, James Madison enjoyed another alliance that served him well. His wife, Dolley Madison, remained a celebrated and influential presence in Washington. Martha Washington and Abigail Adams were both women of means and education, the latter more outspoken than the former, but neither took such an active role in contributing to her husband's successful tenure in office. The widower Jefferson looked to his daughter and to Dolley Madison for assistance in entertaining and maintaining a public household in the capital. The term "First Lady," along with "Presidentress," first appeared, however, to describe Dolley Madison. By the time James Madison became chief executive, his wife had a good sense of what the role could be. Taller and seventeen years younger than her husband, Mrs. Madison dressed like a queen and entertained like an ambassador. A born diplomat, she tirelessly arranged receptions and dinners that allowed key officials from the United States and abroad to interact in a comfortable, nonthreatening environment. Her natural political instinct allowed her to facilitate meetings and choreograph events to the benefit of her husband's administration. Even after Madison's retirement, Mrs. Madison's home remained a center of activity for the nation's leaders.

Perhaps the most memorable mental image of the Madison administration remains that of the First Lady, fleeing British troops as they swarmed Washington, D.C., evacuating the burning White House, carrying the portrait of George Washington and saving it from the flames. The picture carries the stigma of war and the embarrassment of invasion, but it also reflects the hope of the survivor and the determination to preserve the U.S. tradition for future citizens. The image in its contradictions serves as a fitting metaphor for the Madison presidency.

Madison began his administration facing the question of nation/state relations thanks to the final stages of a court case dating back to the War of Independence. An old Pennsylvania dispute had made its way to the U.S. Supreme Court as *Olmstead v. the Executrices of the Late David Rittenhouse* and been decided in 1803. The defendant's estate owed thousands of dollars to the plaintiff. The debt fell to the late defendant's two elderly daughters, however, and the governor of Pennsylvania promised the widows protection. When a federal marshal came for the two sisters, the governor deployed the state militia to defend them. The militia soldiers in turn were indicted for their actions. A standoff followed and Madison intervened. The president diffused the situation by pardoning the indicted members of the militia for their efforts under Pennsylvania law but contrary to the decision of the U.S. Supreme Court. By siding with the state against the national legislature, Madison maintained his support of the decentralization of the extended republic, the balance between state and national powers, against Federalist efforts to centralize governmental authority.

In contrast to his position in the *Olmstead* scenario, Madison exploited his executive power—beyond constitutional limits, his critics believed—when pressed to resolve the issue of Florida. Though Jefferson believed Florida became a U.S. possession through the Louisiana Purchase, clear title seemed uncertain. The land was settled by a variety of peoples from Spaniards and native Americans to runaway slaves and pirates. Some settlers grew agitated and sought proper annexation with the United States. Madison, worried that Great Britain might seize the unresolved situation as an opportunity to take over the area, ordered troops to occupy West Florida. He then counted West Florida as part of the Orleans Territory organized under its territorial governor. Careful after receiving criticism for acting without constitutional authority, Madison followed proper procedure with regard to East Florida and submitted his plans for congressional approval before he acted. The legislature approved further occupation and Madison claimed East Florida for the United States as well. The question of means aside, Madison denied the British a military opportunity that might have seriously compromised the United States. He also preserved the tradition of territorial expansion begun in the Jefferson administration.

The chief preoccupation and primary event of Madison's presidency was the War of 1812. Earlier presidents had endured quasi wars with Great Britain but avoided official warfare. By Madison's time, true battle seemed inevitable in order to protect domestic and foreign trade. Critics, however, feared that a war for commerce would result in a loss of international consumers of U.S. goods and a devastated national economy. Congress answered Madison's call with a declaration of war nonetheless. In the darkest moments of battle for the United States, Great Britain invaded and sacked Washington, D.C., and Madison absorbed much of the blame. The tide of war turned, however, and peace came with the Treaty of Ghent in 1814. The opponents of war were wrong in their first criticism, for trade resumed quickly. They proved partially correct in their fears for the economy, though. The war took its toll on the financial health of the United States.

Such concerns led Madison to one of the most significant reversals of his career in public service. Madison had fought the chartering of the First Bank of the United States during the Washington administration and even penned a potential veto announcement for the president. Despite Madison's efforts, Washington eventually approved of Alexander Hamilton's comprehensive economic plan, including the bank. Madison did not see the creation and maintenance of a national bank among the powers enumerated in the U.S. Constitution. As a strict constructionist, he tried to hold himself and others accountable to the letter of the law. When Congress passed a bill to recharter the bank during the War of 1812, Madison vetoed it. Less than a year later, as he struggled with the sluggish postwar economy, the president changed his mind and supported the Second Bank of the United States. He did not believe the bank to be constitutional in a strict sense, but the urgency of the times caused him to consider the ends—reviving public credit, providing a national medium of circulation, and assisting the Treasury—rather than the means. In the national bank issue, Madison was his own greatest opponent.

Madison ended his second term much as he began his first, wrestling with the issues of national/state relations and seeking to preserve the delicate balance of the extended republic. On his last day in office, the president vetoed the so-called Bonus Bill, which provided national funds for internal improvements such as roads and canals. He feared that the legislature recklessly expanded the "general welfare" clause of the Constitution in order to justify national involvement in regional and local projects. His opponents argued that the effects of such projects would benefit the entire country by speeding commerce, information, and military forces across the young nation. Madison was not convinced. The precedent of using "general welfare" to justify any potentially useful endeavor seemed like a slippery slope to him. In the end, the bill failed to garner enough votes to overturn the veto and Madison's decision stood.

The president entered office with two primary goals: to preserve the Jeffersonian legacy and to keep the United States out of war. In the first endeavor, he succeeded. He pressed the territorial claims of the Louisiana Purchase and completed its unfinished business in Florida. He supported a strict construction of the U.S. Constitution when he could, as in the case of internal improvements, and states rights when he was able, such as in the *Olmstead* affair. Yet, like Jefferson, he also drew power to the executive and expanded its influence to (or, at times, beyond) constitutional limits. The ideals and party of Democratic-Republicanism fared reasonably well during his two terms.

Though Madison did not keep the United States out of war, he did the next best thing. When war came the United States held its own—

arguably more by luck than ability. Though the nation and its commander in chief suffered embarrassments, Madison saw events through until peace was achieved and he was heralded as a hero. The United States emerged from war with restored domestic and international trade and a rocky but improving economy. If war was inevitable, Madison showed satisfactory results. As the middle man in the Virginia Dynasty, delivering the momentum of the Revolution of 1800 into successor James Monroe's hands, bridging Jeffersonianism and the Era of Good Feelings, Madison could have done far worse.

Madison's reputation as president has suffered from a variety of modern prejudices. As a man, Madison possessed few of the glamorous attributes that make historical figures fascinating to mainstream audiences; he was short, small, quiet, with an intellectual wit and scholarly personality, with few vices, sexual or otherwise, to capture the imagination. As a leader, he suffered from unfortunate timing; a war that had been brewing for years erupted during his administration, and scholars often equate war with failure. Madison's own brilliant wife overshadows him in public perception, as does the image of his closest friend, Thomas Jefferson. The values he embraced as Father of the U.S. Constitution and Democratic-Republican—the rigor of strict constructionism, the balance of state and national governments—are not emphasized by many in the current political debate.

Madison nevertheless proved to be a competent steward of the nation and tradition he had inherited. He carried the country through the fire of warfare and delivered it intact to his chosen successor. Without Madison, Jefferson's two terms would have reflected an aberration in the history of the presidency rather than the foundation of a dynasty in the White House. Jefferson lit the fire; Madison carried the torch.

STATE/NATIONAL GOVERNMENT RELATIONS

One of the first challenges to face President James Madison was a humorous farce of a problem that nonetheless raised a very serious issue: the relation between state and national governments. The story began decades earlier. The case first hit Pennsylvania courts in 1778, and eventually went to the U.S. Supreme Court in 1803 as *Olmstead v. the Executrices of the Late David Rittenhouse*. In this case, plaintiffs sued for prizes earned during a capture at sea in the War of Independence. The Court found in favor of the claim and demanded that the money and accrued interest be paid; the defendant by this time had died, however, and his elderly, widowed daughters had inherited his estate. When the governor of Pennsylvania, Simon Snyder, learned that the Court had ordered the two sisters to pay $15,000, he and the state legislature promised them protection and indemnity. Eventually a federal marshal came to arrest the two elderly ladies. In response, the governor deployed the state militia to protect the Rittenhouse sisters. The marshal, in turn, threatened to call a posse to confront the militia. A regular showdown developed, one on the side of the law of the land and the other on the side of two old and defenseless women.

Governor Snyder appealed to the president to intervene. This placed Madison in a difficult position, wedged between a Democratic-Republican governor and Federalist John Marshall, chief justice of the U.S. Supreme Court. The governor of Pennsylvania, by failing to respect the court's decision, was acting against not only the judiciary but also the U.S. Constitution. To further complicate matters, the state legislature backed up the governor's stand by passing a bill supporting the militia's actions and setting aside the funds to cover the Rittenhouse debt. But the other side would not back down. The commanding officer of the Pennsylvania state militia, General Michael Bright, and seven of his men faced a federal indictment for protecting the sisters. At this point, Madison made his move to diffuse the situation. He used his executive power and pardoned Bright and his men, noting "it is considered that the offences committed in this case proceeded rather from a mistaken sense of duty, than from a spirit of disobedience to the authority and laws of the United States." The state of Pennsylvania celebrated. A Philadelphia dinner even honored the eight pardoned members of the state militia as heroes.

What played well in Philadelphia did not play well in Washington, D.C., at least in the U.S. Supreme Court. John Marshall fumed over Madison's interference and apparent blessing for Pennsylvania's disobedient and unlawful conduct. He argued that such an event as the Pennsylvania debacle threatened the entire fate of the Union. A state legislature could not, he argued, annul the decision of the Court—and yet in Pennsylvania it did, and got away with it. If a state could overturn the ruling of the national judiciary, Marshall continued, then "the Constitution itself becomes a solemn mockery."

The *Rittenhouse* case turned out to be a one-time, awkward, rather ridiculous interlude. Many of its causes sprang from particular moments in time. It was a decades-old case that referred to events that occurred when the colonies broke free from Great Britain, and it had survived in the courts of two governmental systems since then. It was, in short, an exception to the rule.

It did, however, underscore the tension between state and national governments in the federal system. Madison, who as the Father of the U.S. Constitution played a seminal role in creating the delicate balance of federalism that made the extended republic possible, in fact liked this tension as a check on powers in both directions. Marshall did not. As a Federalist, he gave priority to the national government and its authority.

He favored a more centralized system, and events such as those in Pennsylvania disturbed him terribly.

In the end, Madison had little choice of what to do. He followed his ideological priorities by backing a state against national power, and he followed his political priorities by backing an ally against the opposition. Most importantly, he ended a tense situation before it could become violent. If he had the opportunity for a little payback to John Marshall for using *Marbury v. Madison* to expand the power of the national judiciary, of course, that was nice as well. The larger issue of state and national relations would remain a key theme of many presidential administrations to come.

THE PRESIDENT'S POSITION: PARDON
(PRO—STATES RIGHTS)

To James Madison
From Michael Leib
Philadelphia, May 3d, 1809

Sir,

Yesterday General Bright and those associated with him in resisting the process of the district court, were sentenced to fine and imprisonment, and accordingly committed to prison. The public sensation on this event is considerable, and is transferring itself from the outrage upon the law, to those who are now suffering under it. A distinction is made between the legality and the justice of the procedure; and it is deemed a hardship, that militia men, acting under the orders of the Governor of Pennsylvania, by the Constitution their commander in chief, should be punished for their obedience, while the principal is wholly exempted from responsibility. As the law is now satisfied by the payment of the money, and the conviction of the offenders, permit me to suggest to you the expediency of pardoning them. I am persuaded that general satisfaction will be given to the people of this State if you interpose in their behalf; and I cannot help adding, that the republican cause will suffer should the sentence be carried into full effect; you will pardon me, therefore, for my solicitude in the case, and for my urgency in favor of an immediate release of General Bright and his associates. With sentiments of sincere respect and regard I am, Sir, Your obedient Servant.

M Leib

See *The Papers of James Madison: Presidential Series*, vol. 1, *1 March–30 September 1809*, ed. Robert A. Rutland (Charlottesville: University Press of Virginia, 1984), p. 159.

To James Madison
From Thomas Leiper
Philadelphia, May 5th, 1809

Dear Sir

General Michael Bright certainly acted against Law when he obeyed the orders of Governor Snyder but at the same time the General did believe he had no discretionary powers but to act as he was ordered. The Grand Jury to my knowledge sixteen out of the nineteen found the Bill and the sixteen were astonished at the three when they pronounced the Bill not true. Their are none who justify the Governor but those in office or expect to be but this can be accounted for as he has the power of turning out at pleasure. But Altho' nine tenth of the thinking men are of the opinion the sentence against General Bright and those under his command is perfectly correct yet notwithstanding nothing would give us *all* more pleasure and satisfaction than to see your Pardon extended to those men. I am with the highest esteem & respect Dear Sir Your most Obedient Servant

Thomas Leiper

See *The Papers of James Madison: Presidential Series*, vol. 1, *1 March–30 September 1809*, ed. Robert A. Rutland (Charlottesville: University Press of Virginia, 1984), p. 172.

Executive Pardon
6 May 1809

James Madison, President of the United States of the America,

To all who shall see these presents, GREETING:

Whereas it has been represented to me that Genl Michael Bright, James Atkinson, William Cole, Charles Westfall, Samuel Wilkins, Abraham Ogden, Daniel Phyle, Charles Hong and John Knipe, all of the state of Pennsylvania, were, at a Circuit Court of the United States lately held for the Pennsylvania District, at Philadelphia, duly and severally convicted of opposing and obstructing the Marshal for that District in the execution of his official duty, and thereupon the said Court sentenced the said Michael Bright to three months imprisonment, and to pay to the United States a fine of fifty dollars. And whereas it is considered that the offences committed in this case proceeded rather from a mistaken sense of duty, than from a spirit of disobedience to the authority and laws of the United States: Now therefore be it known, that I James Madison President of the United States of America for these and other good causes and considerations me thereunto moving, do by these presents pardon and remit to the several persons above named the offences as aforesaid by them committed, and the fines respectively incurred by them; requiring that all prosecutions and judicial proceedings for and on account thereof be forthwith stayed and discharged.

In testimony whereof, I have hereunto set my hand, and caused the Seal of the United States to be affixed to these presents the Sixth day of May in the year of our Lord 1809; and of the Independence of the United States the Thirty third.

James Madison

By the President,
   R Smith   Secretary of State.

See *The Papers of James Madison: Presidential Series*, vol. 1, *1 March–30 September 1809*, ed. Robert A. Rutland (Charlottesville: University Press of Virginia, 1984), pp. 173–174.

SUPREME COURT DECISION IN FAVOR OF THE NATIONAL GOVERNMENT

United States v. Peters (1809)

Mr. Chief Justice MARSHALL delivered the opinion of the Court.

With great attention, and with serious concern, the Court has considered the return made by the Judge for the District of Pennsylvania to the mandamus directing him to execute the sentence pronounced by him in the case of *Gideon Olmstead and others v. Rittenhouse's Executrixes*, or to show cause for not so doing. The cause shown is an act of the Legislature of Pennsylvania, passed subsequent to the rendition of his sentence. This act authorizes and requires the Governor to demand, for the use of the State of Pennsylvania, the money which had been decreed to Gideon Olmstead and others, and which was in the hands of the executrixes of David Rittenhouse; and, in default of payment, to direct the Attorney General to institute a suit for the recovery thereof. This act further authorizes and requires the Governor to use any further means he may think necessary for the protection of what it denominates "the just rights of the State," and also to protect the persons and properties of the said executrixes of David Rittenhouse, deceased, against any process whatever, issued out of any federal Court in consequence of their obedience to the requisition of the said act.

If the legislatures of the several States may, at will, annul the judgments of the courts of the United States, and destroy the rights acquired under those judgments, the Constitution itself becomes a solemn mockery, and the nation is deprived of the means of enforcing its laws by the instrumentality of its own tribunals. So fatal a result must be deprecated by all, and the people of Pennsylvania, not less than the citizens of every other State, must feel a deep interest in resisting principles so destructive of the union, and in averting consequences so fatal to themselves.

The act in question does not, in terms, assert the universal right of the State to interpose in every case whatever, but assigns, as a motive for its interposition in this particular case, that the sentence the execution of which it prohibits was rendered in a cause over which the federal Courts have no jurisdiction.

If the ultimate right to determine the jurisdiction of the courts of the Union is placed by the Constitution in the several State legislatures, then this act concludes the subject; but if that power necessarily resides in the supreme judicial tribunal of the nation, then the jurisdiction of the District Court of Pennsylvania over the case in which that jurisdiction was exercised ought to be most deliberately examined, and the act of Pennsylvania, with whatever respect it may be considered, cannot be permitted to prejudice the question. . . .

It is contended that the federal Courts were deprived of jurisdiction, in this case by that amendment of the Constitution which exempts States from being sued in those Courts by individuals. This amendment declares that the judicial power of the United States shall not be construed to extend to any suit, in law or equity, commenced or prosecuted against one of the United States by citizens of another State, or by citizens or subjects of any foreign State.

The right of a State to assert, as plaintiff, any interest it may have in a subject which forms the matter of controversy between individuals in one of the courts of the United States is not affected by this amendment, nor can it be so construed as to oust the Court of its jurisdiction, should such claim be suggested. The amendment simply provides that no suit shall be commenced or prosecuted against a State. The State cannot be made a defendant to a suit brought by an individual, but it remains the duty of the courts of the United States to decide all cases brought before them by citizens of one State against citizens of a different State where a State is not necessarily a defendant. In this case, the suit was not instituted against the State or its Treasurer, but against the executrixes of David Rittenhouse, for the proceeds of a vessel condemned in the Court of Admiralty, which were admitted to be in their possession. If these proceeds had been the actual property of Pennsylvania, however wrongfully acquired, the disclosure of that fact would have presented a case on which it was unnecessary to give an opinion; but it certainly can never be alleged, that a mere suggestion of title in a State to property in possession of an individual must arrest the proceedings of the court, and prevent their looking into the suggestion and examining the validity of the title.

If the suggestion in this case be examined, it is deemed perfectly clear that no title whatever to the certificates in question was vested in the State of Pennsylvania.

By the highest judicial authority of the nation, it has been long since decided that the Court of Appeals erected by Congress had full authority to revise and correct the sentences of the Courts of Admiralty of the several States in prize causes. That question, therefore, is at rest. Consequently, the decision of the Court of Appeals in this case annulled the sentence of the Court of Admiralty, and extinguished the interest of the State of Pennsylvania in the *Active* and her cargo which was acquired by that sentence. The full right to that property was immediately vested in the claimants, who might rightfully pursue it into whosoever hands it might come. These certificates, in the hands, first, of Matthew Clarkson, the Marshal, and afterwards of George Ross, the Judge, of the Court of Admiralty, were the absolute property of the claimants. Nor did they change their character on coming into the possession of David Rittenhouse. . . .

Since, then, the State of Pennsylvania had neither possession of nor right to the property on which the sentence of the District Court was pronounced, and since the suit was neither commenced nor prosecuted against that State, there remains no pretext for the allegation that the case is within that amendment of the Constitution which has been cited, and, consequently the State of Pennsylvania can possess no Constitutional right to resist the legal process which may be directed in this cause.

It will be readily conceived that the order which this Court is enjoined to make by the high obligations of duty and of law is not made without extreme regret at the necessity which has induced the application. But it is a solemn duty, and therefore must be performed. A peremptory mandamus must be awarded.

In U.S. Supreme Court Collection. <http://supct.law.cornell.edu/supct/>.

EXECUTIVE POWER

One of the unresolved lingering issues left by the Louisiana Purchase was the fate of Florida. Jefferson assumed that the area was included in the transaction but possession never reverted to the United States. Instead, an amalgam of Spanish forces, U.S. citizens, native Americans, runaway slaves, and others occupied a kind of gray area outside of any clear jurisdiction. Jefferson's plan, and then Madison's, was to wait for an end to hostilities between France and Great Britain and then settle the issue through negotiation. The peacetime they anticipated did not come; in fact, the United States itself seemed to move closer to war with Great Britain.

In the meantime, some settlers in Florida grew restless to resolve the situation. They wrote letters to the president asking for annexation in the United States, either as part of a preexisting state or as an independent one. A group of insurgents even claimed to liberate the area and elect their own president in order to conduct talks with Madison about annexation. Others who had established land titles under the Spanish worried about whether their property rights would be protected under U.S. law. As concerns grew louder, Madison felt that he had to make a decision. The people's unrest was troublesome, but Madison's greatest concern was that Great Britain might move in and try to take the unclaimed area for its own.

Citing the 1803 treaty with France as his justification, Madison ordered a military occupation of West Florida on October 27, 1810, and he instructed the governor of the Orleans Territory to assume control of West Florida. Less than three months later, he asked Congress for the right to occupy East Florida as well. After a heated dispute the legislators agreed. Eventually the lands officially became annexed as territories and then became states.

Madison moved on West Florida on his own authority, but asked for congressional blessings on the East Florida action. In the interim, violent opposition had appeared in the legislature and elsewhere about Madison and his so-called bully tactics in Florida. The military presence seemed like overkill to some; more importantly, others questioned where Madison gained the power to use troops at all. Leaders such as Senator Outerbridge Horsey of Delaware voiced objections loudly. Much as Jefferson had been criticized after the Louisiana Purchase, Madison faced allegations of unconstitutional conduct.

The central constitutional argument against Madison had two parts. First, Madison moved troops in the vicinity of other non-U.S. soldiers (the Spanish, for example) in order to establish dominance and control. To some opponents of the president, this sounded uncomfortably close to a warlike situation. The U.S. Constitution provided that only Congress could declare war. The president had no authority to use soldiers for military means. Madison, some argued, had done just that.

Second, the West Florida action in effect annexed the area as a territory and established a governor to oversee the territory. These provisions for the maintenance and oversight of West Florida seemed more like making law, the legislators' power, than executing law, the president's power. If the president's decisions made legislation, then they violated the U.S. Constitution. Critics of Madison believed had his decisions had done just that.

Madison adopted a pragmatic approach to the situation. In essence— again, much like Jefferson with the Louisiana Purchase—he agreed with his critics. He had been uncomfortable acting in Florida for the very reasons they articulated. On the other hand, however, Madison did not want a bad situation, such as unrest in Florida, to become a worse one, such as facing war with Britain on North American soil if the British controlled Florida. After acting impulsively regarding part of the lands, Madison felt confident that he could do more through the proper channels. A contrite but resolute Madison asked Congress for permission to expand the occupation to include East Florida, and the legislators rewarded him with an affirmative answer.

The lands never again left U.S. control and eventually joined the Union. Frustration over the handling of the situation paled in the face of war with Great Britain, which soon eclipsed other issues of concern. The Florida scenario reflected the tension between the need for quick responses and the more methodical pace of constitutional government— it is, after all, faster to get one person to agree on policy than a roomful of people. On the other hand, the fact that legislators and other critics called Madison on his behavior reflected the checks and balances of the government at work. The interlude also underscored how very Jeffersonian Madison indeed was; though a supporter of limited government, Madison, too, could expand the authority of his office beyond the law when he believed the ends justified the means.

THE PRESIDENT'S POSITION: ANNEXATION OF FLORIDA

James Madison, Proclamation on West Florida
27 October 1810

Whereas the territory south of the Mississippi Territory and eastward of the river Mississippi, and extending to the river Perdido, of which possession was not delivered to the United States as pursuance of the treaty concluded at Paris on the 30th April 1803, has at all times, as is well known, been considered and claimed by them as being within the colony of Louisiana conveyed by the said treaty in the same extent that it had in the hands of Spain and that it had when France originally possessed it; and

Whereas the acquiescence of the United States in the temporary continuance of the said territory under the Spanish authority was not the result of any distrust of their title, as has been particularly evinced by the general tenor of their laws and by the distinction made in the application of those laws between that territory and foreign countries, but was occasioned by their conciliatory views and by a confidence in the justice of their cause and in the success of candid discussion and amicable negotiation with a just and friendly power; and

Whereas a satisfactory judgment, too long delayed, without the fault of the United States, has for some time been entirely suspended by events over which they had no control; and

Whereas a crisis as at length arrived subversive of the order of things under the Spanish authorities, whereby a failure of the United States to take the said territory into its possession may lead to events ultimately contravening the views of both parties, whilst in the meantime the tranquillity and security of our adjoining territories are endangered and new facilities given to violations of our revenue and commercial laws of those prohibiting the introduction of slaves;

Considering, moreover, that under these peculiar and imperative circumstances a forbearance on the part of the United States to occupy the territory in question, and thereby guide against the confusions and contingencies which threaten it, might be construed into a dereliction of their title or an insensibility to the importance of the stake; considering that in the hands of the United States it will not cease to be a subject of fair and friendly negotiation and adjustment; considering, finally, that the acts of Congress, though contemplating a present possession by a foreign authority, have contemplated also an eventual possession of the said territory by the United States, and are accordingly so framed as in that case to extend in their operation to the same:

Now be it known that I, James Madison, President of the United States of America, in pursuance of these weighty and urgent considerations, have deemed it right and requisite that possession should be taken of the said territory in the name and behalf of the United States. William C.C. Claiborne, governor of the Orleans Territory, of which the said Territory is to be taken as part, will accordingly proceed to execute the same and to exercise over the said Territory the authorities and functions legally appertaining to his office; and the good people inhabiting the same are invited and enjoined to pay due respect to him in that character, to be obedient to the laws, to maintain order, to cherish harmony, and in every manner to conduct themselves as peaceable citizens, under full assurance that they will be protected in the enjoyment of their liberty, property, and religion. . . .

J.F. Watts and Fred L. Israel, eds., *Presidential Documents: The Speeches, Proclamations, and Policies That Have Shaped the Nation from Washington to Clinton* (New York: Routledge, 2000), pp. 41–42.

SENATE OPPOSITION TO ANNEXATION

Mr. Horsey, Address to the Senate
December 28, 1810

Mr. Horsey addressed the Senate as follows:

Mr. President: The bill under consideration contains two important provisions. The first in effect incorporates with the Territory of Orleans the province of West Florida east of the Mississippi, as far as the river Perdido; the second extends to that part of the province thus incorporated the laws now in force within the said Territory.

These provisions naturally involve two questions: first, whether the United States have a good title to that part of the province described in the bill; and secondly, whether it would be expedient for the Government of the United States to take possession of it by force.

Before I proceed to consider these questions, I beg leave, Mr. President, to advert what may be considered a preliminary question. I refer to the authority of the President of the United States to issue his proclamation and the accompanying orders of the 27th of August last, directing the forcible occupation of that territory. I deem it material to consider this point, because, if the proclamation were unauthorized, then Congress are not committed by it, nor are they bound to give it their attention.

If the President had any authority to issue this proclamation, that authority must have been derived either under the Constitution of the United States or under some act or acts of Congress. The President has no power which does not proceed from one or the other of these sources. The Constitution has given to Congress the exclusive power of making laws and declaring war—to the President the power of executing the laws of the Union. The powers of the one are legislative, of the other executive. The question then would be, whether the President in issuing this proclamation has not transcended the limits of his powers.

Sir, what is the nature and import of this proclamation? In my humble conception both legislation and war. War—because it directs the occupation of this territory by a military force. The regular troops of the United States are ordered to march, and if they should not be found adequate to the object, the Governors of the Orleans and Mississippi Territories are directed to call out the militia of their respective territories, to co-operate with the regular forces. But we shall be told, sir, that the President, in issuing this proclamation, has taken the precaution to direct that in any case any particular place, however small, should remain in possession of a Spanish force, the commanding officer is not to proceed to employ force against it, but to make immediate report thereof to the Secretary of State. Suppose while your commanding officer is making this report, the Spanish force sallies out and makes an attack upon your army, or suppose a Spanish army . . . should march from East Florida with the view of repelling the invasion of this territory; what are Governor Claiborne and his army to do? Ground their arms and surrender themselves prisoners of war: or are they, sir, to drop their muskets and take to their heels? These are the only alternatives presented—they must either surrender, run, or fight. And who will doubt which of these alternatives the gallantry of an American army would impel them to choose? Sir, a conflict would be inevitable!

. . . But, sir, this proclamation is not only war, it is an act of legislation too. It annexes the territory in question to the Orleans Territory; it creates a governor; it enacts laws, and appropriates money. . . . This proclamation is substantially the bill under discussion, except that it goes much further. The first section of the bill only contains an annexation of the territory in question to the Orleans Territory—this the proclamation has already done. The second section only extends the laws of that territory to the particular territory in question—and this too the proclamation has already done. The only material difference in fact existing between the proclamation and the bill is, that the proclamation contains the further and important provision for raising the troops and the money necessary for carrying it into execution. And here, sir, I will take the liberty to remark that I do not consider this bill the only one intended on the subject. This is a mere entering wedge—when this is passed, Congress are committed to pass another, providing the necessary military and pecuniary means to carry this act into execution; and indeed I should not be surprised, if, before the close of the session, a bill were introduced to take possession of East as well as West Florida. . . .

See *Annals of Congress*, Library of Congress. <http://memory.loc.gov/cgi-bin/ampage>.

WAR OF 1812

John Adams and Thomas Jefferson both had postponed war with Great Britain, leaving it to James Madison in 1812. There were many reasons for the war, but the majority of them involved the issue of trade. Critics argued from a financial perspective as well, saying that the war waged for commerce ultimately would bankrupt the nation and alienate the chief market for U.S. goods.

Many justifications led to Madison's war message to Congress on June 1, 1812. British forces in Canada played upon native American resentment at U.S. encroachment and treatment by encouraging border raids against U.S. towns. Great Britain allied with Spain, so many U.S. citizens blamed the British for the continued presence of the Spanish in Florida. British ships also continued to harass U.S. vessels on the high seas. At times British sailors boarded U.S. ships and removed alleged "deserters," a number of whom were actually U.S. citizens, and impressed them into service. This treatment was not just relegated to the high seas, either; British ships patrolled near the U.S. coasts and interfered with entering and departing vessels. The British thus endangered U.S. citizens and hindered U.S. commerce. Madison believed the nation could not grow financially or politically at home or in the eyes of other countries until the British problem was solved.

War hawks in Congress such as John C. Calhoun and Henry Clay organized and gained control of Congress. Their desire for a fight whipped up increasing support of the idea within the legislature and the U.S. citizenry. By the time Madison requested a declaration of war against Great Britain, Congress was happy to comply.

Others proved less ecstatic about the possibility of war. Critics pointed out that, despite past hostilities with Great Britain, the United States still did more business with the British and their allies than any other people. Fighting your own consumer was not good business, they argued. Other opponents of fighting speculated about the possible cost of such a venture. Could the United States really afford war? Some said no.

The war began nonetheless. U.S. forces quickly abandoned a short and disastrous three-pronged offensive against Canada. A fleet of U.S. ships on Lake Erie then managed to defeat British forces and create the opportunity for a successful U.S. invasion of Canada. After early victories against British warships, U.S. vessels fell back into home ports where the British blockaded them. The most lasting image of the war remains the British armada sailing up Chesapeake Bay and sacking and burning Washington, D.C. The First Lady left the capital only a short time earlier, saving George Washington's portrait from the flames. The humiliation and destruction haunted Madison who, in the midst of war, had quietly won reelection. War hawks lost their positions to leaders who favored peace and sneered at "Mr. Madison's War."

Then, just as quickly, the tide of war changed and Madison became a hero. Peace came on Christmas Eve of 1814 with the Treaty of Ghent. Both sides accepted a return to peaceful trade and exchanged all wartime conquests to their original owners. The news came from New Orleans that U.S. forces (including a collection of pirates, Creoles, and blacks) led by Andrew Jackson defeated a large invasion force, though neither side knew that the war had been over for two weeks. The thrilling victory added fuel to celebratory spirits.

Critics proved mistaken in their predictions of terrible failure. The war had been costly in terms of lives, funds, and property, but the economy survived and trade resumed without problem. The unforeseen effect of the war was the final death of the Federalist Party. Leaders such as Daniel Webster had blocked the Madison administration's efforts in the war. Federalists had even met on December 15, 1814, in the Hartford Convention to protest the growing influence of the South and West and the shrinking power of the New England states. The attendees threatened nullification and even secession if their voices were not heard about the war and other policies. The peace that came less than ten days later made the Federalists and their message seem irrelevant. Never again would the party enjoy a fraction of the power of its past.

Madison emerged far less scathed than he could have, although by personality and principle he was not the ideal candidate for a wartime commander in chief. The U.S. citizenry seemed to appreciate peace all the more because the war had hit so close to home—home itself, for James and Dolley Madison. The president would not face international hostilities again in office.

THE PRESIDENT'S POSITION: IN FAVOR OF WAR WITH GREAT BRITAIN

War Message to Congress
Washington, June 1, 1812

To the Senate and House of Representatives of the United States

I communicate to Congress certain documents, being a continuation of those heretofore laid before them on the subject of our affairs with Great Britain.

Without going back beyond the renewal in 1803 of the war in which Great Britain is engaged, and omitting unrepaired wrongs of inferior magnitude, the conduct of her Government presents a series of acts hostile to the United States as an independent and neutral nation.

British cruisers have been in the continued practice of violating the American flag on the great highway of nations, and of seizing and carrying off persons sailing under it, not in the exercise of a belligerent right founded on the law of nations against an enemy, but of a municipal prerogative over British subjects. British jurisdiction is thus extended to neutral vessels in a situation where no laws can operate but the law of nations and the laws of the country to which the vessels belong, and a self-redress is assumed which, if British subjects were wrongfully detained and alone concerned, is that substitution of force for a resort to the responsible sovereign which falls within the definition of war. Could the seizure of British subjects in such cases be regarded as within the exercise of a belligerent right, the acknowledged laws of war, which forbid an article of captured property to be adjudged without a regular investigation before a competent tribunal, would imperiously demand the fairest trial where the sacred rights of persons were at issue. In place of such a trial these rights are subjected to the will of every petty commander.

The practice, hence, is so far from affecting British subjects alone that, under the pretext of searching for these, thousands of American citizens, under the safeguard of public law and of their national flag, have been torn from their country and from everything dear to them; have been dragged on board ships of war of a foreign nation and exposed, under the severities of their discipline, to be exiled to the most distant and deadly climes, to risk their lives in the battles of their oppressors, and to be the melancholy instruments of taking away those of their own brethren.

Against this crying enormity, which Great Britain would be so prompt to avenge if committed against herself, the United States have in vain exhausted remonstrances and expostulations, and that no proof might be wanting of their conciliatory dispositions, and no pretext left for a continuance of the practice, the British Government was formally assured of the readiness of the United States to enter into arrangements such as could not be rejected if the recovery of British subjects were the real and sole object. The communication passed without effect.

British cruisers have been in the practice also of violating the rights and the peace of our coasts. They hover over and harass our entering and departing commerce. To the most insulting pretensions they have added the most lawless proceedings in our very harbors, and have wantonly spilt American blood within the sanctuary of our territorial jurisdiction. The principles and rules enforced by that nation, when a neutral nation, against armed vessels of belligerents hovering near her coasts and disturbing her commerce are well known. When called on, nevertheless, by the United States to punish the greater offenses committed by her own vessels, her Government has bestowed on their commanders additional marks of honor and confidence. . . .

Such is the spectacle of injuries and indignities which have been heaped on our country, and such the crisis which its unexampled forbearance and conciliatory efforts have not been able to avert. It might at least have been expected that an enlightened nation, if less urged by moral obligations or invited by friendly dispositions on the part of the United States, would have found its true interest alone a sufficient motive to respect their rights and their tranquility on the high seas; that an enlarged policy would have favored that free and general circulation of commerce in which the British nation is at all times interested, and which in times of war is the best alleviation of its calamities to herself as well as to other belligerents; and more especially that the British cabinet would not, for the sake of a precarious and surreptitious intercourse with hostile markets, have persevered in a course of measures which necessarily put at hazard the invaluable market of a great and growing country, disposed to cultivate the mutual advantages of an active commerce. . . .

We behold, in fine, on the side of Great Britain, a state of war against the United States, and on the side of the United States a state of peace toward Great Britain.

Whether the United States shall continue passive under these progressive usurpations and these accumulating wrongs, or, opposing force to force in defense of their national rights, shall commit a just cause into the hands of the Almighty Disposer of Events, avoiding all connections which might entangle it in the contest or views of other powers, and preserving a constant readiness to concur in an honorable reestablishment of peace and friendship, is a solemn question which the Constitution wisely confides to the legislative department of the Government. In recommending it to their early deliberations I am happy in the assurance that the decision will be worthy the enlightened and patriotic councils of a virtuous, a free, and a powerful nation. . . .

See James Madison, *Writings*, ed. Jack N. Rakove (New York: Literary Classics, 1999), pp. 685–686, 690–692.

OPPOSITION TO THE WAR

"They Call It a War for Commerce!"
New York Evening Post, 26 January 1812

Look for yourselves, good people all—The administration tell me that the object for which they are going to war with Great Britain, is to secure our commercial rights; to put the trade of the country on a good footing; to enable our merchants to deal with Great Britain on full as favorable terms as they deal with France, or else not deal at all. Such is the declared object for which all further intercourse is to be suspended with Great Britain and her allies, while we proceed to make war upon her and them until we compel her to pay more respect to American commerce: and, as Mr. Stow truly observed in his late excellent speech, the anxiety of members of Congress to effect this object is always the greater in proportion to the distance any honorable member lives from the seaboard. To enable you, good people, to judge for yourselves, I have only to beg of you to turn your eyes to Mr. Gallatin's letter in a succeeding column, stating the amount of the exports of the United States for the last year; the particular country to which these exports were sent, and specifying the amount received from us by each. If you will just cast a glance at this document, you will find of the articles of our own growth or manufactures we in that time carried or sent abroad (in round numbers) no less than $45,294,000 worth. You will next find that out of this sum, all the rest of the world (Great Britain and her allies excepted) took about $7,719,366, and that Great Britain and her allies took the remainder, amounting to $38,575,627. Now, after this, let me ask you what you think of making war upon Great Britain and her allies, for the purpose of benefiting commerce?

See Declaration of the War of 1812. <http://www.hillsdale.edu/dept/History/ Documents/War/America/1812/1812-Newspapers-Declaration.htm>.

"An Address to the People of the Eastern States"
New York Evening Post, 21 April 1812

In a war with England we shall need numerous armies and ample treasuries for their support. The war-hounds that are howling for war through the continent are not to be the men who are to force entrenchments, and scale ramparts against the bayonet and the cannon's mouth; to perish in sickly camps, or in long marches through sultry heats or wastes of snow. These gowned warriors, who are so loudly seconded by a set of fiery spirits in the great towns, and by a set of office hunters in the country, expect that their influence with the great body of the people, the honest yeomanry of our country, is such that every farmer, every mechanic, every laborer, will send off his sons, nay, will even shoulder his firelock himself and march to the field of blood. While these brave men who are "designing or exhorting glorious war," lodged safe at Monticello or some other secure retreat, will direct and look on; and will receive such pay for their services as they shall see fit to ask, and such as will answer their purposes.

Citizens, if pecuniary redress is your object in going to war with England, the measure is perfect madness. You will lose millions when you will gain a cent. The expense will be enormous. It will ruin our country. Direct taxes must be resorted to. The people will have nothing to pay. We once had a revenue;—that has been destroyed in the destruction of our commerce. For several years past you have been deceived and abused by the false pretenses of a full treasury. That phantom of hope will soon vanish. You have lately seen fifteen millions of dollars wasted in the purchase of a province we did not want, and never shall possess. And will you spend thousands of millions in conquering a province which, were it made a present to us, would not be worth accepting? Our territories are already too large. The desire to annex Canada to the United States is as base an ambition as ever burned in the bosom of

Alexander. What benefit will it ever be to the great body of the people, after their wealth is exhausted, and their best blood is shed in its reduction?—"We wish to clear our continent of foreign powers." So did the Madman of Macedon wish to clear the world of his enemies, and such as would not bow to his sceptre. So does Bonaparte wish to clear Europe of all his enemies; yea, and Asia too. Canada, if annexed to the United States, will furnish offices to a set of hungry villains, grown quite too numerous for our present wide limits; and that is all the benefit we ever shall derive from it.

These remarks will have little weight with men whose interest leads them to advocate war. Thousands of lives, millions of money, the flames of cities, the tears of widows and orphans, with them are light expedients when they lead to wealth and power. But to the people who must fight, if fighting must be done,—who must pay if money be wanted—who must march when the trumpet sounds, and who must die when the "battle bleeds,"—to the people I appeal. To them the warning voice is lifted. From a war they are to expect nothing but expenses and sufferings; —expenses disproportionate to their means, and sufferings lasting as life.

In our extensive shores and numerous seaports, we know not where the enemy will strike; or more properly speaking, we know they will strike when a station is defenceless. Their fleets will hover on our coasts, and can trace our line from Maine to New Orleans in a few weeks. Gunboats cannot repel them, nor is there a fort on all our shores in which confidence can be placed. The ruin of our seaports and loss of all vessels will form an item in the list of expenses. Fortifications and garrisons numerous and strong must be added. As to the main points of attack or defence, I shall only say that an efficient force will be necessary. A handful of men cannot run up and take Canada, in a few weeks, for mere diversion. The conflict will be long and severe: resistance formidable, and the final result doubtful. A nation that can debar the conqueror of Europe from the sea, and resist his armies in Spain, will not surrender its provinces without a struggle. Those who advocate a British war must be perfectly aware that the whole revenue arising from all British America for the ensuing century would not repay the expenses of that war.

See Declaration of the War of 1812. <http://www.hillsdale.edu/dept/History/Documents/War/America/1812/1812-Newspapers-Declaration.htm>.

THE NATIONAL BANK

Critics of the War of 1812 feared that fighting for commerce was a self-defeating proposition. War, they claimed, could only alienate consumers of U.S. exports and destroy the domestic economy. The opponents of the president proved wrong on the first count; trade with Great Britain resumed—more freely than before—immediately after the war. The hostilities did weaken the U.S. economy, however. In the aftermath of battle, Madison and Congress looked for ways to support the injured finances of the United States and its citizens. The final conclusion included a complete reversal for the president. In this case Madison himself, at one time or another in 1815, personally provided both sides to the ongoing debate about the national bank.

One of the proposed solutions to economic problems was the rechartering of the U.S. National Bank. Few issues created such political schizophrenia in the early presidents as did the national bank question. George Washington could not decide whether to allow the institution or veto it. Eventually, he asked Alexander Hamilton to prepare one document supporting the bank and James Madison to write one justifying a veto of it. In the eleventh hour he opted to go with Hamilton's advice and support the bank, which became a centerpiece for Hamilton's economic program. Madison's veto explanation was never used.

Madison remained firmly anti–national bank for years. Many members of Congress came around to his opinion that the government had no constitutional authority to create and support such an institution. In 1811, the legislature refused to recharter the First Bank of the United States, and it ceased to exist. Four years later, many leaders no longer concerned themselves about questions of constitutionality. They simply wondered if a national bank could assist in rebuilding the wartime economy. War seemed to justify whatever methods officials used, as long as those methods worked. Congress passed a bill to replace the dissolved bank and sent it to Madison.

On January 30, 1815, Madison vetoed the bill meant to create the Second Bank of the United States. For the president, nothing had changed since George Washington had considered the bank years earlier. The U.S. Constitution had not been altered to enumerate the power for Congress to create such an institution. Moreover, Madison did not believe the bank would do what its proponents claimed, namely, revive public credit, provide a national medium of circulation, and assist the Treasury. Instead, Madison saw the possibility for an opportunistic monopoly to follow its own interest without accountability. Too much remained in flux during times of war, he suggested. The bank was not only unconstitutional, but also financially risky. He wanted no part of it.

A year more of war, however, was enough to make even the staunch Madison change his mind. The economy continued to suffer and no policy was in place to remedy its ills. Quickly running out of ideas to revitalize U.S. finances, Madison finally allowed himself to consider what Congress had proposed months earlier. In the president's annual message of December 5, 1815, he admitted that if the state banks could not restore a standard national currency, "the probable operation of a national bank will merit consideration." Though the words were unimpressive, and his enthusiasm was less than glowing, Madison's statement was very significant, since it marked an abandonment of a policy he had embraced for his entire career. Thomas Jefferson, a fellow opponent of the national bank during the Washington administration, even stepped forward and endorsed Madison's new position. Congressmen followed suit and the debate turned from questions of constitutionality to questions of efficacy. "Should it exist?" was replaced with "will it work?" Once again, means became less important than ends.

Congress eventually took the president up on his new willingness to consider the bank and offered Madison another recharter bill; this time the president signed it. The Second Bank of the United States opened on January 1, 1817. In most ways it was similar to the original bank Hamilton had created. It grew to include twenty-five branches throughout the nation. The economy rebounded and allowed the next president to enjoy an era of great prosperity. Little debate remained about the bank. Its existence stood testament to the fact that, in times of extreme duress or excitement, Madison followed Jefferson's lead and opted for short-term solutions with long-term costs. With each unconstitutional act, Madison threatened the delicate balance of federalism and the very compact that he had designed decades earlier.

THE PRESIDENT'S POSITION: FOR THE SECOND NATIONAL BANK

James Madison, Seventh Annual Message to Congress
Washington, December 5, 1815

. . . Although the embarrassments arising from the want of an uniform national currency have not been diminished since the adjournment of Congress, great satisfaction has been derived in contemplating the revival of the public credit and the efficiency of the public resources. The receipts into the Treasury from the various branches of revenue during the nine months ending on the 30th of September last have been estimated at $12,500,000; the issues of Treasury notes of every denomination during the same period amounted to the sum of $14,000,000, and there is also obtained upon loan during the same period a sum of $9,000,000, of which the sum of $6,000,000 was subscribed in cash and the sum of $3,000,000 in Treasury notes. With these means, added to the Treasury on the 1st day of January, there has been paid between the 1st of January and the 1st of October on account of the appropriations of the preceding and of the present year (exclusively of the amount of the Treasury notes subscribed to the loan and of the amount redeemed in the payment of duties and taxes) the aggregate sum of $33,500,000, leaving a balance then in the Treasury estimated at the sum of $3,000,000. Independent, however, of the arrearages due for military services and supplies, it is presumed that a further sum of $5,000,000, including the interest on the public debt payable on the 1st of January next, will be demanded at the Treasury to complete the expenditures of the present year, and for which the existing ways and means will sufficiently provide.

The national debt, as it was ascertained on the 1st of October, last, amounted in the whole to the sum of $120,000,000, consisting of the unredeemed balance of the debt contracted before the late war ($39,000,000), the amount of the funded debt contracted in consequence of the war ($64,000,000), and the amount of the unfounded and floating debt, including the various issues of Treasury notes, $17,000,000, which is in a gradual course of payment. There will probably be some addition to the public debt upon the liquidation of various claims which are depending, and a conciliatory disposition on the part of Congress may lead honorably and advantageously to an equitable arrangement of the militia expenses incurred by the several States without the previous sanction or authority of the Government of the United States; but when it is considered that the new as well as the old portion of the debt has been contracted in the assertion of the national rights and independence, and when it is recollected that the public expenditures, not being exclusively bestowed upon subjects of a transient nature, will long be visible in the number and equipments of the American Navy, in the military works for the defense of our harbors and our frontiers, and in the supplies of our arsenals and magazines the amount will bear a gratifying comparison with the objects which have been attained, as well as with the resources of the country.

The arrangements of the finances with a view to the receipts and expenditures of a permanent peace establishment will necessarily enter into the deliberations of Congress during the present session. It is true that the improved condition of the public revenue will not only afford the means of maintaining the faith of the Government with its creditors inviolate, and of prosecuting successfully the measures of the most liberal policy, but will also justify an immediate alleviation of the burdens imposed by the necessities of the war. It is, however, essential to every modification of the finances that the benefits of an uniform national currency should be restored to the community. The absence of the precious metals will, it is believed, be a temporary evil, but until they can again be rendered the general medium of exchange it devolves on the wisdom of Congress to provide a substitute which shall equally engage the confidence and accommodate the wants of the citizens throughout the Union. If the operation of the State banks can not produce this result, the probable operation of a national bank will merit consideration; and if neither of these expedients be deemed effectual it may become necessary to ascertain the terms upon which the notes of the Government (no longer required as an instrument of credit) shall be issued upon motives of general policy as a common medium of circulation. . . .

See James Madison, *Writings*, ed. Jack N. Rakove (New York: Literary Classics, 1999), pp. 712–714.

THE PRESIDENT'S VETO OF THE SECOND BANK

James Madison, Veto of the Second Bank of the United States
January 30, 1815

. . . Having bestowed on the bill entitled "An act to incorporate the subscribers to the Bank of the United States of America" that full consideration which is due to the great importance of the subject, and dictated by the respect which I feel for the two Houses of Congress, I am constrained by a deep and solemn conviction that the bill ought not to become a law to return it to the Senate, in which it originated, with my objections to the same.

Waiving the question of the constitutional authority of the Legislature to establish an incorporated bank as being precluded in my judgment by repeated recognitions under varied circumstances of the validity of such an institution in acts of the legislature, executive, and judicial branches of the Government, accompanied by indications, in different modes, of a concurrence of the general will of the nation, the proposed bank does not appear to be calculated to answer the purposes of reviving the public credit, of providing a national medium of circulation, and of aiding the Treasury by facilitating the indispensable anticipations of the revenue and by affording to the public more durable loans. . . .

Public credit might indeed be expected to derive advantage from the establishment of a national bank, without regard to the formation of its capital, if the full aid and cooperation of the institution were secured to the Government during the war and during the period of its fiscal embarrassments. But the bank proposed will be free from all legal obligation to cooperate with the public measures, and whatever might be the patriotic disposition of its directors to contribute to the removal of those embarrassments, and to invigorate the prosecution of the war, fidelity to the pecuniary and general interest of the institution according to their estimate of it might oblige them to decline a connection of their operations with those of the National Treasury during the continuance of the war and the difficulties incident to it. Temporary sacrifices of interest, though overbalanced by the future and permanent profits of the charter, not being requirable of right in behalf of the public, might not be gratuitously made, and the bank would reap the full benefit of the grant, whilst the public would lose the equivalent expected from it; for it must be kept in view that the sole inducement to such a grant on the part of the public would be the prospect of substantial aids to its pecuniary means at the present crisis and during the sequel of the war. It is evident that the stock of the bank will on the return of peace, if not sooner, rise in the market to a value which, if the bank were established in a period of peace, would authorize and obtain for the public a bonus to a very large amount. In lieu of such a bonus the Government is fairly entitled to and ought not to relinquish or risk the needful services of the bank under the pressing circumstances of war. . . .

On the whole, when it is considered that the proposed establishment will enjoy a monopoly of the profits of a national bank for a period of twenty years; that the monopolized profits will be continually growing with the progress of the national population and wealth; that the nation will during this same period be dependent on the notes of the bank for that species of circulating medium whenever the precious metals may be wanted, and at all times for so much thereof as may be an eligible substitute for a specie medium, and that the extensive employment of the notes in the collection of the augmented taxes will, moreover, enable the bank greatly to extend its profitable issues of them without the expense of specie capital to support their circulation, it is as reasonable as it is requisite that the Government, in return for these extraordinary concessions to the bank, should have a greater security for attaining the public objects of the institution than is presented in the bill, and particularly for every practicable accommodation, both in the temporary advances necessary to anticipate the taxes and in those more durable loans which are equally necessary to diminish the resort to taxes.

In discharging this painful duty of stating objections to a measure which has undergone the deliberations and received the sanction of the two Houses of the National Legislature, I console with the reflection that if they have not the weight which I attach to them they can be constitutionally overruled, and with a confidence that in a contrary event the wisdom of Congress will hasten to substitute a more commensurate and certain provision for the public exigencies.

See J.F. Watts and Fred L. Israel, eds., *Presidential Documents: The Speeches, Proclamations, and Policies That Have Shaped the Nation from Washington to Clinton* (New York: Routledge, 2000), pp. 48–50.

THE NATIONAL GOVERNMENT'S ROLE IN INTERNAL IMPROVEMENTS

When Congress penned the one thousand eight hundred and sixteen charter of the Second Bank of the United States, it left $1.5 million bonus dollars to the legislature for unspecified use. Speaker of the House Henry Clay followed up on this by writing a bill appropriating the windfall for internal improvements such as roads and canals. Such improvements, he and his supporters argued, would stimulate commerce and better defense thanks to added efficiency and greater mobility at less expense. The so-called Bonus Bill passed the legislature and moved to the desk of President Madison, already packing his bags to return home and cede the White House to his successor, James Monroe.

The proponents of the bill noted that only the national legislature had access to the kind of funds that could finance long-term, large-scale improvements to make one nation of many separate states. Supporters distinguished between local projects that would benefit only small groups of citizens and great endeavors that would benefit the extended community. Only the latter, roads and canals that could speed commerce and military interests, would be recipients of the bonus funds, they argued. They imagined open waterways and efficient roads speeding information, goods, and even troops to every end of the country. The Bonus Bill backers relied heavily on justification rather than authorization. In other words, they hoped the good of the potential results overshadowed the fact that the legislature might not be authorized to make such plans in the first place.

In the final days of his tenure, Madison could not let pass the opportunity to revive strict construction of the U.S. Constitution once again. The Bonus Bill, he argued, had no basis in the Constitution; for Congress to allot federal funds for regional projects, a constitutional amendment would be needed to give that power to the legislature. The "general welfare" clause the bill seemed to invoke was not sufficient authorization. The clause was not intended, he argued, to be a catchall phrase embracing every purpose not enumerated in the Constitution. Such loose interpretation would make the judiciary's role of watching the boundary between state and federal legislation impossible, Madison believed. On his very last day in office Madison vetoed the bill. Speaker of the House Henry Clay called for votes to overturn the veto, but the bill ultimately failed to gain a sufficient degree of support to pass.

So Madison ended his second term much as he began his first term, focusing on issues of constitutionality and national/state governmental relations. The lesson he wanted to provide to Congress about constitutional powers did not stick; James Monroe would face the same question of internal improvements during his own presidency. The full circle

Madison made underscored his core consistency, however. Though sometimes inclined to trade means for ends, Madison at heart was a clockmaker, and the gears and pulleys of the U.S. Constitution were his ultimate achievement. His fears for the balance between national power and state sovereignty proved in the long run to be justified. During his time as the chief executive, however, he honestly tried—tried and failed, many times, with himself to blame in some cases—to maintain and defend the system he had created.

Madison's veto on his last day also set a new cycle in motion for future presidents. Thomas Jefferson, for example, was loath to invoke the veto power. Perhaps Madison would have chosen a different means of opposing the idea had the bill been debated earlier in his administration. As a parting shot, however, Madison could not resist the veto and the explanation he attached to it. Others after him, most notably Andrew Jackson, would use the veto opportunity often.

THE PRESIDENT'S POSITION: VETO OF INTERNAL IMPROVEMENTS BILL

James Madison, Veto Message to Congress
March 3, 1817

To the House of Representatives of the United States:

Having considered the bill this day presented to me entitled "An act to set apart and pledge certain funds for internal improvements," and which sets apart and pledges funds "for constructing roads and canals, and improving the navigation of water courses, in order to facilitate, promote, and give security to internal commerce among the several States, and to render more easy and less expensive the means and provisions for the common defense," I am constrained by the insuperable difficulty I feel in reconciling the bill with the Constitution of the United States to return it with that objection to the House of Representatives, in which it originated.

The legislative powers vested in Congress are specified and enumerated in the eighth section of the first article of the Constitution, and it does not appear that the power proposed to be exercised by the bill is among the enumerated powers, or that it falls by any just interpretation within the power to make laws necessary and proper for carrying into execution those or other powers vested by the Constitution in the Government of the United States.

"The power to regulate commerce among the several States" can not include a power to construct roads and canals, and to improve the navigation of water courses in order to facilitate, promote, and secure such a commerce without a latitude of construction departing from the ordinary import of the terms strengthened by the known inconveniences which doubtless led to the grant of this remedial power to Congress.

To refer the power in question to the clause "to provide for the common defense and general welfare" would be contrary to the established and consistent rules of interpretation, as rendering the special and careful enumeration of powers which follow the clause nugatory and improper. Such a view of the Constitution would have the effect of giving to Congress a general power of legislation instead of the defined and limited one hitherto understood to belong to them, the terms "common defense and general welfare" embracing every object and act within the purview of a legislative trust. It would have the effect of subjecting both the Constitution and laws of the several States in all cases not specifically exempted to be superseded by laws of Congress, it being expressly declared "that the Constitution of the United States and laws made in pursuance thereof shall be the supreme law of the land, and the judges of every State shall be bound thereby, anything in the constitution or laws of any State to the contrary notwithstanding." Such a view of the Constitution, finally, would have the effect of excluding the judicial authority of the United States from its participation in guarding the boundary between the legislative powers of the General and the State Governments, inasmuch as questions relating to the general welfare, being questions of policy and expediency, are unsusceptible of judicial cognizance and decision.

A restriction of the power "to provide for the common defense and general welfare" to cases which are to be provided for by the expenditure of money would still leave within the legislative power of Congress all the great and most important measures of Government, money being the ordinary and necessary means of carrying them into execution.

If a general power to construct roads and canals, and to improve the navigation of water courses, with the train of powers incident thereto, be not possessed by Congress, the assent of the States in the mode provided in the bill cannot confer the power. The only cases in which the consent and cession of particular States can extend the power of Congress are those specified and provided for in the Constitution.

I am not unaware of the great importance of roads and canals and the improved navigation of water courses, and that a power in the National Legislature to provide for them might be exercised with signal advantage to the general prosperity. But seeing that such a power is not expressly given by the Constitution, and believing that it can not be deduced from any part of it without an inadmissible latitude of construction and a reliance on insufficient precedents; believing also that the permanent success of the Constitution depends on a definite partition of powers between the General and the State Governments, and that no adequate landmarks would be left by the constructive extension of the powers of Congress as proposed in the bill, I have no option but to withhold my signature from it, and to cherishing the hope that its beneficial objects may be attained by a resort for the necessary powers to the same wisdom and virtue in the nation which established the Constitution in its actual form and providently marked out in the instrument itself a safe and practicable mode of improving it as experience might suggest.

See James Madison, *Writings*, ed. Jack N. Rakove (New York: Literary Classics, 1999), pp. 718–720.

IN SUPPORT OF THE BILL

Mr. Morrow, Address to the Senate
February 6, 1816

Mr. Morrow, from the committee appointed on so much of the Message of the President of the United States, as relates to roads and canals, made a report in part, which was read, together with a bill, making appropriation for the construction of roads and canals; and the bill was read, and passed to the second reading.;

The report and bill are as follows:

That a view of the extent of territory, the number and magnitude of navigable lakes, rivers, and bays; the variety of climate, and consequent diversity of productions embraced by the United States, cannot fail to impose the conviction, that a capacity exists in this country to maintain an extensive internal commerce. The variety of productions peculiar to the several parts, invites to the prosecution of a commerce of the most interesting kind. A commerce internal, subject solely to the regulations of the country, not dependent on, or materially affected by the vicissitudes of foreign competition or collisions; the profits on which will rest in the country, and make an addition to the wealth of the nation. Such a commerce will, in its natural tendency, create interests and feelings, consonant with the great interests of the community. Any practicable scheme, therefore, for improvement of roads and inland navigation, having for its object the encouragement and extension of a commerce so beneficial, has strong claims to the attention and aid of Government, constituted to promote the general welfare.

Such improvements, executed on an extensive scale, would unquestionably contribute to the general interest and increase of wealth in the nation, for, whatever tends to accelerate the progress of industry, in its various and particular branches, or to remove the obstacles to its full exertion, must, in the result, produce that effect. The contemplated improvement in roads and canals, by extending the communication for commercial and personal intercourse, to the interior and distant parts of the Union, would bestow common benefits, and give an enlarged faculty to the great branches of national industry, whether agricultural, commercial, or manufacturing.

The agricultural products, which at present, from inconvenient distance, their weight, or bulk, are unportable, could then be carried to a distant market; the reduction on the charge for transportation would become an addition to the price; and a ready market, and increased price, enhance the value of the lands from which the products were drawn.

The general commerce of the country would thereby receive a proportional advantage from the increase of the quantity of articles for exportation, the facility and extension to the vending of imported commodities, as also from a more general consumption arising from an increased ability in the community to purchase such commodities. To manufacturers a reduction on the charge for transportation of the raw material, and wrought commodity, would be highly beneficial. The beneficial effects on individual interests, and the general wealth in society, arising from a system of cheap conveyance, by artificial roads and canals, does not rest on speculative opinion or abstract reasonings for confirmation; all doubts as to the advantages, have been removed by the test of experience in every country, where such improvements have been executed on a liberal scale. . . .

It is believed that improvements so important to the political and general interest of society, stand strongly recommended to the attention of the National Legislature. The General Government alone possess the means and resources to give direction to works calculated for general advantage, and to insure their complete execution.

The particular objects of this kind, to which public aid should be given, the means to be employed, and the mode of applying the public moneys remain to be considered.

The objects are, such artificial roads and canals as are practicable of execution, and which promise a general or extensive advantage to the community; others, of minor importance, that are local in their nature, and will produce only local benefits, will, more properly, be left for execution to the means and enterprise of individuals, or to the exertions of particular States. It is, indeed, a political maxim, well attested by experience, that wherever private interests are competent to the provision and application of their own instruments and means, such provisions and means should be left to themselves.

The great works which are calculated for national advantage, either in a military or commercial view, their execution must depend (at least for aid) on the General Government. Wherever great obstacles are to be overcome, great power and means must be employed. To such works the means of associated individuals are incompetent, and the particular States may not have a sufficient interest in the execution of works of the most essential advantage to other parts of the community. In other cases, where interest might be sufficiently operative, the means or the power may not be possessed, their territorial jurisdiction being limited short of the whole extent of the work. . . .

See *Annals of Congress*, Library of Congress. <http://memory.loc.gov/cgi-bin/ampage>.

RECOMMENDED READINGS

Heidler, David S., and Jeanne T. Heidler, ed. *Encyclopedia of the War of 1812*. Santa Barbara, Calif.: ABC-CLIO, 1997.

Hickey, Donald R. *The War of 1812: A Forgotten Conflict*. Urbana: University of Illinois Press, 1989.

Jefferson, Thomas, and James Madison. *The Republic of Letters: The Correspondence between Thomas Jefferson and James Madison, 1776–1826*. New York: Norton, 1995.

Ketcham, Ralph. *James Madison: A Biography*. New York: Macmillan, 1971.

———. *Presidents Above Party: The First American Presidency, 1789–1829*. Chapel Hill: University of North Carolina Press, 1984.

Madison, James. *The Papers of James Madison: Presidential Series*. Edited by Robert A. Rutland. 4 vols. Charlottesville: University Press of Virginia, 1984.

McCoy, Drew. *The Last of the Fathers: James Madison and the Republican Legacy*. Cambridge: Cambridge University Press, 1989.

Rosen, Gary. *American Compact: James Madison and the Problem of Founding*. Lawrence: University Press of Kansas, 1999.

Rutland, Robert Allen. *James Madison and the Search for Nationhood*. Washington, D.C.: Library of Congress, 1981.

———. *James Madison: The Founding Father*. New York: Macmillan, 1987.

———. *The Presidency of James Madison*. Lawrence: University Press of Kansas, 1990.

Schultz, Harold. *James Madison*. New York: Twayne, 1970.

Wait, Eugene M. *America and the War of 1812*. Commack, N.Y.: Kroshka Books, 1999.

5

JAMES MONROE

(1817–1825)

INTRODUCTION

As the final Virginia Dynasty president, James Monroe assured his predecessors their place in history. His administration marked a moment of tremendous national unity and pride. From the recent experience of war and depression, the nation rebounded with a growing commercial economy, rapid westward expansion, and increasing confidence on the world stage. Monroe's two terms were so popular, in fact, that the years became known as "The Era of Good Feelings." He won his first term handily and his second without opposition at all. If the Virginia Dynasty had to end, it ended on a high note.

Monroe began his presidency with a nearly sixteen-week tour of the United States, including the former Federalist stronghold of New England. During this journey he also became the first president to visit the West; his presence on the other side of the mountains seemed to reassure and encourage settlers that they, too, were members of the Union. He cultivated the nationalism that had grown with the Louisiana Purchase and fanned the flames of manifest destiny.

For all the newness he symbolized—new western lands, new commercialism, new national power—the understated Monroe also invoked the past. As the last president to have served in the War of Independence, Monroe wore simple knee-buckled breeches and three-pointed, Revolution-era hats. He traveled simply and recalled the Washingtonian image of the executive as simply another citizen among citizens. Some critics argued that he lacked the mental capacity of a Jefferson or a Madison, which was hardly a fair comparison considering their luminary intellects. Many called him plain; he lacked the charisma of Jefferson, and his First Lady could not compensate for him as Dolley Madison did for her husband James. Nevertheless, Monroe held his own as he spoke extemporaneously to the crowds he met along his journey's path. He also restored a formality to the White House reminiscent of the first presidential administration.

President Monroe was all too aware of his membership in the Virginia Dynasty. It concerned him that all former presidents with the exception of John Adams had called the same state home; what began as a coincidence, he feared, might become a precedent. Much of Monroe's agenda centered around issues of inclusion, and he did not want the U.S. citizenry to assume that only Virginians were able to lead the country. As his secretary of state and implied successor, then, Monroe chose a New Englander: John Quincy Adams. Adams not only had defected from the withering Federalist Party to join the Republicans, but also was the son of the second president of the United States. Adams, like Monroe, had particular strong experience in foreign affairs. After years of impressive assignments overseas, he had chaired the U.S. peace commission responsible for the Treaty of Ghent that ended the War of 1812. Since then, he had served as minister to Great Britain. Adams would prove invaluable in the administration and its most important achievement, the Monroe Doctrine.

Monroe balanced the northern appointment with a southern one (William H. Crawford as secretary of the treasury). He completed his cabinet with John C. Calhoun as secretary of war, Benjamin Crowninshield as secretary of the navy, and William Wirt as attorney general. New York governor Daniel D. Tomkins served as Monroe's vice president for both terms, which added to the geographic breadth of the executive branch. Monroe relied on his cabinet to inform and advise him. When opinions differed between officials, he listened to the different sides of the debate much as Washington had done. While Monroe maintained good relationships with his advisors, he could not say the same for congressmen. Together, the members of the Monroe administration struggled to work with a divided, factious legislature.

Although Congress, like the rest of the nation, represented something of a Democratic-Republican consensus, this did not make for harmony. In fact, the pulls of party infrastructure, discipline, and leadership meant less now that almost everyone was on the same side. As Justice Joseph Story commented, "The Government has been carried on so long by mere party spirit, that I expect our rulers will be somewhat perplexed to carry it on by any other principle."[1] Leaders filled the void left by party affiliation with new divisions: traditional agricultural interests versus new commercial interests, and northern versus southern, often antislavery versus proslavery, loyalties.

Many of the challenges facing President Monroe were not of his making. He inherited several issues left unresolved by earlier administrations. At times, the hardworking Monroe made strides in settling the issues; at other times he postponed them further for his successors to handle. The first of these involved the question of the military chain of command. General Andrew Jackson, made famous by his success at the Battle of New Orleans during (technically, after) the War of 1812, protested the fact that the secretary of war under President Madison issued a direct order to a major under Jackson's command. He was so angry that standard procedure—the order going first to the general, and then from the general to the major—had been abandoned, that he instructed his troops not to obey orders that did not come through traditional channels. In other words, he told his soldiers to disobey direct orders from the commander in chief and his highest ranking staff.

Monroe handled the problem well, striking a compromise with Jackson that spared the general's pride but also removed his block on direct orders. The situation grew more complicated, though, when Jackson interpreted directions to engage and subdue the Seminoles in Florida as authorization to capture Spanish forts and declare U.S. control over Pensacola. Monroe blamed Jackson for acting without authorization. Jackson claimed his orders gave him the latitude to make command decisions. Again, Monroe handled the situation with skill. He managed not only to keep the United States out of war due to Jackson's reckless actions, but also to convince Spain to sell its Florida lands and set defined boundaries to remaining territories. Jackson went free by riding public opinion, but Monroe emerged quite well himself. The Pensacola problem promised international danger, but Monroe's final resolution was a popular and political success.

The next problem Monroe inherited stemmed from the issue of slavery. Slaveholding and non-slaveholding interests were perfectly balanced in the Senate when Missouri, a slaveholding territory, applied for statehood in 1819 and threatened to tip numbers in favor of the southern contingency in the Senate. As legislators debated what to do, the northern part of Massachusetts, a non-slaveholding area, applied for statehood as Maine. Though the two would cancel out each other's Senate votes and therefore preserve fragile balance between the two competing factions, this development promised only to table the issue for a finite period. The solution was temporary at best.

Monroe worried about the regionalism he saw tearing apart the legislature. As a southerner, he believed that northerners did not understand the economic and political realities of southern life. He urged southerners to take the initiative and approve Maine's application. By doing so, they would take the high ground against their own interests and divorce the two applications from each other. Surely northern interests would accept Missouri from a sense of fair play, he believed.

Monroe's efforts did not succeed. Instead, Henry Clay's compromise prevailed. Missouri and Maine gained admittance to the Union together, and slavery was forbidden in the Louisiana Territory lands north of Missouri's topmost border. Monroe continued to worry about the constitutionality of changing the process for entering states and imposing new restrictions on territories, but the compromise insured peace for the short term.

Monroe capitalized on his strengths and those of his secretary of state by repositioning the United States on the world stage via the Monroe Doctrine. In light of many Latin American revolutions against colonial powers, added to hostilities in Europe that threatened to play out in the Americas, Monroe believed it was time to end ambivalence on the question of the role of the United States in foreign affairs. In an address penned by John Quincy Adams, Monroe promised neutrality in European issues but announced that European powers could no longer colonize in the Western Hemisphere. In effect, he declared the Americas a "hands off zone" that would be protected by the United States.

Some felt that limiting the attention of the United States to Latin America abandoned the nation's role as a worldwide champion of liberty. Whig leader Daniel Webster, for example, called for active U.S. support of the Greek revolution and its resulting independent nation. Others, however, feared that such action would be overextending the young nation and its capabilities. Despite critique of the policy, the doctrine stood. Monroe did voice support for the Greeks but chose not to act on it. The Monroe Doctrine set a precedent for a century of U.S. policy and afforded the nation years without significant international entanglements.

Like Madison, Monroe faced the issue of how to fund internal improvements. Congress wanted to allocate national funds for regional works that, although located in only some states, would nonetheless benefit the entire country. Monroe agreed with the legislators in principle. He saw that key roads, for example, would produce benefits that would touch every part of the nation. But Monroe, like his two most recent predecessors, tried to construct the U.S. Constitution strictly. He feared that using the vague phrase "general welfare" to justify internal improvements would be careless and costly. He countered with his own suggestion: why not add an amendment to the Constitution to enable internal improvements? That way, the projects would go forward and the "general welfare" clause would not be stretched out of shape.

Monroe's suggestion seemed too slow and complicated for the eager legislators, however. They had little time for due procedure as they watched the West expand and commerce move with it. Roads and canals were needed to help the nation keep up with its unprecedented growth.

Eventually, Congress wore down the president. He signed two internal improvement bills into law before the end of his second term. Monroe slid down the slippery slope Madison had predicted, and the "general welfare" stretched beyond the Republicans' wildest imaginations.

One of the last challenges of Monroe's presidency was the question of the Georgia Compact of 1802. This agreement promised that the U.S. government would extinguish the property rights of the American Indians living within the borders of Georgia. Over twenty years later, however, many native Americans remained on their lands and refused to sell. Monroe did not approve of coerced removal. He did, however, believe that the Amerindians would be safer and happier in the U.S. West or outside of the United States altogether. He feared for their rights if they remained in Georgia; he doubted they could be adequately protected. He urged officials to persuade the native American nations to relocate in peace. Georgia would get its land and the Amerindians would be out of danger.

Some peoples, such as the members of the Cherokee Nation, did not intend to give up their claims to lands they and their ancestors had inhabited for thousands of years. They pointed out that they had made many changes in language, business, and culture in order to get along with their new neighbors. Some had even adopted Christianity. They believed their future was in Georgia or nowhere at all. With the continued protection of the United States, they could continue to flourish; without it, they would perish. Native American leaders such as Elias Boudinot played on racial assumptions to plead with U.S. citizens to respect the rights of Amerindians.

The president avoided forced removal during his administration, but the issue was far from settled. The unresolved question of the Georgia Compact of 1802 left the door open for coercion and bloodshed in the near future. The "Indian Civilization Campaign" era created by Jefferson was coming to a tragic end.

Monroe may not have solved some long-standing problems, but he did not create many, either. The presidency reflected the man: understated, subtle, and careful. Monroe avoided war and salvaged public opinion when officers exceeded their authority. He reimagined U.S. foreign policy when the world became more complicated. He erred on the side of compromise and postponed quandaries that seemed to have no clear solution.

As an administrator, the president chose able advisors and listened to them. As a leader, he brought his office full circle to play to a Washingtonian tune. His dress was plain and antiquated. His demeanor was formal and thoughtful. He urged his officials to debate and he considered their conflicting opinions. He traveled in simple style as a citizen among fellow citizens. His actions, or perhaps at times inactions, fostered a national unity and hopefulness bolstered by a great expansion, growing economy, and stronger sense of power on the international stage.

Also, like Washington, Monroe had a flair for the symbolic. The end of the Virginia Dynasty was not his failure; in fact, it was his design. Worried that too many Virginia presidents would start an exclusive and inappropriate precedent, Monroe groomed his New Englander secretary of state, John Quincy Adams, to succeed him and he did. Monroe enjoyed closer relations with Adams than Washington experienced with his father, John Adams. The succession of a new Adams brought the Virginia Dynasty to a close even as it maintained the dynasty's final legacy, the Era of Good Feelings.

NOTE

1. Joseph Story. Recounted to Ezekiel Bacon. March 12, 1818. See William W. Story, ed., *Life and Letters of Joseph Story*, vol. 1 (Boston: Charles E. Little and James Brown, 1851), p. 311.

PENSACOLA SEIZURE

One of the first challenges to face President James Monroe dealt with the former hero of the Battle of New Orleans, General Andrew Jackson. Jackson headed the southern division of the army and shouldered the burden of securing and maintaining peace in the region for the United States. At the end of Madison's administration, Jackson challenged the secretary of war regarding the proper chain of command in the army. Monroe inherited the problem of addressing Jackson and his protest. Monroe's uneasy first exchange with Jackson proved prophetic, as Jackson further earned his reputation as a loose cannon by acting without what Monroe considered to be adequate authorization when he seized Pensacola and nearly ignited an international incident.

Monroe's presidential relationship with Jackson began with correspondence regarding Jackson's nullification of direct orders from Washington. The general wrote to the new president and outlined his view of the problems facing the military; chief among these was a loss of respect for the chain of command, and thus an invitation to insubordination and chaos. He cited, for example, the fact that the secretary of war recently had given special commands directly to a major in the Corps of Topographical Engineers, despite the fact the major served under Jackson. Jackson noted that proper subordination rules required that the order come through Jackson, not from the secretary of war straight to a major. After the incident Jackson took the matter into his own hands. He went so far as to forbid obedience to any orders from the War Department that did not come through traditional channels.

Monroe responded to Jackson by saying that, although the general was quite correct about the general efficiency of the chain of command, some situations required urgent and immediate action. The secretary of war spoke with the authority of the president, Monroe explained, and since the secretary represented the commander in chief, his orders required obedience. Monroe strived for a conciliatory tone toward Jackson, however, and promised that commanding officers would receive copies of orders that bypassed normal channels if and when they were issued. Jackson was mollified.

It seemed Monroe had navigated a delicate situation successfully and ended his problems with Jackson. This was not the case. He sent the general into Georgia to take control of military actions against Seminoles there with admonitions not to enter Florida unless in pursuit of Seminoles and, if he did, to respect the remaining Spanish. Instead, Jackson entered Florida, seized the Spanish fort at St. Marks, and executed two men as British spies allegedly involved with inciting the Seminoles to war. He continued on to force the surrender of Fort Carlos de Barrancas and claim American authority over all of Pensacola. By the time Monroe learned of what had happened, officials from Spain, Great Britain, and elsewhere were demanding explanations.

Monroe wrote to Jackson in the effort to understand why the general had pursued an unauthorized course of action that looked to many like a declaration of war against Spain and possibly others. Jackson responded by refusing to take personal responsibility for events; he believed he had acted while fulfilling his broad orders against the Seminoles, and therefore was justified in the command decisions he had made. Many letters followed, as Monroe renounced Jackson's actions and the general defended them. The two talked past each other.

In the end, Monroe avoided international hostilities by blaming Jackson for events and distancing the presidency from the Pensacola fiasco. On the domestic front, Jackson's actions remained quite popular—so much so, in fact, that he escaped arrest and censure due to public support. To Monroe's credit, the president turned the situation to the advantage of the United States. The seizure proved Spain could not protect its remaining Florida lands, and the administration took the chance not only to quell the possibility of war, but also to open negotiations with Spain. On February 22, 1819, Spain transferred all authority over the Floridas to the United States in exchange for the U.S. assumption of $5 million in Spanish debts to U.S. merchants. The Adams-Onis Treaty also marked the first time officials recognized the Pacific Ocean as the western border of the United States. Like Madison before him, Monroe continued to complete the details of Jefferson's vision for an expanded U.S. nation. That vision later would be championed by another larger-than-life president: Andrew Jackson.

THE PRESIDENT'S POSITION: AGAINST SEIZURE
OF PENSACOLA

James Monroe to Andrew Jackson
Washington, July 19th, 1818

Dear Sir,— . . . In reply to your letter I shall express myself with freedom and candor which I have invariably used in my communication with you. I shall withold nothing in regard to your attack of the Spanish posts, and occupancy of them, particularly Pensacola, which you ought to know; it being an occurrence of the most delicate and interesting nature, and which without a service circumspect and cautious policy, looking to all the objects which claim attention, may produce the most serious and unfavorable consequences. It is by a knowledge of all the circumstances and a comprehensive view of the whole subject that the danger to which this measure is exposed may be avoided and all the good which you have contemplated by it, as I trust, be fully realized.

In calling you into active service against the Seminoles, and communicating to you the orders which had been given just before to General Gaines, the views and intentions of the Government were fully disclosed in respect to the operations in Florida. In transcending the limit prescribed by those orders you acted on your own responsibility, on facts and circumstances which were unknown to the Government when the orders were given, many of which, indeed, occurred afterward, and which you thought imposed on you the measure, as an act of patriotism, essential to the honor and interests of your country.

The United States stand justified in ordering their troops into Florida in pursuit of their enemy. They have this right by the law of nations, if the Seminoles were inhabitants of another country and had entered Florida to elude pursuit. Being inhabitants of Florida with a sovereignty over that part of the territory, and a right to the soil, our right to give such an order is the most complete and unquestionable. It is not an act of hostility to Spain. In the less so, because her government is bound by treaty to restrain, by force of arms if necessary, the Indians there from committing hostilities against the United States.

But an order by the government to attack a Spanish post would assume another character. It would authorize war, to which, by the principles of our Constitution, the Executive is incompetent. Congress alone possesses the power. I am aware that cases may occur where the commanding general, acting on his own responsibility, may with safety pass this limit, and with essential advantage to his country. The officers and troops of the neutral power forget the obligations incident to their neutral character; they stimulate the enemy to make war; they furnish them with arms and munitions of war to carry it on; they take an active part in their favor; they afford them an asylum in their retreat. The general obtaining victory pursues them to their post, the gates of which are shut against him; he attacks and carries it, and rests on those acts for justification. The affair is then brought before his government by the power whose post has been thus attacked and carried. If the government whose officer made the attack had given an order for it, the officer would have no merit in it. He exercised no discretion, nor did he act on his own responsibility. The merit of the service, if there be any in it, would not be his. This is the ground on which the occurrence rests. I will now look to the future.

The foreign government demands:—was this your act? or did you authorize it? I did not: it was the act of the general. He performed it for reasons deemed sufficient himself, and on his own responsibility. I demand, then, the surrender of the post, and his punishment. The evidence justifying the conduct of the American general, and proving the misconduct of those officers, will be embodied to be laid before the Sovereign, as the ground on which their punishment will be expected.

If the Executive refused to evacuate the posts, especially Pensacola, it would amount to a declaration of war, to which it is incompetent. It would be accused of usurping the authority of Congress, and giving a deep and fatal wound to the Constitution. By charging the offence on the officers of Spain, we take the ground which you have presented, and we look to you to support it. You must aid in procuring the documents necessary for this purpose. Those which you sent by Mr. Hambly were prepared in too much haste, and do not I am satisfied, do justice to the cause. This must be attended to without delay.

Should we hold the posts, it is impossible to calculate all the consequences likely to result from it. It is not improbable that war would immediately follow. Spain would be stimulated to declare it; and, once declared, the adventurers of Britain and other countries, would under the Spanish flag, privateer on our commerce. . . . Why risk these consequences? . . .

See *The Writings of James Monroe: Including A Collection of His Public and Private Papers and Correspondence Now For the First Time Printed*, vol. 6, 1817–1823, ed. Stanislaus Murray Hamilton (New York: G.P. Putnam's Sons, 1902), pp. 54–58.

ANDREW JACKSON DEFENDS THE SEIZURE
OF PENSACOLA

Andrew Jackson to James Monroe
Nashville, August 19th, 1818

Dr. Sir

Your letter of the 19th. July apprising me of the course to be persued in relation to the Floridas, has been received. In a future communication, it is my intention to submit my views of all the questions springing from the subject, with the fullness and candeur which the importance of the topic, and the part I have acted in it, demand. At present, I will confine myself to a consideration of a part of your letter which has a particular bearing on myself, and which seems to have originated in a misconception of the import of the order, under which I commenced the Seminole campaign. In making this examination, I will use all the freedom which is courted by your letter; and which I deem necessary to afford you a clear view of the construction which was given to the order and the motives under which I proceeded to execute its intentions.

It is stated in the second paragraph of your letter, that I *transcended the limits of my order*, and that I *acted on my own responsibility*.

To these two points I mean at present to confine myself. But before entering on the proof of their inapplicability to my acts in Florida, allow me fairly to state that the assumption of responsibility will never be shrunk from, when the Public interest can be thereby promoted. I have passed through difficulties and exposures for the honor & benefit of my country—and whenever still, for this purpose, it shall become necessary to assume a further liability, no scruple will be urged or felt. But when it shall be required of me to do so, and the result shall be danger and injury to that country, the inducement will be lost, and my consent will be wanting.

This principle is held to be incontrovertible—That an order generally, to perform a certain service, or effect a certain object, without any specification of the means to be adopted, or the limits to govern the executive officer—leaves an *entire discretion* with the officer as to the choice and application of means, but preserves the responsibility, for his acts in the authority from which the order emanated. Under such an order *all the acts* of the inferior are the acts of the superior—and in no way can the subordinate officer be impeached for his measures, except on the score of deficiency in Judgment and skill. It is also a grammatical truth that the limits of such an order cannot be *transcended* without an entire desertion of the objects it contemplated. For as long as the main legitimate design is kept in view the policy of the measures, adopted, to accomplish it, is alone to be considered. If these be adopted as the proper rules of construction, and we apply them to my order of Decbr 26th. 1817: it will be at once seen, that, both in discription, and operative, principle, they embrace that order exactly. The requisitions of the order are, for the comdg. Genl to assume the immediate command at Fort Scott—to concentrate all the contiguous and disposable force of the Division on that quarter, to call on the executives of adjacent states for an auxiliary militia force, and concludes with this general, comprehensive command—"with this view, you may be prepared to concentrate your forces, and adopt the necessary measures to terminate a conflict which it has ever been the desire of the President, from motives of humanity, to avoid, but which is now made necessary by their settled hostility."

In no part of this document, is there a reference to any previous order, either to myself, or another officer, with a view to point to me, the measures thought advisable, or the limits of my power in choosing and effecting them. It states that Genl Gains had been ordered to Amelia Island; and then proceeds to inform me that "subsequent orders have been given (him) to Genl Gains (of which copies *will be* furnished you) that you would be directed to take the command, and directing him to reassume, should he deem the public interest to require it, the command at Fort Scott untill you should arrive there"—lastly, it mentions that "he was instructed to penetrate the Seminole Towns through the floridas, provided the strength of his command at amelia, would Justify his engageing in offensive operations.["] The principle determining the weight of *refferences*, in subsequent orders, to instructions previously given, is well settled. . . .

How then can it be said, with propriety, that I have *transcended the limits* of *my orders* or *acted on my own responsibility*? My order was as comprehensive as it could be, and contained neither minute original instructions, or a reference to others, previously given, to guide and govern me. The fullest discretion was left with me. . . .

It will afford me pleasure to aid the Government in procuring any testimony that may be necessary to prove the hostility of the officers of Spain, to the United States. I had supposed that the evidence furnished had established that fact. . . . I trust on view of all my communications (copies of which have been forwarded by Capt Gadsden) you will find that they do not bear the construction you have given them. . . .

See *The Papers of Andrew Jackson*, vol. 4, *1816–1820*, ed. Harold D. Moser, David R. Hoth, and George H. Hoemann (Knoxville: University of Tennessee Press, 1994), pp. 236–238.

MISSOURI COMPROMISE

The question of slavery had plagued the United States since the Constitutional Convention of 1787. All attempts to solve the problem during the creation of the U.S. Constitution and in administrations since then were stopgap measures rather than real solutions. One of the most significant debates during the Monroe administration, one tied directly to the issue of slavery, challenged the president as both a national leader and a southerner.

In 1819, the Missouri Territory applied for statehood. The application marked a historic milestone; Missouri was the first of the territories from the Louisiana Purchase lands to organize and seek admission to the United States as a state. At the time, the U.S. Senate membership divided equally between those representing slaveholding and non-slaveholding interests. Any new state would send representatives who would tip the scales in favor of one group or the other. As a southern territory, one in which the practice of slavery was already well entrenched, Missouri provoked a vicious power struggle when it applied for statehood. Slaveholding states supported admission and non-slaveholding states did not.

As the struggle continued, the northern part of Massachusetts applied for separate admission as Maine. As a non-slaveholding state, Maine offered the opportunity for leaders to postpone answering the problem of slavery yet again by maintaining perfect balance in the Senate. House Speaker Henry Clay organized a combination of the two bids for statehood, and an additional compromise meant to pacify the representatives: a prohibition of slavery in the remaining Louisiana Territory lands above the northern boundary of Missouri (latitude 36 degrees 30').

President Monroe watched events unfold with great unease. First and foremost, he feared the factionalism the issue ignited—leaders saw themselves as northerners or southerners, antislavery or proslavery, rather than as fellow citizens of the United States. An "us versus them" mentality developed—and the president fell victim to it just as other officials did. As a southerner, Monroe felt that northern leaders did not understand and appreciate the southern way of life, including slavery. In short, Monroe felt threatened.

Monroe also feared establishing arbitrary standards and procedures for admitting new states to the Union. He believed that all territories should follow the same precedents for inclusion in the United States that previous territories had used. By making Missouri's admittance dependent on Maine's, for example, Clay and his compromise changed the rules whereby territories became states. By outlawing slavery in the territories north of Missouri, Clay and his compromise denied territorial citizens the right to choose their own system, a right enjoyed by other citizens in the past.

In an effort to end the divisiveness of the Missouri question, Monroe supported the idea of approving Maine's application immediately. This would end talk of a combined application making Maine dependent on Missouri and vice versa. It would also give southerners who backed Maine's candidacy against their own regional interests a kind of moral authority to call then for the admission of Missouri with no strings attached. He believed the "olive branch" approach would not only allow both territories into the Union, but would also negate any need for extra prohibitions on the remaining territorial lands. Perhaps most importantly, the act would foster cooperation in place of faction. Monroe did not see his plan come to pass, however.

Clay's compromise satisfied both parties and passed the House. Monroe, despite his concerns over the issues and the emotions they sparked, as well as the constitutional basis for restrictions against future states, signed the compromise into law. The roar of debate quieted for a time. Many leaders, however, realized the action as the short-term solution it was. It answered no real questions, and it left the balance of power all-too-delicately balanced between proslavery and antislavery factions. It would take war to settle the issue of slavery in the United States. Thomas Jefferson foresaw the impending crisis clearly when he remarked about the Missouri controversy, "This momentous question, like a fire-bell in the night, awakened and filled me with terror, I considered it at once as the knell of the Union. It is hushed, indeed, for the moment. But this is a reprieve only, not a final sentence."[1]

NOTE

1. Thomas Jefferson. Letter to John Holmes, April 22, 1820. See Paul L. Ford, ed., *The Works of Thomas Jefferson*, vol. 12 (New York: G.P. Putnam's Sons, 1904), p. 158.

THE PRESIDENT'S POSITION: AGAINST THE MISSOURI COMPROMISE

James Monroe to Thomas Jefferson
Washington, February 7, 1820

Dear Sir,—I send you by this days mail, the documents of greatest interest, which have been presented to Congress during the present Session. On our concerns with Spain we have nothing new, and little reason to expect a Minister here from that country, during the Session, Mr. Vivas, said to have been appointed some months ago, being under quarantine, within a few leagues of Madrid, in consequence of passing on his way thither, through some town infected with disease. The Missouri question, absorbs by its importance, and the excit'ment it has produc'd, every other and there is little prospect, from present appearances of its being soon settled. The object of those, who brought it forward, was undoubtedly to acquire power, and the expedient well adapted to the end, as it enlisted in their service, the best feelings of all that portion of our Union, in which slavery does not exist, and who are unacquainted with the condition of their Southern brethren. The same men, in some instances, who were party to the project in 1786, for closing the mouth of the Mississippi for 25 years, may be consider'd as the Authors of this. The dismemberment of the Union by the Allegheny Mountains, when then believ'd to be their object; and although a new arrangement of powers, is more particularly sought on this occasion, yet it is believ'd, that the anticipation, of even that result, would not deter its Authors from the pursuit of it. I am satisfied that the bond of Union, is too strong for them, and that the better their views are understood, throughout the whole Union, the more certain will be their defeat in every part. It requires, however, great moderation, firmness, and wisdom, on the part of those opposed to the restriction, to secure a just result. These great and good qualities, will I trust, not be wanting. . . .

See *The Writings of James Monroe: Including A Collection of His Public and Private Papers and Correspondence Now For the First Time Printed*, vol. 6, *1817–1823*, ed. Stanislaus Murray Hamilton (New York: G.P. Putnam's Sons, 1902), pp. 113–114.

James Monroe to Thomas Jefferson
Washington, February 19, 1820

Dear Sir,—I forward to you by this days Mail a copy of the Journal of the Convention which formed the Constitution of the U States. By the Act of Congress providing for the distribution of them, one is allowed to you, and likewise to Mr. Madison and to Mr. Adams.

The *Intelligencer* will communicate to you some account of the proceedings of Congress on the Missouri Question, and particularly of the late votes taken on different propositions in the Senate. It seems, that a resolution was adopted on the 17th, which establishes a line, to commence, from the western boundary of Missouri, in Lat: 36.30 and run westward indefinitely, north of which slavery should be prohibited; but permitted South of it. Missouri and Arkansas, as is presum'd, to be admitted, without restraint. By the terms applied to the restriction "for ever" it is inferr'd that it is intended, that the restraint should apply to territories, after they become States, as well as before. This will increase

the difficulty incident to an arrangement of this subject, otherwise sufficiently great, in any form, in which it can be presented. Many think
that the right exists in one instance and not in the other. I have never
known a question so menacing to the tranquility and even the continuance of our Union as the present one. All other subjects have given way
to it, and appear to be almost forgotten. As however there is a vast
portion of intelligence and virtue of the people, and the bond of Union
has heretofore prov'd sufficiently strong to triumph over all attempts
against it, I have great confidence that this effort will not be less unavailing. . . .

See *The Writings of James Monroe: Including a Collection of His Public and Private
Papers and Correspondence Now For the First Time Printed*, vol. 6, *1817–1823*, ed.
Stanislaus Murray Hamilton (New York: G.P. Putnam's Sons, 1902), pp. 115–116.

James Monroe to James Madison
Washington, November 16, 1820

. . . The contest for the chair, and the result, indicate a disposition to
review the Missouri question in the temper displayed in the last session.
The clause in the Constitution of that State authorizing an inhibition of
free Negroes from emigrating into it is understood to be that which will
more particularly be laid hold of. Unfavorable [surmises] are formed of
the result. It is undoubtedly to be regretted that the State furnished any
pretext for such [surmises]. It is urged by some favorable to the immediate admission of the State into the Union that, as the Constitution [nul-
lifies] all parts of State Constitutions repugnant to it, then in force, so it
will nullify any part of the Constitution of a new State which may be
admitted, it being necessary that the incorporation should be complete
in every case or clause, the same as to the new as well as the original
States, and not a compact, or treaty between separate communities, as it
would otherwise be: that Congress, in its legislative character, can make
no compact which would deprive the Supreme Court of its right to declare such article in the Constitution of the new State void: that if, however, it has such a right, a declaration by Congress disapproving that
clause, and protesting against it would deprive it of such sanction and
leave it to the decision of the court. . . .

See *The Writings of James Monroe: Including A Collection of His Public and Private
Papers and Correspondence Now For the First Time Printed*, vol. 6, *1817–1823*,
ed. Stanislaus Murray Hamilton (New York: G.P. Putnam's Sons, 1902), pp. 160–
161.

FOR THE MISSOURI COMPROMISE

Journal of the Senate of the United States of America, 1789–1873
Saturday, December 9, 1820

Mr. Tichenor communicated the following resolutions of the legislature of the state of Vermont; which were read:

STATE OF VERMONT.

IN GENERAL ASSEMBLY,
Nov. 15, 1820.

The committee, to whom was referred so much of his excellency's speech as relates to the admission of the territory of Missouri into the Union as a state, submit the following report:

The history of nations demonstrates that involuntary servitude not only plunges the slave into the depths of misery, but renders a great proportion of community dependant and wretched, and the remainder tyrannic and indolent.

Opulence, acquired by the slavery of others, degenerates its possessors, and destroys the physical powers of government. Principles so degrading are inconsistent with the primitive dignity of man, and his natural rights.

Slavery is incompatible with the vital principles of all free governments, and tends to their ruin. It paralizes industry, the greatest source of national wealth, stifles the love of freedom, and endangers the safety of the nation.

It is prohibited by the laws of nature, which are equally binding on governments and individuals. The right to introduce and establish slavery in a free government does not exist.

The Declaration of Independence declares, as self-evident truths, "that all men are created equal; that they are endowed by their Creator with certain unalienable rights; that among these are life, liberty, and the pursuit of happiness; that, to secure these rights, governments are instituted among men, deriving their just powers from the governed; that whenever any form of government becomes destructive of these ends, it is the right of the people to alter or abolish it."

The constitution of the United States, and of the several states, have recognized these principles as the basis of their governments: and have expressly inhibited the introduction or extension of slavery, or impliedly disavowed the right.

The powers of Congress to require the prohibition of slavery in the constitution of a state, to be admitted as one of the United States, is confirmed by the admission of new states according to the ordinance of 1787, and by a constitutional "guarantee to every state in the Union of a republican form of government." This power in Congress is also admitted in the act of March 6, 1820, which declares, that, in all that territory ceded under the name of Louisiana, which lies north of 36 deg. 30 min. north latitude, "slavery and involuntary servitude shall be forever prohibited."

Where slavery existed in the states, at the time of the adoption of the constitution of the United States, a spirit of compromise, or painful necessity, may have excused its continuance; but can never justify its introduction into a state to be admitted from the territories of the United States.

Though slavery is not expressly prohibited by the constitution, yet, that invaluable instrument contains powers, first principles, and self-evident truths, which bring us to the same result, and lead us to Liberty and Justice, and the equal rights of man, from which we ought never to depart. "In it is clearly seen a deep and humiliating sense of slavery," and a cheering hope that it would, at some future period, be abolished—and even a determination to do it.

It is apparent that servitude produces, in the slave-holding states, peculiar feelings, local attachments, and separate interests; and, should it be extended into new states, "it will have a tendency to form a combination of power, which will control the measures of the general government;" and which cannot be resisted, except by the physical force of the nation. . . .

If Missouri be permitted to introduce and legalize slavery by her constitution, and we consent to her admission, we shall justly incur the charge of insincerity in our civil institutions, and in all our professions of attachment to liberty. It will bring upon the constitution and Declaration of Independence, a deep stain, which cannot be forgotten, or blotted out. "It will deeply affect the Union in its resources, political interests, and character."

The admission of another new state into the Union, with a constitution which guarantees security and protection to slavery, and the cruel and unnatural traffic of any portion of the human race, will be an error which the Union cannot correct, and an evil which may endanger the freedom of the nation.

Congress never ought, and we trust never will, plant the standard of the Union in Missouri, to wave over the heads of involuntary slaves, "who have nothing they can call their own, except their sorrows and their sufferings," and a life beyond the grave, and who can never taste the sweets of liberty, unless they obtain it by force or by flight. Nor can a community made up of masters and slaves ever enjoy the blessings of liberty, and the benefits of a free government: these enjoyments are reserved for a community of freemen, who are subject to none, but to God and the laws. . . .

See *Annals of Congress*, Library of Congress. http://memory.loc.gov/ammem/amlaw/lawhome.html.

INTERNAL IMPROVEMENTS

President James Madison used his final day in office to veto the so-called Bonus Bill, a bill for national funding of internal improvements. The bill's supporters lacked the numbers to override the veto. This did not end the issue of internal improvements, however. President James Monroe faced the same question during his administration. Like his predecessor before him, Monroe wrestled with the constitutional questions such potential funding raised.

There was no doubt in anyone's mind that internal improvements were needed in the growing nation to allow speedy and efficient transfer of goods, information, and people. Construction of the Cumberland Road offered an excellent example. Attempted passage over mountains and streams led to many injuries and discouraged many would-be travelers from making the trek from the Atlantic states to the West. A well-constructed road would not only prevent damages, but would also actively encourage travel and commerce. Monroe pondered the question of how to fund the road. Would it be fair to ask each of the states to pay for the part of the road that fell within its borders? In essence, that would force local interests to fund national goods—the regions would not be the only ones to benefit from the road, so why should they be the only ones to pay for it? If the road contributed to commerce and movement on a national scale, should the nation not fund it directly and oversee its consistent, standardized construction across the many states?

Monroe believed that the national government should fund the Cumberland Road because of the benefits the road would provide. He did not, however, see that the U.S. Constitution allowed such an investment. Like Madison before him, Monroe feared that applying the "general welfare" clause of the Constitution to the subject of general improvements would stretch the clause's meaning beyond all shape and open the door for constant congressional actions with little or no authority. In other words, he feared that interpreting the clause loosely would, in effect, allow Congress to do anything it pleased.

The president suggested that leaders begin by drafting a constitutional amendment that would clearly allow the Congress to take action on internal improvements. Then the amendment would go to the states for ratification. This would allow strict constructionists to rest assured that the U.S. Constitution remained respected, but it also would allow important work to be done. Monroe offered a compromise, but Congress was not interested.

To many legislators, the process Monroe described seemed long and painstaking. After all, they wanted a road, not a new addition to the Constitution. They complained that other acts for "the general welfare" seemed uncontroversial; the Constitution made no specific mention of lighthouses, trade houses, post offices, and other such buildings, and yet no one seemed concerned that legislators had authorized them under the "general welfare" clause. And had not James Madison ultimately supported a national bank? Why should the bank be any more acceptable than a road?

In a way, Monroe fell victim to the very phenomenon Madison had foreseen years earlier when he explained to Washington why the first national bank should not be created. Once Congress interprets "general welfare" broadly, Madison had explained, more and more things could be justified under its umbrella. Madison rationalized the second bank to himself as president, and this continued the slippery slope leading to an expanded reading of the clause. Monroe had a valid point but an unpopular one. He eventually gave in to the inevitable, as earlier presidents had done, and signed both a general survey bill and a bill authorizing the Cumberland Road's extension from Wheeling, Virginia, to Zanesville, Ohio.

THE PRESIDENT'S POSITION: IN FAVOR OF A
CONSTITUTIONAL AMENDMENT

James Monroe, Views on the Subject of Internal
Improvements
1822

The situation of the Cumberland road requires the particular and early attention of Congress. Being formed over very lofty mountains and in many instances over deep and wide streams, across which valuable bridges have been erected, which are sustained by stone walls, as are many other parts of the road, all these works are subject to decay, have decayed, and will decay rapidly unless timely and effectual measures are adopted to prevent it.

The declivities from the mountains and all the heights must suffer from the frequent and heavy falls of water and its descent to the valleys, as also from the deep congelations during our severe winters. Other injuries have also been experienced on this road, such as the displacing of the capping of the walls and other works, committed by worthless people either from a desire to render the road impassable or to have the transportation in another direction, or from a spirit of wantonness to create employment for idlers. These considerations show that an active and strict police ought to be established over the whole road, with power to make repairs when necessary, to establish turnpikes and tolls as the means of raising money to make them, and to prosecute and punish those who commit waste and other injuries.

Should the United States be willing to abandon this road to the States through which it passes, would they take charge of it, each of that portion within its limits, and keep it in repair? It is not to be presumed that they would, since the advantages attending it are exclusively national, by connecting, as it does, the Atlantic with the Western States, and in a line with the seat of National Government. The most expensive parts of this road lie within Pennsylvania and Virginia, very near the confines of each State and in a route not essentially connected with the commerce of either.

If it is thought proper to vest this power in the United States, the only mode in which it can be done is by an amendment of the Constitution. The States individually can not transfer the power to the United States, nor can the United States receive it. The Constitution forms an equal and the sole relation between the General Government and the several States, and it recognizes no change in it which shall not in like manner apply to all. If it is once admitted that the General Government may form compacts with individual States not common to the others, and which the others might even disapprove, into what pernicious consequences might it lead? Such compacts are utterly repugnant to the principles of the Constitution and of the most dangerous tendency. The States through which this road passes have given their sanction only to the route and the acquisition of the soil by the United States, a right very different from that of jurisdiction, which can not be granted without an amendment to the Constitution, and which need not be granted for the purposes of this system except in the limited manner heretofore stated. On full consideration, therefore, of the whole subject I am of opinion that such an amendment ought to be recommended to the several States for their adoption.

I have now essentially executed that part of the task which I imposed on myself of examining the right of Congress to adopt and execute a system of internal improvement, and, I presume, have shown that it does not exist. It is, I think, equally manifest that such a power vested in Congress and wisely executed would have the happiest effect on all the great interests of our Union. It is, however, my opinion that the power should be confined to great national works only, since if it were unlimited it would be liable to abuse and might be productive of evil. For all minor improvements the resources of the States individually would be fully adequate, and by the States such improvements might be made with greater advantage than by the Union, as they would understand better such as their more immediate and local interests required. . . .

See *The Writings of James Monroe: Including a Collection of His Public and Private Papers and Correspondence Now For the First Time Printed*, vol. 6, *1817–1823*, ed. Stanislaus Murray Hamilton (New York: G.P. Putnam's Sons, 1902), pp. 276–278.

REPRESENTATIVE JOSEPH HEMPHILL AGAINST A CONSTITUTIONAL AMENDMENT

Annals of Congress
January 1823

Mr. Hemphill rose, and addressed the Chair as follows:

Mr. Chairman: It was my intention to offer some remarks in favor of the present bill at some stage of its progress, and I thank the honorable gentleman from Tennessee (Mr. Cocke) for affording me this early opportunity, by calling on me to state the reasons why the measure recommended should be adopted, and to show that Congress possesses the power to accomplish this object. I cheerfully comply, as I consider the measure of such high concern to this country as any other which could be introduced here for discussion. It is equally interesting to the present generation and to posterity; it contains nothing that is either new or romantic; it is a subject which, on many occasions, has received the consideration of Congress, and it is one which never will be abandoned— nothing but success can terminate its repeated debates on this floor. The importance of it is universally acknowledged; indeed we cannot read of improvements, even in foreign countries, without being infinitely gratified. Great works, of a permanent character are every where admired, and yet it seems extraordinary that any thing like a general system of improvements has to encounter, in the beginning, a powerful opposition. It is not a century since the erection of toll gates was spiritedly resisted in England; and, if my recollection is correct, it is less than thirty years since the first turnpike road in the United States, from Philadelphia to Lancaster, was violently opposed.

The local jealousies and prejudices which are so fatal to improvements have entirely subsided in England, as respects both roads and canals; and there is scarcely a spot in that island which is not within a reasonable distance of a water transportation along canals.

The immense undertaking in the State of New York, which would do honor to any age of nation, had similar prejudices to overcome; but I sincerely hope that we have now arrived at a period in which there is a concurrence of opinion among a large majority of the people on this interesting subject.

I will not, Mr. Chairman, detain the Committee, by going into any tedious detail on the capacity of the country for improvements. There is a general knowledge on this subject, which we all equally possess; waters, we know, may be connected by short portages in instances innumerable; the country (if I may be allowed the expression) can be converted into convenient islands, each containing a capacity within itself of water communications, traversing in almost every direction. . . .

It is the design of the bill to obtain accurate information, with plans and estimates, for the purpose of commencing a general system of internal improvement. The committee which reported the bill, at the last session, selected some of the most prominent objects, leaving a discretionary power with the President to cause plans and estimates to be made in any other places which he might deem important, in a commercial or military point of view.

This is part of the subject which will present difficulties and create local jealousies; as every portion of the country cannot apparently be benefited alike. But such obstacles must be subdued by the good sense and dispassionate deliberation of those in power. It will, however, be recollected that the object now is merely to obtain information to enable a future Congress to say when and where the works shall be commenced. . . .

It is curious to witness the alarm which is occasionally excited concerning the exercise of constructive powers, when Congress is never in session a week without acting upon them. We have only to look at the statute book for instances—see the law relating to fugitives who are held to service or labor in any of the States; the laws regulating the carrying of the mail; the Bank of the United States; the Military Academy; lighthouses, and trading houses among the Indians, are all creatures of constructive power. . . . Yes, Mr. Chairman, we not only make laws which are the mere offspring of constructive powers, but we enforce those laws by high penalties, and the sanguinary punishment of death.

Congress has power to establish post offices and post roads, and there is not another word on this subject in the Constitution; but Congress has passed laws for the carrying of the mail, and for a violation of these laws mail robbers have been executed. . . . I think there is an error in the reasoning against the Cumberland road bill. . . .

See *Annals of Congress*, Library of Congress. <http://memory.loc.gov/ammem/amlaw/lawhome.html>.

MONROE DOCTRINE

No previous president enjoyed as much diplomatic experience and knowledge of international relations as did James Monroe. He had served as minister to France under Washington and then as minister to England under Jefferson, and conducted special missions to France and Spain under Jefferson as well. Monroe was poised particularly well to appreciate the importance of the national revolutions spreading throughout Latin America as former colonies refused to accept the rule of new Napoleonic governments in Europe and the restored rulers who succeeded them. Monroe was eager to recognize newly independent lands such as Buenos Aires and make sure that they remained unmolested by their former colonizers.

His consistent excitement over the revolutions was tainted by the realization that he had to remain somewhat uninvolved, at least while trying to settle boundary questions with Spain regarding Louisiana Purchase lands. The president expressed his support of the rebellions but otherwise erred on the side of impartial neutrality. After treaties with Spain were signed, Monroe recognized the new nations in Latin America publicly.

At the same time Latin American colonies rebelled, Russia and Great Britain appeared to be considering pressing claims to the Pacific coast south of Canada. To complicate matters, war raged between France and Spain and threatened to spill over into Spanish lands in North America. Monroe believed that the United States should remain neutral in European affairs, but he also felt Europeans had no business in the United States or Latin America. As Monroe looked to articulate these assumptions, he also considered his legacy as president. If he could create the guidelines for U.S. relations with other nations, and theirs with the United States, he could solve many future problems for his successors.

On December 2, 1823, Monroe offered his seventh annual address to both houses of Congress. In it, he combined moral support of Latin American revolutions with the practical self-interest of the United States. The so-called Monroe Doctrine advised Europeans that they should no longer view any part of the Western Hemisphere as potential lands for colonization. Monroe implied that Europe could do what it wished with Europe, but the United States would oversee, protect, and defend its hemisphere. In effect, Monroe extended the nation's backyard to include Central and South America and the Caribbean. His tone was paternalistic but not colonial; independent nations would remain independent. The Monroe Doctrine ushered in a thirty-year span in which the United States remained free of serious international involvement, a welcome change from the years of quasi war and direct war former presidents had known. The doctrine also shaped centuries of U.S. policies with regard to Latin America. The precedent-setting announcement remained the most important accomplishment of the Monroe administration.

Some U.S. leaders did not believe that the doctrine went far enough, however. By limiting U.S. attention to the Western Hemisphere, they argued, the policy abandoned U.S. moral responsibility to liberty across the world. For example, the Greeks were fighting for their own independence at the same time Latin American nations were overthrowing their colonizers. Did not the United States, as the world's example of a nation that claimed and achieved its own freedom, owe it to Greece as well as to Latin America to support struggles for liberty? Leaders such as Daniel Webster believed so. Webster worried that Monroe's emphasis on Latin America would blind the nation to worthy causes around the globe. Indeed, the first draft of the Monroe Doctrine included a bold endorsement of the Greek revolution and even an appointment of a special U.S. agent to independent Greece, but Secretary of State John Quincy Adams edited this out of the final version and retained only vague support for the Greek cause. In order to maintain peace with Europe, Adams believed, the United States needed to be as quiet on European affairs as the nation expected Europe to be on affairs in the Americas. In the end, popular support for the Monroe Doctrine not only overwhelmed criticisms against it, but also assured Monroe a permanent legacy as president.

THE PRESIDENT'S POSITION: THE MONROE DOCTRINE

James Monroe, Seventh Annual Address to Congress
December 2, 1823

. . . At the proposal of the Russian Imperial Government, made through the minister of the Emperor residing here, a full power and instructions have been transmitted to the minister of the United States at St. Petersburg to arrange by amicable negotiation the respective rights and interests of the two nations on the northwest coast of this continent. A similar proposal has been made by His Imperial Majesty to the Government of Great Britain, which has likewise been acceded to. The Government of the United States has been desirous by this friendly proceeding of manifesting the great value which they have invariably attached to the friendship of the Emperor and their solicitude to cultivate the best understanding with his Government. In the discussions to which this interest has given rise and in the arrangements by which they may terminate the occasion has been judged proper for asserting, as a principle in which the rights and interests of the United States are involved, that the American continents, by the free and independent condition which they have assumed and maintain, are henceforth not to be considered as subjects for future colonization by any European powers. . . .

It was stated at the commencement of the last session that a great effort was then making in Spain and Portugal to improve the condition of the people of those countries, and that it appeared to be conducted with extraordinary moderation. It need scarcely be remarked that the results have been so far very different from what was then anticipated. Of events in that quarter of the globe, with which we have so much intercourse and from which we derive our origin, we have always been anxious and interested spectators. The citizens of the United States cherish sentiments the most friendly in favor of the liberty and happiness of their fellow-men on that side of the Atlantic. In the wars of the European powers in matters relating to themselves we have never taken any part, nor does it comport with our policy to do so. It is only when our rights are invaded or seriously menaced that we resent injuries or make preparation for our defense. With the movements in this hemisphere we are of necessity more immediately connected, and by causes which must be obvious to all enlightened and impartial observers. The political system of the allied powers is essentially different in this respect from that of America. This difference proceeds from that which exists in their respective Governments; and to the defense of our own, which has been achieved by the loss of so much blood and treasure, and matured by the wisdom of their most enlightened citizens, and under which we have enjoyed unexampled felicity, this whole nation is devoted. We owe it, therefore, to candor and to the amicable relations existing between the United States and those powers to declare that we should consider any attempt on their part to extend their system to any portion of this hemisphere as dangerous to our peace and safety. With the existing colonies or dependencies of any European power we have not interfered and shall not interfere. But with the Governments who have declared their independence and maintain it, and whose independence we have, on great consideration and on just principles, acknowledged, we could not view any interposition for the purpose of oppressing them, or controlling in any other manner their destiny, by any European power in any other light than as the manifestation of an unfriendly disposition toward the United States. In the war between those new Governments and Spain we declared our neutrality at the time of their recognition, and to this we have adhered, and shall continue to adhere, provided no change shall occur which, in the judgement of the competent authorities of this Government, shall make a corresponding change on the part of the United States indispensable to their security.

The late events in Spain and Portugal shew that Europe is still unsettled. Of this important fact no stronger proof can be adduced than that the allied powers should have thought it proper, on any principle satisfactory to themselves, to have interposed by force in the internal concerns of Spain. To what extent such interposition may be carried, on the same principle, is a question in which all independent powers whose governments differ from theirs are interested, even those most remote, and surely none of them more so than the United States. Our policy in regard to Europe, which was adopted at an early stage of the wars which have so long agitated that quarter of the globe, nevertheless remains the same, which is, not to interfere in the internal concerns of any of its powers; to consider the government de facto as the legitimate government for us; to cultivate friendly relations with it, and to preserve those relations by a frank, firm, and manly policy, meeting in all instances the just claims of every power, submitting to injuries from none. But in regard to those continents circumstances are eminently and conspicuously different.

It is impossible that the allied powers should extend their political system to any portion of either continent without endangering our peace and happiness; nor can anyone believe that our southern brethren, if left to themselves, would adopt it of their own accord. It is equally impossible, therefore, that we should behold such interposition in any form with indifference. If we look to the comparative strength and resources of Spain and those new Governments, and their distance from each other, it must be obvious that she can never subdue them. It is still the true policy of the United States to leave the parties to themselves, in hope that other powers will pursue the same course. . . .

The Avalon Project at Yale Law School, 1997. William C. Fray and Lisa A. Spar, co-directors. <http:www.yale.edu/lawweb/avalon.monroe.htm/>.

DANIEL WEBSTER: IN FAVOR OF EXTENDING U.S. PROTECTION TO GREECE

Daniel Webster to Edward Everett
Washington, December 5 [1823]

My dear Sir
. . . I have spoken to several Gentlemen on the subject of a motion respecting Greece, & all of them approve of it. My only doubt, at present,

is as to the manner. The object which I wish to bring about, and which I believe may be brought about, is the appointment of a Commissioner to go to Greece. Two modes present themselves. A motion to that effect, & a speech in support of it, giving some account of the rise & progress of the Greek Revolution, & shewing the propriety & utility of the proposed mission.

The other is, to raise a Com[mitt]ee on the subject, & let there be a report, containing the same matter. The first would be the easier to be done; the last would be the more grave & imposing. Whichever may be adopted, your communications are invaluable; & I wish you would tell me frankly how far I can use them without injury to your January Article in N.A.* We can wait until that article is *out*, if you think best—but my impression is we should do well to bring forward the subject within ten or twelve days from this time, while the House is not yet much occupied, & while the Country feels the warmth communicated by the Presidents Message. . . .

I shall send you every thing, in the shape of a document, that is printed this session. These are interesting times—let us improve them. . . .

Note: This refers to "The Life of Ali Pacha" in *The North American Review*, New Series, 9 (January 1824): 106–140.

See *The Papers of Daniel Webster: Correspondence*, vol. 1, ed. Charles M. Wiltse (Hanover, N.H.: University Press of New England, 1974), pp. 338–339.

Daniel Webster to Edward Everett
Washington, December 6 [1823]

My D Sir

There was, as I believe a meeting of the members of Administration yesterday; at which, inter alia, they talked of Greece. The *pinch* is, that in the Message the President has taken, as is supposed, pretty high ground as to *this Continent*; and is afraid of the appearance of interfering in the concerns of the *other continent* also. This does not weigh greatly with me—I think we have as much Community with the Greeks, as with the inhabitants of the Andes, & the dwellers on the borders of the Vermilion Sea. It was, or I am not well informed, stated, yesterday, that there ought to be a Commiss[ione]r, & that you ought to be persuaded to go. Go you will—and go you shall—if you chuse to do so.

If nothing should occur to alter my present purpose, I shall bring forward a motion on the subject *on Monday*—& shall propose to let it lie on the table for a fortnight.

If you can find any tolerable map of Modern Greece, I wish you would send it to me, for *Mr. Calhoun*. I write this at his request, who desires me to say to you that he is as friendly to the Greeks as yourself.

I am glad to see that you publish in the Daily your narrative. It will be well recd—& do much good.

There seems to be here a good natured & liberal spirit, on all subjects. . . .

See *The Papers of Daniel Webster: Correspondence*, vol. 1, ed. Charles M. Wiltse (Hanover, N.H.: University Press of New England, 1974), p. 339.

Joel Roberts Poinsett to Daniel Webster
[1823?]

Dear Sir

I saw the President and shewed him the modification you proposed. He still objects on the ground, that such measures ought to originate with the Executive,* and that your resolution proposes to go further than he wishes. He intended only to express his wishes for the success of the Greeks. I think it important to the cause you advocate that some expression favorable to the Greeks should pass the house, and propose to offer a substitute for your resolution. If the Friends of a positive measure in their favor are most numerous your resolution will pass, if on the contrary the majority are of the opinion we ought to confine ourselves to an expression of sympathy and interest in their cause, mine will be adopted. . . .

Note: This refers to Webster's December 8 proposal that the United States send a special commissioner to Greece.

See *The Papers of Daniel Webster: Correspondence*, vol. 1, ed. Charles M. Wiltse (Hanover, N.H.: University Press of New England, 1974), p. 344

AMERICAN INDIAN REMOVAL

Along with the question of internal improvements, James Monroe inherited another difficult issue from his predecessors: what to do with native Americans. Though a Jeffersonian with clear sympathies for the rights of Amerindians, Monroe also faced the legacy of the ill-advised Georgia Compact of 1802. This agreement ceded western Georgia lands to the U.S. national government in return for extinguished Amerindian land titles within Georgia state borders. How and when American Indians would lose the rights to their lands in Georgia was unclear. The problem fell to the U.S. government. Over twenty years after the compact became law, the problem remained.

Some indigenous nations had agreed to exchange their Georgia properties for others in the West. Others, such as the Cherokee Nation, had no intention of moving from the ancestral lands they had occupied for thousands of years. Monroe faced an uneasy question: should he continue to negotiate, or should he buckle to popular pressure and forcibly remove the remaining native nations in Georgia?

Monroe did not favor forced removal. In the final analysis, he believed the American Indian lands belonged to the Amerindians and were theirs to control. He did not believe the United States had the authority to uproot and force the people from their homes. He did, however, think all persuasion should be used to convince the native Americans to leave Georgia and perhaps the United States altogether. Jefferson had hoped the lines separating Amerindians from the US mainstream would crumble and disappear so that the American Indians would eventually be assimilated into the U.S. citizenry. Monroe did not share the former president's optimism. He believed the native Americans would be safer, and therefore happier, far away from the general U.S. population. In effect, he admitted that he could not control U.S. citizens and their actions against Amerindians. He viewed removal as the best protection he could offer the native nations.

Some Amerindians disagreed with Monroe's assessment of the situation. Vocal leaders such as Elias Boudinot of the Cherokee Nation (later editor of the influential newspaper *Cherokee Phoenix*) believed their people's best hope for survival and advancement was to remain in their traditional lands and learn from U.S. culture. A close relationship with mainstream U.S. citizens allowed for trade and education, whereas distant removal promised illness and poverty. Christianized and culturally assimilated Amerindians such as Boudinot played upon the missionary zeal of the religious movement known as the second Great Awakening and the economic power of the Era of Good Feelings in order to show how much the native Americans could gain from remaining in their homelands—and, in return, the rewards Georgians and others could reap by teaching and cultivating their indigenous neighbors.

Boudinot used common racial stereotypes to gain the sympathies of listeners and readers, but his core message was clear: Cherokees neither wanted nor intended to give up their lands in Georgia. He knew that without national U.S. protection, however, native American property rights would be violated and the native nations would disappear. Whereas Monroe believed that voluntary removal was the only hope for the future of native Americans, Boudinot and others believed the opposite. Their positions ended with a temporary stalemate. Monroe postponed the question for a later administration.

In a matter of a few years, the question would return with violent finality and leave a permanent scar on the face of the United States. President Andrew Jackson would prove quite willing to resort to violence in order to take Cherokee lands and others for the state of Georgia. Monroe would not live to see removal at its most coercive and bloody; Boudinot would ultimately embrace it in a last attempt to save his people and be murdered for his part in the infamous Cherokee Trail of Tears (1838–1839).

THE PRESIDENT'S POSITION: FOR VOLUNTARY REMOVAL
OF NATIVE AMERICANS

James Monroe, Address to Congress on Removal of
Indians
Washington, March 30, 1824

To the Senate and House of Representatives of the United States:

I transmit to Congress several papers enumerated in a report from the Secretary of War, relating to the compact between the United States and the State of Georgia entered into in 1802, whereby the latter ceded to the former a portion of the territory then within its limits on the conditions therein specified. By the fourth article of that compact it was stipulated that the United States should at their own expense extinguish for the use of Georgia the Indian title to all the lands within the State as soon as it might be done *peaceably* and on *reasonable* conditions. These papers show the measures adopted by the Executive of the United States in fulfillment of the several conditions of the compact from its date to the present time, and particularly the negotiations and treaties with the Indian tribes for the extinguishments of their title, with an estimate of the number of acres purchased and sums paid for lands they acquired. They show also the state in which this interesting concern now rests with the Cherokees, one of the tribes within the State, and the inability of the Executive to make any further movement with this tribe without the special sanction of Congress.

I have full confidence that my predecessors exerted their best endeavors to execute this compact in all its parts, of which, indeed, the sums paid and the lands acquired during their respective terms in fulfillment of its several stipulations are a full proof. I have also been animated since I came into this office with the same zeal, from an anxious desire to meet the wishes of the State, and in the hope that by the establishment of these tribes beyond the Mississippi their improvement in civilization, their security and happiness would be promoted. By the paper bearing date on the 30th of January last, which was communicated to the chiefs of the Cherokee Nation in this city, who came to protest against any further appropriations of money for holding treaties with them, the obligation imposed on the United States by the compact with Georgia to extinguish the Indian title to the right of soil within the State, and the incompatibility with our system of their existence as a distinct community within any State, were pressed with the utmost earnestness. It was proposed to them at the same time to procure and convey to them territory beyond the Mississippi in exchange for that which they hold within the limits of Georgia, or to pay them for its value in money. To this proposal their answer, which bears date 11th of February following, gives an unqualified refusal. By this it is manifest that at the present time and in their present temper they can be removed only by force, to which, should it be deemed proper, the power of the Executive is incompetent.

I have no hesitation, however, to declare it as my opinion that the Indian title was not affected in the slightest circumstance by the compact with Georgia, and that there is no obligation on the United States to remove the Indians by force. The express stipulation of the compact that their title should be extinguished at the expense of the United States when it may be done *peaceably* and on *reasonable* conditions is a full proof that it was the clear and distinct understanding of both parties to it that the Indians had a right to the territory, in the disposal of which they were to be regarded as free agents. An attempt to remove them by force would, in my opinion, be unjust. In the future measures to be adopted in regard to the Indians within our limits, and, in consequence, within the limits of any State, the United States have duties to perform and a character to sustain to which they ought not to be indifferent. At an early period in their development in the arts of civilized life was made an object with the Government, and that has since been persevered in. This policy was dictated by motives of humanity to the aborigines of the country, and under a firm conviction that the right to adopt and pursue it was equally applicable to all the tribes within our limits.

My impression is equally strong that it would promote essentially the security and happiness of the tribes within our limits if they could be prevailed on to retire west and north of our States and Territories on lands to be procured for them by the United States, in exchange for those on which they now reside. Surrounded as they are, and pressed as they will be, on every side by the white population, it will be difficult if not impossible for them, with their kind of government, to sustain order among them. Their interior will be exposed to frequent disturbances, to remedy which the interposition of the United States will be indispensable, and thus their government will gradually lose its authority until it is annihilated. . . . I submit the subject to your consideration, in full confidence that you will duly weigh the obligations of the compact with Georgia, its import in all its parts, and the extent to which the United States are bound to go under it. I submit it with equal confidence that you will also weigh the nature of the Indian title to the territory within the limits of any State, with the stipulations in the several treaties with this tribe respecting territory held by it within the State of Georgia, and decide whether any measure on the part of Congress is called for at the present time, and what such measure shall be if any is deemed expedient.

See *The Writings of James Monroe: Including A Collection of His Public and Private Papers and Correspondence Now For the First Time Printed*, vol. 7, 1824–1831, ed. Stanislaus Murray Hamilton (New York: G.P. Putnam's Sons, 1903), pp. 14–17.

ELIAS BOUDINOT: AGAINST AMERICAN INDIAN REMOVAL

"An Address to the Whites, Delivered in the First Presbyterian Church, on the 26th of May, 1826, by Elias Boudinott, A Cherokee Indian"

To those who are unacquainted with the manners, habits, and improvements of the Aborigines of this country, the term *Indian* is pregnant with ideas the most repelling and degrading. But such impressions, originating as they frequently do, from infant prejudices, although they hold too true when applied to some, do great injustice to many of this race of beings.

Some there are, perhaps even in this enlightened assembly, who at the bare sight of an Indian, or at the mention of the name, would throw back their imaginations to ancient times, to the ravages of savage warfare, to the yells pronounced over the mangled bodies of women and children, thus creating an opinion, inapplicable and highly injurious to those for whose temporal interest and eternal welfare, I come to plead.

What is an Indian? Is he not formed of the same materials with yourself? For "of one blood God created all the nations that dwell on the face of the earth" [Acts 17:26]. Though it be true that he is ignorant, that he is heathen, that he is savage; yet he is no more than all others have been under similar circumstances. Eighteen centuries ago what were the inhabitants of Great Britain? . . .

. . . My design is to offer a few disconnected facts relative to the present improved state, and to the ultimate prospects of that particular tribe called Cherokees to which I belong.

The Cherokee nation lies within the charted limits of the states of Georgia, Tennessee, and Alabama. Its extent as defined by treaties is about 200 miles in length from East to West, and about 120 in breadth. This country which is supposed to contain about 10,000,000 exhibits great varieties of surface, the most part being hilly and mountainous, affording soil of no value. The vallies, however, are well watered and afford excellent land, in many parts particularly on the large streams, that of the first quality. The climate is temperate and healthy, indeed I would not be guilty of exaggeration were I to say, that the advantages which this country possesses to render it salubrious, are many and superior. Those lofty and barren mountains, as placed there only to exhibit omnipotence, contribute to the healthiness and beauty of the surrounding plains, and give to us that free air and pure water which distinguish our country. These advantages, calculated to make the inhabitants healthy, become interesting. And there can be no doubt that the Cherokee Nation, however obscure and trifling it may now appear, will finally become, if not under its present occupants, one of the Garden spots of America. And here, let me be indulged in the fond wish, that she may thus become under those who now possess her; and ever be fostered, regulated and protected by the generous government of the United States. . . .

There are, with regard to the Cherokees and other tribes, two alternatives; they must either become civilized and happy, or sharing the fate of many kindred nations, become extinct. If the General Government continue its protection, and the American people assist them in their humble efforts, they will, they must rise. Yes, under such protection, and with such assistance, the Indian must rise like the Phoenix, after having wallowed for ages in ignorance and barbarity. But should this Government withdraw its care, and the American people their aid, then, to use the words of a writer, "they will go the way that so many tribes have gone before them; for the hordes that still linger about the shores of Huron, and the tributary streams of the Mississippi, will share the fate of those tribes that once lorded it along the proud banks of the Hudson; of that gigantic race that are said to have exist on the borders of the Susquehanna; of those various nations that flourished about the Potomac and the Rhappahannoc, and that peopled the forests of the vast valley of Shenandoah. They will vanish like a vapour from the face of the earth, their very history will be lost in forgetfulness, and the places that now know them will know them no more."*

There is, in Indian history, something very melancholy, and which seems to establish a mournful precedent for the future events of the few sons of the forest, now scattered over this vast continent. . . . Shall this precedent be followed? I ask you, shall red men live, or shall they be swept from the earth? With you and this public at large, this decision chiefly rests. Must they perish? Must they all, like the unfortunate Creeks, (victims of the unchristian policy of certain persons,) go down in sorrow to their grave?

They hang upon your mercy as to a garment. Will you push them from you, or will you save them? Let humanity answer.

*From Washington Irving, "Traits of Indian Character," *The Analectic Magazine* (February 1814): 145–156.

See Theda Perdue, ed., *Cherokee Editor: The Writings of Elias Boudinot* (Athens, Ga: University of Georgia Press, 1996).

RECOMMENDED READINGS

Ammon, Harry. *James Monroe: A Bibliography*. Westport, Conn.: Meckler, 1991.

———. *James Monroe: The Quest for National Identity*. New York: McGraw-Hill, 1971.

Coffin, Tristam Potter. *Missouri Compromise*. Boston: Little, Brown & Company, 1947.

Cresson, W.P. *James Monroe*. Chapel Hill: University of North Carolina Press, 1946.

Cunningham, Noble E., Jr. *The Presidency of James Monroe*. Lawrence: University Press of Kansas, 1996.

Dangerfield, George. *The Era of Good Feelings*. Chicago: Ivan R. Dee, Inc., 1989.

Elliot, Ian, ed. *James Monroe, 1758–1831: Chronology, Documents, Bibliographical Aids*. Dobbs Ferry, N.Y.: Oceana Publications, 1969.

Jameson, John F. *James Monroe: With a Bibliography of Writings Pertinent to the Monroe Doctrine*. New York: AMS Press, 1972.

Ketcham, Ralph. *Presidents Above Party: The First American Presidency, 1789–1829*. Chapel Hill: University of North Carolina Press, 1984.

May, Ernest R. *The Making of the Monroe Doctrine*. Cambridge, Mass.: Harvard University Press, 1992.

Moore, Glover. *The Missouri Controversy, 1819–1821*. Lexington: University of Kentucky Press, 1953.

Styron, Arthur. *The Last of the Cocked Hats: James Monroe and the Virginia Dynasty*. Norman: University of Oklahoma Press, 1945.

BIBLIOGRAPHY

Adams, John. *Papers of John Adams*. Edited by Robert J. Taylor. 10 vols. Cambridge, Mass.: Belknap Press of Harvard University Press, 1977.

Ammon, Harry. *James Monroe: A Bibliography*. Westport, Conn.: Meckler, 1991.

————. *James Monroe: The Quest for National Identity*. New York: McGraw-Hill, 1971.

Annals of Congress. Library of Congress. <http://memory.loc.gov/ammem/amlaw/lawhome.html>.

Bradley, Harold W. "The Political Thinking of George Washington." *Journal of Southern History* 9 (1945): 469–486.

Brookhiser, Richard. *Founding Father: Rediscovering George Washington*. New York: Free Press, 1996.

Brown, David S. *Thomas Jefferson: A Biographical Companion*. Santa Barbara, Calif.: ABC-CLIO, 1998.

Brown, Ralph Allen. *The Presidency of John Adams*. Lawrence: University Press of Kansas, 1975.

Brown, Walt. *John Adams and the American Press: Politics and Journalism at the Birth of the Republic*. Jefferson, N.C.: McFarland & Company, 1995.

Callahan, North. *Thanks, Mr. President: The Trail-Blazing Second Term of George Washington*. New York: Cornwall Books, 1991.

Cappon, Lester J., ed. *The Adams-Jefferson Letters: The Complete Correspondence*. Chapel Hill: University of North Carolina Press, 1988.

Coffin, Tristam Potter. *Missouri Compromise*. Boston: Little, Brown & Company, 1947.

Cresson, W.P. *James Monroe*. Chapel Hill: University of North Carolina Press, 1946.

Cunningham, Noble E., Jr. *The Presidency of James Monroe*. Lawrence: University Press of Kansas, 1996.

Dangerfield, George. *The Era of Good Feelings*. Chicago: Ivan R. Dee, Inc., 1989.

DeConde, Alexander. *Entangling Alliance: Politics and Diplomacy Under George Washington*. Durham, N.C.: Duke University Press, 1958.

Elkins, Stanley, and Eric McKitrick. *The Age of Federalism*. New York: Oxford University Press, 1993.

Elliot, Ian, ed. *James Monroe, 1758–1831: Chronology, Documents, Bibliographical Aids*. Dobbs Ferry, N.Y.: Oceana Publications, 1969.

Ellis, Joseph J. *American Sphinx: The Character of Thomas Jefferson*. New York: Alfred A. Knopf, 1997.

———. *Passionate Sage: The Character and Legacy of John Adams*. New York: Norton, 1993.

———, ed. *Thomas Jefferson: Genius of Liberty*. New York: Viking Press, 2000.

Ferling, John E. *John Adams: A Life*. New York: Holt, 1996.

———. *John Adams: A Bibliography*. Westport, Conn.: Greenwood, 1994.

Flexner, James Thomas. *Washington: The Indispensable Man*. New York: Signet, 1969.

The George Washington Papers at the Library of Congress. <http://memory.loc.gov/ammem/gwhtml/gwhome.html>.

Gregg, Gary L., II, and Matthew Spalding, eds. *Patriot Sage: George Washington and the American Political Tradition*. Wilmington, Del.: ISI Books, 1999.

Heidler, David S., and Jeanne T. Heidler, ed. *Encyclopedia of the War of 1812*. Santa Barbara, Calif.: ABC-CLIO, 1997.

Hickey, Donald R. *The War of 1812: A Forgotten Conflict*. Urbana: University of Illinois Press, 1989.

Hutson, James H. "John Adams' Title Campaign." *The New England Quarterly: A Historical Review of New England Life and Letters* (March 1968): 30–39.

Israel, Fred L., ed. *Major Presidential Decisions*. New York: Chelsea House, 1980.

Jameson, John F. *James Monroe: With a Bibliography of Writings Pertinent to the Monroe Doctrine*. New York: AMS Press, 1972.

Jefferson, Thomas. *Thomas Jefferson, Political Writings*. Edited by Joyce Appleby and Terence Ball. New York: Cambridge University Press, 1999.

Jefferson, Thomas, and James Madison. *The Republic of Letters: The Correspondence between Thomas Jefferson and James Madison, 1776–1826*. New York: Norton, 1995.

Kaplan, Lawrence S. *Thomas Jefferson: Westward the Course of Empire*. Wilmington, Del.: S Books, 1999.

Ketcham, Ralph. *James Madison: A Biography*. New York: Macmillan, 1971.

———. *Presidents Above Party: The First American Presidency, 1789–1829*. Chapel Hill: University of North Carolina Press, 1984.

Kurtz, Stephen G. *The Presidency of John Adams: The Collapse of Federalism, 1795–1800*. New York: A.S. Barnes and Company, 1961.

Madison, James. *The Papers of James Madison: Presidential Series*. Edited by Robert A. Rutland. 4 vols. Charlottesville: University Press of Virginia, 1984.

Malone, Dumas. *Jefferson and His Time*. 6 Vols. Boston: Little, Brown, 1948–1981.

May, Ernest R. *The Making of the Monroe Doctrine*. Cambridge, Mass.: Harvard University Press, 1992.

Mayer, David N. *The Constitutional Thought of Thomas Jefferson*. Charlottesville: University Press of Virginia, 1994.

McCoy, Drew. *The Last of the Fathers: James Madison and the Republican Legacy.* Cambridge: Cambridge University Press, 1989.

McDonald, Forrest. *The Presidency of George Washington.* Lawrence: University Press of Kansas, 1974.

———. *The Presidency of Thomas Jefferson.* Lawrence: University Press of Kansas, 1976.

McLaughlin, Jack, ed. *To His Excellency Thomas Jefferson: Letters to a President.* New York: W.W. Norton & Company, 1991.

Milkis, Sydney M., and Michael Nelson. *The American Presidency: Origins and Development, 1776–1998.* 2nd ed. Washington, D.C: Congressional Quarterly Books, 1999.

Miller, John C. *Crisis in Freedom: The Alien and Sedition Acts.* Boston: Little, Brown, and Company, 1951.

Moore, Glover. *The Missouri Controversy, 1819–1821.* Lexington: University of Kentucky Press, 1953.

Onuf, Peter S., ed. *Jeffersonian Legacies.* Charlottesville: University Press of Virginia, 1993.

Peterson, Merrill D. *Thomas Jefferson and the New Nation: A Biography.* New York: Oxford University Press, 1970.

Phelps, Glenn A. *George Washington and American Constitutionalism.* Lawrence: University Press of Kansas, 1993.

Prucha, Francis Paul. *The Great Father: The United States Government and the American Indians.* Lincoln: University of Nebraska Press, 1986.

Randall, Willard Sterne. *George Washington: A Life.* New York: Henry Holt, 1997.

Rasmussen, William M.S., and Robert S. Tilton. *George Washington: The Man behind the Myths.* Charlottesville: University Press of Virginia, 1999.

Risjord, Norman K. *Thomas Jefferson.* Madison, Wis.: Madison House, 1994.

Rosen, Gary. *American Compact: James Madison and the Problem of Founding.* Lawrence: University Press of Kansas, 1999.

Rosenfeld, Richard N. *American Aurora: A Democratic-Republican Returns, The Suppressed History of Our Nation's Beginnings and the Heroic Newspaper That Tried to Report It.* New York: St. Martin's Press, 1997.

Rozell, Mark J., William D. Pederson, and Frank J. Williams, eds. *George Washington and the Origins of the American Presidency.* Westport, Conn.: Praeger, 2000.

Rutland, Robert Allen. *James Madison and the Search for Nationhood.* Washington, D.C.: Library of Congress, 1981.

———. *James Madison: The Founding Father.* New York: Macmillan, 1987.

———. *The Presidency of James Madison.* Lawrence: University Press of Kansas, 1990.

Schultz, Harold. *James Madison.* New York: Twayne, 1970.

Sheldon, Garrett Ward. *The Political Philosophy of Thomas Jefferson.* Baltimore: Johns Hopkins University Press, 1991.

Smith, Page. *John Adams.* 2 vols. New York: Doubleday, 1962.

Smith, Richard Norton. *Patriarch: George Washington and the New American Nation.* Boston: Houghton Mifflin, 1993.

Spalding, Matthew, and Patrick J. Garrity. *A Sacred Union of Citizens: George Wash-*

ington's Farewell Address and the American Character. Lanham, Md.: Rowan and Littlefield, 1996.

Styron, Arthur. *The Last of the Cocked Hats: James Monroe and the Virginia Dynasty*. Norman: University of Oklahoma Press, 1945.

Tansill, Charles Callan. *The United States and Santo Domingo, 1798–1873: A Chapter in Caribbean Diplomacy*. Baltimore: Johns Hopkins Press, 1938.

The Thomas Jefferson Papers at The Library of Congress. <http://memory.loc.gov/ammem/mtjhtml/mtjhome.html>.

Thompson, C. Bradley. *John Adams and the Spirit of Liberty*. Lawrence: University Press of Kansas, 1998.

Wait, Eugene M. *America and the War of 1812*. Commack, N.Y.: Kroshka Books, 1999.

Washington, George. *The Papers of George Washington: Presidential Series*. Edited by Dorothy Twohig. 9 vols. Charlottesville: University Press of Virginia, 1987.

Yarbrough, Jean M. *American Virtues: Thomas Jefferson on the Character of a Free People*. Lawrence: University Press of Kansas, 1998.

INDEX

About the Author

AMY H. STURGIS is an independent scholar who specializes in early national U.S. history and Amerindian studies. She is Editor-in-Chief of *Humane Studies Review* for the Institute of Humane Studies. She has published in a number of scholarly journals and presented at national and international conferences in history, political science, and ethnic studies.